T0305652

Project and Program Excellence

Motivational Leadership for Breakthrough Results

Project and Program Excellence

Motivational Leadership for Breakthrough Results

Thomas Pavelko

CRC Press
Taylor & Francis Group
Boca Raton London New York

CRC Press is an imprint of the
Taylor & Francis Group, an **informa** business

AN AUERBACH BOOK

The views presented in this book are those of the author. They are not the views of any of the author's prior employers, of any organization with which the author has done business, or of Lockheed Martin. All outlines and checklists in the figures are copied from open source examples.

Material in this book is taken from the following book written by the author, with permission from Taylor & Francis Group: *Project and Program Turnaround* / ISBN: 9781138626805 / 2017.

First Edition published 2022
by CRC Press
6000 Broken Sound Parkway NW, Suite 300, Boca Raton, FL 33487-2742

and by CRC Press
2 Park Square, Milton Park, Abingdon, Oxon, OX14 4RN

ISBN: 978-1-032-18637-5 (hbk)
ISBN: 978-1-032-12076-8 (pbk)
ISBN: 978-1-003-25615-1 (ebk)

DOI: 10.1201/9781003256151

Trademark Used in This Publication

BAND-AID is a registered trademark of Johnson & Johnson in New Brunswick, NJ.

Dedication

This book is dedicated to all program team members who believe an extraordinary level of team performance is achievable. It is!

Contents

Dedication   *vii*

Contents   *ix*

List of Illustrations   *xv*

List of Tables   *xix*

Preface   *xxi*

Acknowledgments   *xxxi*

About the Author   *xxxiii*

Chapter One   Program Performance Breakthrough   **1**
- 1.1   Paradox Observed—Being "On-Step"   1
- 1.2   Current Success Level   9
  - 1.2.1   Struggle to Be Better   9
  - 1.2.2   Why Let the Best Go?   12
  - 1.2.3   Program Use History   13
- 1.3   Past Successful Program Elements   18
  - 1.3.1   Program Success Elements   18
  - 1.3.2   Elements When On-Step   19
- 1.4   Chapter Highlights   23

Chapter Two   Why Motivation-Based Leadership   **25**
- 2.1   The "Secret Sauce"?   25
- 2.2   Applies "Pull," not "Push"   27

2.3   Frees Creativity   28
2.4   Distributes Vigilance   28
2.5   Improves Known On-Step Elements   28
2.6   Identifies and Guides Team-Member Development   29
2.7   Accelerates Learning What You Do Best   29
2.8   Respects Personal Esteem   29
2.9   Provides a Fair, Positive, and Fulfilling Environment   30
2.10   Increases Customer Satisfaction   30
       2.10.1 Satisfaction of Current Customer for Future Work   30
       2.10.2 Providing Traits Customers Want   32
2.11   Chapter Highlights   33

Chapter Three   Motivation Model to Be First Place   **35**
3.1   Connecting Human Motivations with First-Place
       Performance   35
3.2   Prehistoric Humans   36
3.3   Modern Theories   38
       3.3.1   Herzberg Factor   39
       3.3.2   Hawthorne Effect   40
       3.3.3   Expectancy   41
       3.3.4   Three-Dimensional Attribution   42
       3.3.5   "X" and "Y" Type Leadership   42
       3.3.6   Self-Determination   43
       3.3.7   Maslow's Human Motivation   44
3.4   Motivations in Modern Teams   48
3.5   Chapter Highlights   49

Chapter Four   Changes in Program Leadership Indicated   **51**
4.1   Traditional versus On-Step   51
4.2   Old versus Modern Leadership   53
4.3   Lessons for New Leaders   53
4.4   Business Culture Realignment   55
4.5   Evaluate and Engage with Added Human Factors   61
4.6   Leaders Must Constantly Adjust   61
4.7   Chapter Highlights   62

Chapter Five   The Impact of Motivation-Based Leadership   **63**
5.1   Improves Existing On-Step Elements   63
5.2   Guides Team Mix   65

5.3   Introduces Two-Step Execution   66
5.4   Suggests Inverted Pyramid Organization Function   66
5.5   Updates Leadership Roles   69
5.6   Provides Leadership Selection Guidance   70
5.7   Provides Guidance for Team-Member Development   71
5.8   Chapter Highlights   71

Chapter Six   Motivation Management Details   73
6.1   Benefits of Maslow Paradigm   73
      6.1.1   Applies Common Sense   73
      6.1.2   Conforms to Real Human Examples   74
      6.1.3   Guides Problem-Oriented/
              Solution-Oriented Classification   78
      6.1.4   Lessons   83
6.2   More About Self-Actualization   85
      6.2.1   A Paradox   85
      6.2.2   Source of High Fulfillment   87
6.3   Guidance for Identifying Team-Member Motivation   88
      6.3.1   Identifying Motivation Level   89
      6.3.2   When Is Self-Actualization Found?   93
      6.3.3   Making Team Assignments   95
      6.3.4   Traditional Leadership Misses Out   96
      6.3.5   New Tools Review   96
6.4   Chapter Highlights   97

Chapter Seven   More on the Two Steps to Success   99
7.1   Details Introduction   99
7.2   Step 1: Organize, Educate, Buy In   103
7.3   Step 2: Facilitate, Remove Barriers, Lead   107
7.4   Two Steps Through Program Life   108
7.5   Fulfilling Motivation Needs for Success   109
7.6   Past Successful Leadership Elements—
      The Natural Consequence   113
7.7   Chapter Highlights   113

Chapter Eight   Step 1 (Setup, Buy In): How to Do It   115
8.1   Starting a Program   115
8.2   Finding a Great Program Manager   115
8.3   Creating a Highly Effective Organization   120

	8.3.1 One Lead Per Task Team	120
	8.3.2 Leading the Task Leads	121
	8.3.3 Complete Task-Team Participation	122
	8.3.4 Well-Partitioned Task Teams	122
	8.3.5 General Operation	125
8.4	Organize for Managing Suppliers	129
8.5	Selecting Excellent Task Leads	132
8.6	Interviewing Prospective Team Members	135
8.7	Determining Best Team Mix	137
8.8	Guidelines for the Work Environment	143
	8.8.1 In-Person Communication	143
	8.8.2 Colocated Facilities	145
8.9	Additional Appeals to Motivation Needs	148
	8.9.1 Milestone Commitments, Not Just Goals	148
	8.9.2 Clarification of Roles	151
	8.9.3 Planning and Tracking Progress Successfully: The Program Plan	156
	8.9.4 Find Faults/Failures Early	159
	8.9.5 Savings with Reuse	162
	8.9.6 Understand All Contracts	165
	8.9.7 Successful Software Development	167
	8.9.8 Valuable Planning and Tracking	173
	8.9.9 Consider a Scheduler	176
	8.9.10 Applying Multiple Books	178
	8.9.11 All Motivated to Clearly Plan	181
8.10	Chapter Highlights	182
Chapter Nine	**Step 2 (Execution): How to Do It**	**185**
9.1	Essential Fulfillment of Motivation Needs During Execution	185
	9.1.1 The Application of In-Person Communication in Program Execution	186
	9.1.2 Strict Adherence to Program Plan	187
	9.1.3 Leadership Removes Barriers	192
	9.1.4 Plan Changes Only via Procedure	195
	9.1.5 Using Metrics Effectively	200
	9.1.6 Conducting Valuable Meetings	203
	9.1.7 Three Traditional Solution Levels	207
	9.1.8 Innovation—Gold at the Door	209

	9.1.9	Incorporating Team Rhythm	214
	9.1.10	Watch the Flank!	217
	9.1.11	Creating Valuable Documents	221
	9.1.12	Insist on Root Cause	228
	9.1.13	Mistakes to Avoid When Controlling Configuration	235
	9.1.14	Code of Conduct Increases Business Success	239
9.2	Motivating High Tempo		244
	9.2.1	They Are Special	244
	9.2.2	Share Early Successes	246
	9.2.3	Growing Dedication and Providing Guidance	248
9.3	Chapter Highlights		263

Chapter Ten   Program Closure **265**

10.1	Criteria	265
10.2	Is It Enough?	266
10.3	Forward Plan for Team Members	266
10.4	Chapter Highlights	268

Chapter Eleven   Building the Sponsor's Reputation **269**

11.1	Establishes a First-Place Portfolio	269
11.2	Gives Enterprise Teams Feeling of Being First Place	269
11.3	Identifies Future Leadership	270
11.4	Provides Improvements and Innovations for Future	270
11.5	Increases Morale and Allegiance	270
11.6	Demonstrates High Capability of the Brand	270
11.7	Chapter Highlights	271

Glossary **273**

Index **275**

List of Illustrations

Figure 1.	Do YOU Want to Be Part of a First-Place Program?	*xxvi*
Figure 2.	Lessons to Come Benefit Many	*xxvii*
Figure 3.	Terms Used Must Be Defined	*xxviii*
Figure 1.1	Big Difference Between the Best and Rest	2
Figure 1.2	On-Step Performance Is Special	3
Figure 1.3	On-Step Team Members Develop Valuable Attributes	3
Figure 1.4	Overview of Steps to a First-Place Program	4
Figure 1.5	Path to This Book's Query	5
Figure 1.6	Author Applied What He Observed to Work	6
Figure 1.7	Team Intensity Clarified Our Needs	7
Figure 1.8	Suspect Human Motivation Is Key	8
Figure 1.9	Program Success Needs Breakthrough	10
Figure 1.10	Modern Talent Is Lost Too Soon	12
Figure 1.11	Mimicking Military Organization Is Suboptimal	15
Figure 1.12	Military Conduct Different from Programs	16
Figure 1.13	Three Levels of Performance	20
Figure 1.14	Turnarounds Taught Success Elements	20
Figure 1.15	Success Actions Were Repeatedly Found	21
Figure 1.16	First-Place Teamwork Is Selfless	22
Figure 1.17	Programs On-Step Remain a Paradox	22
Figure 2.1	Suspected Addressing Human Motivation Is Key	26
Figure 2.2	Motivation-Based Leadership Has Favorable Consequences	26
Figure 2.3	This Book Reveals the "Secret Sauce"	27
Figure 2.4	Team Members Achieving Self-Actualization Make Sacrifices	31
Figure 3.1	What Is the Foundation for On-Step Teamwork?	36
Figure 3.2	Prehistoric Motivations Are Premature	37

Figure 3.3   Process Should Not Counter Common Sense   39
Figure 3.4   Contemporary Theories Are More Relevant   40
Figure 3.5   Maslow—Cornerstone of Modern Motivation Theory   45
Figure 3.6   Maslow Maps to Real Experience   45
Figure 3.7   Each Motivation Level Has Special Desires   46
Figure 4.1   Military Compared to Modern Programs—Very Different   52
Figure 4.2   On-Step Leaders Need Courage   54
Figure 4.3   Effect of Ignoring Motivation   56
Figure 4.4   There Are Important Factors When Managing Motivation   58
Figure 4.5   Some Lessons Are Counterintuitive   58
Figure 4.6   The PM Supports the Team   59
Figure 4.7   Self-Actualization—Developing or One of Six Destinations   61
Figure 4.8   Modern Leader's Role Is Constantly Supportive   62
Figure 5.1   Valuing Individual Motivation Is Key   63
Figure 5.2   On-Step Elements—Learned from Past   64
Figure 5.3   Teams Need Mix of Two Types   65
Figure 5.4   Two Steps to Create First-Place Program   67
Figure 5.5   The PM Works for the Teams   68
Figure 5.6   Modern Role of Leadership Expanded   70
Figure 6.1   Good Motivation Management Process
              Appeals to Common Sense   74
Figure 6.2   Motivations Differ and Evolve   75
Figure 6.3   Team Types Have Valuable Attributes   79
Figure 6.4   Team Types Have Weaknesses   79
Figure 6.5   Motivation Is Used to Sort Staff   81
Figure 6.6   Factors Pertain to All Team Members During Evaluation   83
Figure 6.7   Lead to Empower Team Members   84
Figure 6.8   Book Supplements Maslow with Six Levels of Self-Actualization   86
Figure 6.9   Facilitating Individual Motivation Allows Members
              to Be Their Best   87
Figure 6.10   Each Level Has Real Examples   90
Figure 6.11   Let's Summarize   96
Figure 7.1   Step 1—Set Up: Organize, Educate, Buy In   100
Figure 7.2   Step 2—Execution: Leadership Executes   101
Figure 7.3   Determine Status and Destination   104
Figure 7.4   Steps Change over Duration   110
Figure 7.5   Feedback Throughout Life of the Work   111
Figure 8.1   Look in Enterprise for PM   116
Figure 8.2   There Are Important Attributes the PM Must Have   117
Figure 8.3   There Is a Method to Establish Independent Pieces   123
Figure 8.4   Physically Separated Teams Must Be Highly Independent   126

Figure 8.5   Important Features When Organizing   127
Figure 8.6   Organizational Attributes for First-Place Program   128
Figure 8.7   Supplier Management Team Must Have
                 Checks and Balances   130
Figure 8.8   Communicate the Supplier Management Process   132
Figure 8.9   Best Task Leaders May Not Be Obvious   134
Figure 8.10 Our Maslow-Based Hierarchy Is a Guiding Discriminator   138
Figure 8.11 Work Content Determines Team Mix   139
Figure 8.12 Recruiting Essentials: Mix Need, Don't Assume   140
Figure 8.13 Recruiting Funnel May Be Used for Large Events   141
Figure 8.14 Mutually Identifying Motivation Is Essential   142
Figure 8.15 In-Person Communication for Fast Progress   144
Figure 8.16 Colocation Facilitates Speed and Accuracy   146
Figure 8.17 Colocated, Face-to-Face Fundamental Need   147
Figure 8.18 Commitments Are Currency of Progress   149
Figure 8.19 Clarifying Roles Increases Team Speed   152
Figure 8.20 Clearly Define Team Roles—Change with Process   153
Figure 8.21 Team-Member Responsibilities Start With Fundamentals   154
Figure 8.22 Balance Strengths of Tracking Tools   160
Figure 8.23 Planning for Success   161
Figure 8.24 Plan Program or Project to Find Faults Early   161
Figure 8.25 Detecting and Correcting Faults Early Needed
                 for First Place   163
Figure 8.26 Reuse Saving Is Often a Fleeting Promise   163
Figure 8.27 Carefully Consider Reuse   164
Figure 8.28 Written Agreements Must Be Complete and Unambiguous   166
Figure 8.29 Software Development Lead Must Be an Ambassador   168
Figure 8.30 Software Application Domains Require Specialists   170
Figure 8.31 Small Amount of Software Cost Is Coding   171
Figure 8.32 SW Development Fundamentals to Be in First Place   172
Figure 8.33 Accurate Plan Depiction—Tracking Essential   174
Figure 8.34 Consider a Scheduler: Part-Time Team Member to Professional   177
Figure 8.35 Multiple Books Can Be Used to Deliver on Time   179
Figure 8.36 "One Step at a Time"   183
Figure 9.1   Facilitate Maximum In-Person Communication   188
Figure 9.2   Program Plan Must Describe All Work   188
Figure 9.3   Program Plan = Operator's Manual   190
Figure 9.4   Leadership Identifies and Removes Delays to Progress   192
Figure 9.5   Program Plan Changes Only with Process   196
Figure 9.6   Process Required to Change Process, Design, Documents   197
Figure 9.7   Process *Input* Metrics Often More Valuable than *Output*   200

Figure 9.8   Input Metrics Often Have Higher Value   201

Figure 9.9   Smart Metrics Can Mitigate Major Cost and Schedule Losses   201

Figure 9.10   Valuable Meetings Require Preparation!   204

Figure 9.11   Strive for Simple, Multipurpose Solutions   207

Figure 9.12   Simple Is Best but Usually Hardest   208

Figure 9.13   Innovations Fuel Faster Completion and Higher Quality   210

Figure 9.14   Encourage Innovations, Process Improvements to Be First Place   212

Figure 9.15   Programs Need Common Beat   215

Figure 9.16   Watch the Flank for Undetected Risks ⇨ Issues   218

Figure 9.17   Encourage Risk Vigilance and Preparation   220

Figure 9.18   Document What's Important and Revise Per Process   222

Figure 9.19   Necessary, Succinct Documents Are Needed to Be First Place   226

Figure 9.20   Root Cause Process Must Be Performed Completely   229

Figure 9.21   Insist on Single *Root* Cause   230

Figure 9.22   Avoid Common Mistakes in Configuration Control   236

Figure 9.23   Watch Out for Configuration Gremlins   236

Figure 9.24   Build the Team Code   240

Figure 9.25   Team Ethics Is Part of Team Code   242

Figure 9.26   Point Out Start of Team Value   245

Figure 9.27   Team Dedication Fosters Special Traits   252

Figure 10.1   Program Closure Must Be Planned   266

Figure 11.1   First-Place Makes an Outstanding Enterprise   271

List of Tables

Table 8.1	Finding a Great Program Manager	119
Table 8.2	Creating a Highly Effective Organization	129
Table 8.3	Organizing for Managing Suppliers	131
Table 8.4	Selecting Excellent Task Leads	135
Table 8.5	Determining Best Team Mix	143
Table 8.6	In-Person Communication	145
Table 8.7	Colocated Facilities	148
Table 8.8	Milestone Commitments, Not Just Goals	151
Table 8.9	Clarification of Roles	155
Table 8.10	Planning and Tracking Progress Successfully	158
Table 8.11	Find Faults/Failures Early	162
Table 8.12	Savings with Reuse	165
Table 8.13	Understand All Contracts	166
Table 8.14	Successful Software Development	173
Table 8.15	Valuable Planning and Tracking	176
Table 8.16	Consider a Scheduler	178
Table 8.17	Apply Multiple Books	181
Table 9.1	Strict Adherence to Plan	191
Table 9.2	Leadership Removes Barriers	195
Table 9.3	Plan Changes Only via Procedure	199
Table 9.4	Using Metrics Effectively	202
Table 9.5	Conducting Efficient Meetings	206
Table 9.6	Three Traditional Solution Levels	209
Table 9.7	Innovation	213
Table 9.8	Incorporating Team Rhythm	217
Table 9.9	Watch the Flank	220

Table 9.10	Creating Valuable Documents	227
Table 9.11	Insist on Root Cause	234
Table 9.12	Mistakes When Controlling Configuration	238
Table 9.13	Code of Conduct Increases Business Success	243
Table 9.14	They Are Special	246
Table 9.15	Share Early Successes	248
Table 9.16	Mentoring	249
Table 9.17	Real Open Door	250
Table 9.18	Strong Dedication	252
Table 9.19	Calm and Have Their Backs	255
Table 9.20	Everyone Gets a Second Chance	257
Table 9.21	Stand Up for Them	261
Table 9.22	See in Them What They May Not	263
Table 10.1	Strict Adherence to Plan and Closure	268

Preface

From a young age, I've been intrigued by programs[1] that performed much better than others. I observed these efforts progress at a much faster rate and solve problems more quickly. The team members were assigned work they did best and enjoyed immensely. All the team members were highly satisfied with their contributions. As a result, the products developed were not only good but brilliant! They greatly advanced the capability of the enterprise and developed their technical, planning, and organizational knowledge as a result.

I have observed that some team members are more interested in thoroughly solving a problem, while others are more focused on bringing a solution to bear—and that a mixture of these two was necessary for the most successful program work. Some team members performed their hard work for basic subsistence and continued income. Some wanted a higher title or wanted to be noted as an expert in their field. Still others wanted to make a contribution to improve society. There were even some who simply wanted to integrate the social fabric of the team and help to make all team members feel happy and fulfilled.

Many times, the occurrence of such an extraordinary team has been attributed to so-called "leadership wisdom," or even just good luck, but I felt in my heart that there was some formula that might reveal why this happened and allow it to repeat, and that this formula appealed to a higher human level than just our intellectual plane—that somehow it addressed the basic motivations of modern professionals.

This formula should allow each individual to free their best creativity. It should distribute vigilance amongst all team members to look out for risks and issues. As

---

[1] As discussed in Definitions on page *xxix,* the term *programs* will be used to mean programs and/or projects.

a result, team members should not only learn what they do best but also discover any hidden talents they may have. They should be given help to develop these talents while their personal esteem is protected and they are treated fairly and are given opportunities to grow.

In this book, I've strived to find the paradigm for creating this magic. My goal is to help programs perform at a higher level in the US and around the world than ever imagined!

The use of programs is only recent. They have been in existence for about 100 years, and society is still refining their design and application.

Every program is competing, sometimes against each other in the same enterprise, sometimes against directly competing or similar efforts in their industry—all trying to be the best.

What is surprising is that, almost always, the first-place competitor is ahead of the others by a larger margin than exists between the other competitors. This phenomenon has been observed and chronicled by numerous business authors. You may have noticed this during your work history.

Most attribute this large first-place margin to one or more suspected factors: Extraordinary team member talent? Long-term team history with the customer? Special leadership wisdom? Good luck? None of these suspected causes have ever been verified, and the rationale for this exceptional performance is left unresolved. It turns out that none of these suspected factors are the reason.

This book explains how to put your program in first place. It provides the theory and the processes to do so. The guidance herein can be applied by leaders of all experience levels, and it starts working the first day it is applied. This process applies to all business genres, product types, and staff seniority levels.

By following the guidance in this book, your team will be in front—by a large margin.

Author's Intrigue

My interest in the special value of programs started early in my life. The first program team I learned about at the young age of four came from the book *Mickey Mouse and His Spaceship*.[2] I remember Chip, Dale, and Goofy spending all night designing their moon rocket. In particular, I remember staring at a cartoon of the garage they were working in, with light shining through its windows. I pondered how a team could develop something so extraordinary, a feat one individual could not do. To design a vehicle capable of landing on the moon! My early

---

[2] Werner, J. (1952). *Mickey Mouse and His Spaceship* (Disney: Mickey Mouse). Illustrated by R. H. Disney. Golden/Disney. ISBN: 9780736436335

curiosity eventually developed into a passion to understand what makes this happen and to help others around world achieve their best.

From the start of my professional career, I noted that there were program teams who performed at an acceptable level (give them a grade of C), those who performed better than average (grade of B), and those who were the best performers (grade of A) (please see Figure 1.1 on page 2 for further details). What amazed me was that A teams performed better than B teams by larger margins than the difference between B and C teams. To me this was counter-intuitive! In other competitions I have watched, first place is better than second place by small margins.

What immediately came to mind was that first-place programs might be operating with a different set of rules. They seem to be "On-Step"—a term I learned as a young boating enthusiast. On-Step meant incorporating a discretely different and superior mode of operation—no longer plowing the water but instead freely skimming over its surface. Throughout my career, I have paid close attention to what placed a program On-Step.

As my career advanced, I started to be assigned to complex aerospace programs to stop them from faltering. Usually, I started by solving embedded computer control and software development problems, but then I would be assigned to lead data system engineering, system engineering, and integration and test, and I eventually became the program manager, with a record of 100% successful programs.

My commitment was not just to stop the failures in the programs I was trying to fix, but also to bring the team up to where they had originally planned to be. This required the team to execute faster than planned to catch up to the original milestones.

My solution to achieving the high speeds needed to catch up was simply to apply those elements I had observed in other successful programs that *were* On-Step.

I later chronicled these success elements in my book entitled *Project and Program Turnaround.*[3] If you follow the recommendations in that book, you will save your failing program.

But for a program to achieve first place from the start, more is required than just executing a set of successful management elements. What appeals to the basic human motivations of the team members must be determined first, so they end up *wanting* to be in first place.

Let's face the facts of our animal origins. We are one of many life forms on this planet. Do first-place programs somehow directly appeal to our most basic

---

[3] Pavelko, T. (2017). *Project and Program Turnaround.* Boca Raton, FL: CRC Press/ Taylor & Francis Group. https://www.taylorfrancis.com/books/mono/10.1201/978 1315212746/project-program-turnaround-thomas-pavelko

human needs? Needs that our species has evolved over the last 200,000+ years? If so, what are they?

In this book, I will discuss a series of recent attempts by science to identify what motivates us to do our best in teams. I will select one theory that provides an excellent starting point for assessing the motivational needs of modern-day team members, then I'll show how to use this information to identify team members and partition the team, determine team mix, select team leadership, and manage the team to be in first place. I will also describe the necessary changes needed in the daily activities of modern leadership, as well as the changes needed in the relationship between leaders and their reports.

As an added dividend, the analytical and process steps you will learn will provide you with the tools to identify and develop the more hidden talents in your team members. The results of this added benefit can be highly beneficial to team members, team leadership, the program, and the sponsoring enterprise.

The guidance that will be presented applies to all business genres, including commercial, government, municipal, educational, and nonprofit. The task being pursued could be, for example, improving test scores for fourth graders, reducing overhead costs for a nonprofit, building a satellite, and many more. This wide range of applications all highly benefit from the information and guidance in this book.

By recognizing and managing motivation, team-member satisfaction will be greatly improved. This kind of satisfaction fosters long-term dedication to the business area and the enterprise. Even 10 years after completion, team members from first-place, On-Step program teams plan reunions and enjoy reminiscing about their success.

Ultimately, it is fun being on a first-place program. It is usually the result of extraordinarily successful team organization, team execution, business achievements, and even technical breakthroughs. Team members are enthusiastic, proud, and end up learning more about successful program dynamics and themselves while remaining vigilant for dangers that can cause them to fall behind.

Being on a first-place team gives us the high state of professional fulfillment we all strive for! Please read on to learn how to achieve this.

Who Benefits from Reading This?

The Frank Question!

Do You Want to Lead or Be a Member of a First-Place Program?

I have asked this question many times in the conferences and seminars I've given, and I've been surprised by the guarded responses I've received.

One might expect the leaders and members of a new program to enthusiastically raise their hands and say, "Yes!" But this doesn't happen. Many in the audience hesitate and contemplate. They are careful about showing a response. Are they being asked to commit to a new approach too soon?

Some listeners believe any talk about applying successful leadership elements or motivation management is somehow a disguise for simply working harder. Some may believe the programs I describe as being turned around simply received extra resources from the enterprise. Again, they may believe the team worked harder, not smarter. Others believe that first-place programs are just lucky. They think that the team members on these programs must have had extraordinary talent. Maybe their customer is sympathetic. Or they believe there were gigantic safety margins in the initial cost, schedule, and performance promises.

Team leaders and participants are afraid of failing. Many of them would rather refrain from what they might feel is a "touchy-feely" approach. To them this approach may appear to be too risky. They often believe it is safer to stick to the conventional processes and metrics.

Many believe that "good enough" performance is acceptable. They know that the program they are supporting is bringing profits to their enterprise, and they are comfortable knowing the work of their team is deemed acceptable. They feel confident in following the known and simple series of execution steps the other programs have used. They may ask, "Why is it so important to be in first place?" (see Figure 1).

In this book, you will learn that being in first place does not require harder work, but rather more consistent thought. It requires frequent examination of each team member's motivational needs and an honest and current evaluation of team progress.

Executing a first-place program requires not simply following a series of standard planning steps, then assuming that your planning obligation is complete. You can participate in and manage an acceptable program in this way, but its performance will not put you in first place amongst your competition. To be a first-place program, its plan must be adaptable and updated throughout its entire lifetime.

Does being the first-place contender sound achievable? It is, and this should be the desire of every program team member.

Good for Many

This book should be of high value to a wide range of reader backgrounds (see Figure 2). The lessons in this book are essential for any program managers who want their team to be in first place.

Do YOU Want to Be Part of a First-Place Program?

- Afraid you must work harder?
- Prefer simple, nonrecurrent leadership steps?
- Believe #1 is just good luck?
  - Extraordinary team talent?
  - Special customer relationship?
  - Easy schedule, requirements, etc.?
- One of the best is ok.
- Just be firm, stick to the numbers, no "touchy-feely"?
- Don't want to fail using a new approach?
- We're not psychologists!

Longer hours . . . or more thought needed?

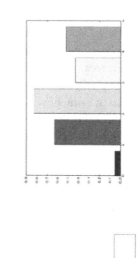

Figure 1. This book is designed to help the reader support and/or lead a first-place program. The author is surprised to observe that many participants are coy about being in first place.

Lessons to Come Benefit Many, Including:

- **Leaders and team members striving to put their program in first place**
- **Leaders/executives of suppliers to programs**
- **Leaders/executives of programs falling behind**
- **Less experienced team members learning to become leaders**
- **Students of program success**
- **Business students**
- **Students of human behavior**

> ***Breadth highlights the appeal to basic humanity.***

Figure 2.   The many parties that benefit from the lessons herein.

This content should also be valuable to individual team members. They can use this information to understand their driving motivations and support their leadership with their growth. In addition, it is very helpful if they plan to eventually be a leader.

This book gives executive management insight into what their program managers must do to be in first place. They can use this information to mentor program managers, especially those within organizations that need to improve.

From reading this book, the customer will better understand the approach and processes used to provide them the very best service and will give them insight on how to help accommodate this approach.

Subcontractors, vendors, and support teams will better support their customers with knowledge of how these organizations achieve first place. They may derive benefits for their own enterprise as well by studying and using this approach.

Students of business who read this book will develop a head start by learning how to lead teams to a high level of success and avoid repeating traditional and often very expensive mistakes.

Students of general motivational psychology will also gain from this book. The highly pragmatic and competitive business arena can assist the development of human motivation theory by demonstrating what makes teams perform with a high level of productivity.

Any person interested in learning how to make teams perform their best and be in first place will benefit from this book. The paradigms and processes provided are proven and successful!

Terms Used Must Be Defined

TERM	DEFINITION
Program	An organization to create a new product or revise an existing product or process. Usually a 3- to 500-member core team, often with additional supplier headcount.
Enterprise	Organization, company, corporation, investment group, etc. the program exists in and is usually funded by.
Program Plan	Documented plan for the program. Includes performance, schedule, cost, and risk requirements. Rigorously kept current via process.
Customer	Individual or agency that has requested the program results. Usually the source of funding.
Program Manager (PM)	Person who organizes and leads the program. Point of contact in the enterprise and for the customer for status.
Program Leadership	The leaders of the program tasks and other support organizations. Usually report directly to the program manager.
Supplier	Parts or service vendor (catalog source) or subcontractor.
Program Commitment(s)	Accomplishments the program promises to achieve. Sometimes one or more of a series of steps to complete.

Figure 3. Terms used to describe programs have yet to be universally defined. These definitions will be used in this book.

Definitions

The terms *program* and *project* are not universally defined (see Figure 3). For example, in some industries a project amongst the employees refers to a home task, such as painting the bathroom. In these particular industries, team efforts are usually referred to as programs. Yet, the "P" in the world-renowned PMI[4] organization stands for "Project." There are some texts that have defined their own hierarchy of tasks, projects, programs, and more. This is valuable within the bounds of their text, but they are not universally recognized.

In this book, the terms *program* and *project* are equivalent and interchangeable. Both labels refer to a team of people who are creating something. This team can be developing a new product, concept, process, study, or more. Or they can be making a sizable change or revision to one of these. Throughout, we will use *program* as meaning both programs and projects.

A program team is defined in this book as containing from three to 500 team members. Larger teams are usually divided into multiple programs.

This maximum size limit is imposed because larger efforts usually require additional layers of leadership between the program manager and the individual contributors. This renders it almost impossible for the program manager to conduct direct contact with team members—contact which is needed for the program to stay in first place.

The age, generation, or cultural background of the team members is irrelevant to the success of motivation management. The human substance addressed in the analysis and processes discussed in this book is common to all humanity.

Summary

- Programs are recent constructs.
- Every program competes externally and internally.
- First-place programs are more ahead of second-place than second are of third, etc.
- This book shows how to be in first place.
- This book benefits team members throughout the range of work genres, team sizes, team-member backgrounds, organizational roles, and more.

Thomas Pavelko
Sunnyvale, CA
May 14, 2021

---

[4] Project Management Institute

Acknowledgments

I wish to thank those individuals who devoted extensive time and effort to review my manuscript and provide highly valuable feedback. They include Professor John Nicholas, PhD; Ronald Watson, MD; and Francis Eynon.

In addition, I wish to thank those executive managers who demonstrated elements of successful motivational management during their brilliant leadership. They include Daniel Tellep, Clarence Johnson, Alfred Smith, Manuel Dimiceli, and Michael Henshaw.

Finally, I want to offer special thanks to John Wyzalek, PhD, of Taylor & Francis and Theron Shreve of DerryField Publishing Services for supporting this book. And most important, to Susan Culligan and Marje Pollack, two outstanding editors/typesetters for their invaluable expertise and patience.

It has been a pleasure and honor to work with everyone.

About the Author

Thomas Pavelko worked for Lockheed Martin for 37 years. During that time, he recruited and led teams to develop embedded high-performance computer systems to perform critical flight controls. He was promoted to System Engineering Manager, Program Manager, and Program Director. He reported to a wide range of divisions including Satellites, Missiles, R&D, Electronics, Propulsion, Advanced Astronautics, Commercial Space, Missile Defense, Human Spaceflight, and Advanced Development Programs (Skunk Works).

He was assigned to large commercial and government programs falling behind, often becoming the new Program Manager. He was directly accountable to customer and corporate leadership for program success. All programs were completed successfully.

Awards

Lockheed Engineer of the Year
Lead Engineer of the Month—Space Systems Division
NOVA Award (Lockheed's highest)—Team Leadership
Team Excellence—Airborne Laser
Team Work Excellence—Commercial Space Systems
Mission Success & Program Excellence—Commercial Space Systems
Special Award—Leading Determination of Orion Reference Mission
Orion Commendation for successful Abort System Launch
Orion Commendation for successful Flight Software PDR
Numerous special awards and performance bonuses—classified programs

Education

Physics	University of California, Riverside
Program Manager 101–102 Series	Santa Clara University
Building Effective Leaders	Paxton Enterprises, San Francisco
Interpersonal Management	Learning International, Stanford, CT
High-Impact Relationships	Linkage Inc., San Francisco, CA
Graduate—Lockheed Management	Santa Clara University, CA
Supervisor Leadership	Lockheed Corp., Sunnyvale, CA
Graduate of Business and Finance Series	DeAnza and Foothill Colleges, CA

Writing, Speaking, Public Service

Author: *Project and Program Turnaround,* Taylor & Francis, 2017

Webinars: IT Metrics and Productivity Institute, Project Management Institute (PMI) worldwide, PMI Book of the Month, IEEE

Public speaking: Keynote—Silicon Valley PMI Symposium, local PMI Chapters, Silicon Valley IEEE, Professional and Technical Consultants Association, San Jose State University staff

Volunteer: BioDesign (Stanford Medical), Fogarty Institute (El Camino Hospital), Heartland Hospice

Licenses

Single-Engine Airplane, Multiengine Airplane, and Glider Pilot
Airline Transport Pilot
Certificated Flight Instructor for airplanes and instruments

Personal

Enjoys traveling the world, writing, and performing music.

Chapter One

Program Performance Breakthrough

1.1 Paradox Observed—Being "On-Step"

You have likely observed three distinct levels of program performance:

1. The first level contains programs that are doing just fine. They are usually a valuable part of their enterprise portfolio. They are making acceptable profits and achieving their commitments. They are frequently referred to as "well run."
2. A second level contains those programs that are, unfortunately, failing. Most people who observe these failing attempts assume that their failure is the result of some kind of basic deficiency. They believe someone will eventually determine what the deficiency is and take care of it.
3. But there is a third category that is both unquestionably evident, yet almost mystifying. This category contains those programs that are far ahead of their second-place competitors—further ahead than the performance differences between second and third place, third and fourth place, etc. As some business authors have written, they are typically a large 10% to 20% ahead of second place via various measurements. Programs in this category almost seem to possess some kind of special grace. You may have encountered teams in this category.

These high-performance programs, which the author refers to as being On-Step, appear to be performing at a discretely much higher level than their competitors. This higher level of performance is achieved with little or no additional energy applied (see Figures 1.1 and 1.2).

It is interesting that being On-Step does not require the program team to work harder. Most first-place, On-Step teams contain team members who are average performers. The members on these teams typically have had little or no prior experience with their customer. There are apparently no circumstances that give them an advantage. Yet, teams On-Step perform better than the rest by a large margin. This book will reveal what their advantage is.

Team members on an On-Step program are usually seen to demonstrate exceptional dedication to the team. Almost all members on such a team are ready to perform any task necessary to keep the team in first place. This includes consistently improving the process they are using and always looking for innovations to simplify their work (see Figure 1.3). And of note, pointless confrontations between team members, demagoguery, or individual laziness are rarely tolerated by the team. In addition, this highly creative environment often becomes a proving ground for candidate supplemental processes to stay On-Step.

Big Difference Between the Best and Rest

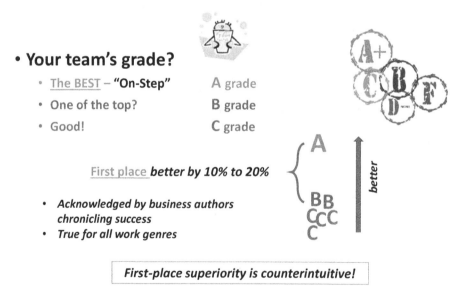

- **Your team's grade?**
  - The BEST – "On-Step"   A grade
  - One of the top?   B grade
  - Good!   C grade

First place **better by 10% to 20%**

- *Acknowledged by business authors chronicling success*
- *True for all work genres*

First-place superiority is counterintuitive!

Figure 1.1 Many authors and industrial leaders have observed that first-place programs are way ahead of competitors and similar programs. What is unique?

On-Step Performance Is Special

ON-STEP!

COMMON WORKS

- **Conservative ROI**
- **Predictable cadence**
- **Most programs and projects**

- **Discreetly faster progress**
- **Superior results**
- **Little added energy**
- **Smarter, not harder?**

Figure 1.2   A watercraft On-Step, skimming on the surface, makes faster progress than one plowing through the water. This is achieved with the right design, not brute power.

On-Step Team Members Develop Valuable Attributes

- **Personal activities take back seat.**
- **Near-term professional gains secondary.**
- **Forges trusted team interdependencies.**
- **Strives for shortest path to completion.**
- **Shares task with best skilled specialists.**
- **Learns more information needed to be successful.**
- **Honors innovations to finish faster.**
- **Will not accept defeat, invents solutions.**
- **Adheres to team code of behavior.**

Figure 1.3   On-Step team members make special sacrifices, are highly inventive, and bond closely with their team members.

What do these programs in this special category do to be in first place, to be On-Step? What are they doing the others are not?

This book identifies what is needed to be On-Step, to be in first place, and shows how to apply them. Figure 1.4 is an introductory summary of these actions, and they will be discussed in further detail throughout this book.

Since the start of the Industrial Revolution in the early to mid-19th century, there have been an assortment of processes and other management elements available to lead the newly conceived programs. Over the decades, successful leaders have chosen to apply a subset of these to perform their best. The author has observed what best practices were found to work well and applied them when leading the recovery of programs that were in trouble. As a result, he was able to successfully save and lead the completion of work for every program he was assigned. Figures 1.5 and 1.6 are a summary of the series of actions that have led to this book.

Overview of Steps to a First-Place Program

- Select PM and initial staff.
- Team review motivation definitions and theory.
- Draft program guidelines.
- Draft organization, team functions, and responsibilities.
- Identify team-member motivation levels.
- Select task leads.
- Educate leads on motivation management.
- Leads document task steps and durations with schedular.
- Create draft program plan.
- Create draft risk analysis plan.
- Estimate resources + facilities.
- Integrate master schedule, determine kick-off.
- Recruit remaining team members.
- Teams review and update program plan.
- Kick off work.
- Feedback Step 2 results to Step 1.
- Update designs, processes, documentation via process.
- Complete work via predetermined closure criteria.

Figure 1.4   These are the basic steps toward building a first-place, On-Step program.

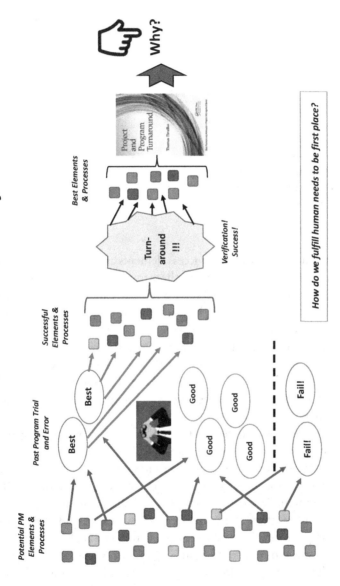

Figure 1.5 Determining the classic program organizational and process success elements included observing what had worked in the past, then testing these elements during the rigors of rejuvenating efforts that were faltering. (*Source:* Book cover image reproduced from Pavelko, T. (2017). *Project and Program Turnaround.* Boca Raton, FL: CRC Press/Taylor & Francis Group, with permission.)

Author Applied What He Observed to Work

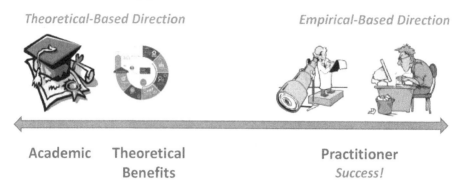

Theoretical-Based Direction   *Empirical-Based Direction*

Academic   Theoretical   Practitioner

Benefits   *Success!*

Figure 1.6 Theoretical justification for organizational and process elements that were successful was certainly required, but acceptance only occurred after the element proved itself in use.

But what in human nature makes the success elements and processes the author has observed so successful? How did they put these troubled programs On-Step?

It is noteworthy that these traditional success elements apply to all team member backgrounds, ages, and generations. There are currently business improvement curriculums that attempt to identify the unique preferences and motivations of the different modern generations. However, the elements provided in this book are derived from our universal basic humanity. These elements are invariant among age groups. Examples include the enhanced communication afforded by in-person team-member contact or the high value of a program team divided into subteams that are highly independent.

The programs the author assumed and was able to save by applying these observed success elements were big, complex, and deeply in trouble (see Figure 1.7). They were formally reviewed weekly by high-level enterprise executives and initially given the unforgiving company rating of RED until back on track. A rating of RED brought probing, even humiliating, but appropriate criticism from the top.

The team members on these programs were bright, eager, and enthusiastic. In most cases their performances were very good but not highly exceptional. They fought to find ways to reduce the time and resources needed to complete the work and carefully abandoned low-value processes and protocols—all while maintaining high product quality.

One such program was valued at over $1 billion. The author was given program leadership mid–calendar year and was informed that the government would cancel the program if it did not achieve a major demonstration

Team Intensity Clarified Our Needs

My Job:

START

WE'RE **BEHIND!**
(Performance, Cost, Schedule, Risk)

Call Tom ...

Fight to Survive!!

SUCCESS!

Figure 1.7 The team environment in a program that is being rejuvenated is intense and pragmatic. It quickly filters out what organizational and process elements are most successful.

milestone by New Year's. This critical milestone was achieved in December by employing observed traditional program success elements. (They will be elaborated on in detail later in this book, along with the rationale that explains why they are successful.) For this program, their application resulted in reorganizing both the integration and test team and the software team and assembling a new program plan including establishing a new integration plan and test flow, updating schedules, redefining the work breakdown, assigning new task leads, and more.

One of the purposes of this book is to find the human basis for these successful management elements (see Figure 1.8). Finding this not only adds to the credibility of these known success elements, but also shows more broadly the way to organize and lead programs to be highly successful and in first place.

Both leading and being a member of a first-place program does take courage. As a first-place contender, you will be admired but sometimes targeted. Leadership must have the courage to immediately attempt implementing good ideas from employees. Some proposed changes may be unconventional, and the program may sometimes need to take a sizable planning step backward before it can then be able to take the much-needed big steps forward.

Leadership may sometimes find powerful executive managers asking why they don't see immediate progress. These executives may recall prior leaders who showed quick, visible progress immediately, but they may not have appreciated that often, in these cases, further details were needed for the long-term work plan that followed.

Suspect Human Motivation Is Key

- Lead with "pull," not "push."
- Supercharges team enthusiasm.
- Increases team and leadership happiness.
- Increases team productivity.
- Guides leadership selections.
- Guides efficient task–team mix.
- Puts an effort On-Step!

Paradigm needed for applying human motivation

Figure 1.8 Appealing to the motivational needs of the team members has long been suspected to be keyed toward being in first place. But this has often been relegated to just "leadership wisdom." This book attempts to provide well-supported motivation structure.

Planning, organizing, and staffing must be thorough from the start. Assessing the core motivations of the individual team members, as you will read, is an additional major involvement during this time. Thorough planning of what is essential always shortens the total duration of the program. Once underway, the execution of a thoroughly planned program will be at a high, On-Step rate. Fast and thorough progress toward completion will be demonstrated, and usually, critical executive attention will then subside.

1.2 Current Success Level

1.2.1 Struggle to Be Better

The development and use of programs to build complicated systems and solve complex problems is only recent. Studying these organizations in depth and learning how to improve their performance is in early stages.

Most readers have been members of our modern industrialized society since their birth. Understandably, we may not realize that planning program work and documenting/tracking it with well-known work products such as organization charts, work breakdown structures, cost and schedule plans, metrics, etc. have been used for only about 100 years.

Society's attempts to improve program performance is still starting. These attempts include experimenting with new management and process emphasis.

Figure 1.9 summarizes documented program performance history. Listed are the methods, attributes, and leadership styles that many modern businesses are employing to improve performance.

What is surprising is that only 75% of programs in the world successfully complete. This low percentage is, of course, disappointing. This does not mean that the remaining 25% are abandoned, but programs in this category have at least stopped and/or gone through one or more reorganizations and replannings. These revisions may include creating a new program plan, changing leadership, re-examining scope of commitments, and more.

Furthermore, of the 75% of programs that do complete, about 65% of them do not achieve all their goals. In other words, these 65% do not achieve what they promised they would do in one or more of the areas of achieving product performances, completing promised milestone work as scheduled, executing within cost restraints, and managing risk.

It must be asserted that the term "goal" will rarely be used in this book. Instead, the term "commitment" is used, the difference being that the latter is a promise, not just an optimistic desire. A commitment is hard to develop and stand behind. Establishing realistic commitments and then achieving them takes

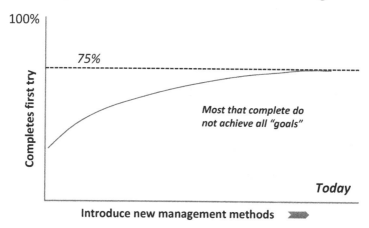

Program Success Needs Breakthrough

100%

75%

Completes first try

*Most that complete do
not achieve all "goals"*

Today

Introduce new management methods ➤➤

Good management remedies not enough

Methods: Waterfall, Critical Path Management, Critical Chain Management, Six Sigma, Earned Value, Lean, Agile, Scrum
Attributes: Excellent communication skills, share clear vision, positive attitude, integrity, competence, calm deposition, problem solving, team building, delegator and decision maker
Styles: Pacesetting, authoritative, affiliative, coaching, coercive, democratic, hybrids

Figure 1.9   First-time program success must improve. This low success rate reflects that principles for complex programs are still evolving.

practice. Leadership must understand and be prepared to forgive commitments that are sincerely asserted after thorough planning but still are not achieved. Successfully completing a well-described piece of work by a promised time is partially dependent on the amount of estimating experience the team member has. Leadership must work with team members to point out where their estimation mistakes occur and to improve their future commitments.

Fundamentally, a good commitment is based on first completely itemizing the work to be done, then adding up the time required for each piece. A discount may be carefully applied for overlapping tasks. If uncertain about the details of the work being planned, the team member should consult with others who have completed similar work. They should compare their own estimate with how long it took these others to complete, then a safety margin should be added to this draft time estimate. An initial margin frequently used is 20% of the initial estimate.

The size of this margin will vary depending on the degree of familiarity the estimator has with the work and the complexity of the work being scheduled.

Usually, for more complicated work, the uncertainty about its completion time is greater, and thus a larger schedule margin must be applied.

If, when the work is executed, the team member exceeds the estimated completion duration, plus schedule margin, they must devote the extra work hours needed to achieve their committed milestone. Team members working on a first-place program, particularly when the team endures the extra uncertainty of developing a new product, must be aware of the potential need to work these extra hours.

Achieving planned milestones on time must be valued as an imperative for both the team as a whole and the team individuals. The work completion times of each team must be synchronized with the completion times for the other teams for programs to complete quickly. Accurate synchronization is necessary for the program to assume and remain in first place.

There are numerous novel management methods that have been developed in recent years and that are actively promoted. Many focus on one of a number of specific needs to manage a team. Some methods are designed to know what the next important task is along the line of tasks that drive the completion date. Some emphasize reducing the cost of development. Some even identify and periodically review the completion of small pieces of work that are accomplished by colocated teams over short periods of time. Most of these methods do improve the performance of the program—many of these improvements are small, but every improvement is of value.

Some of these program management enhancements require a strict series of steps the user must follow. They often further invite the user to purchase special reading material, seminars, posted reminders, and other aids. Many times, the names of these new methods are quoted in the annual report of the enterprise using them. This may partially be an attempt by executive management to demonstrate to their investors and business partners that their processes are up to date. It is instructive to observe that many times these references and the performance improvements they were designed to provide are not discussed in following years. The author fears that many of these suggested enhancements offer hope for improvements in team performance by suggesting a novel process. In many cases, a concise description of what these methods are remedying and how their approach was derived is not presented.

More important, there is very little *analysis* of what was commonly used in past extraordinarily successful programs. Excellent books have chronicled the characteristics of these programs, but what leadership approach was common amongst them that made them that way? What are the basics of getting the best performance from a human team and team participant? Is it important for a program to be On-Step? Is there a theoretical starting point for evaluating these basics? Is there a paradigm that describes basic human motivation and its need to be fulfilled? If so, what is it?

1.2.2 Why Let the Best Go?

The average lifetime of professionals in our world is growing. For a US male it is now 77 years, for a female, 81 years. Fifty years ago, the average for a US male was only 71 years.

The long-standing retirement age of 65 may now be too young. Some enterprises and their leadership are starting to believe that professionals with extraordinary talent and at the peak of their performance are retiring too soon. This includes professionals from a wide variety of expertise. But most disturbing is that many of these professionals *want* to retire, despite their passion for their profession (see Figure 1.10).

Somehow, for many, their work experience has become abusive and disappointing. Often high-performance experts in medicine, business, engineering, leadership, etc. comment, "It's time to get off the treadmill," "It's time to enjoy my life," "I want to stop fighting the war," "Let the younger folks take over."

Modern Talent Is Lost Too Soon

- **Physicians**
  - **Medical groups**
  - **Armed forces**
- **Senior Engineers**
  - **Material specialists**
  - **EEs**
  - **New system concepts**
- **Business Professionals**
  - **Legal**
  - **Contracts specialist**
- **Leadership**
  - **Enterprise**
  - **Program and project**
  - **Training**

"It's time . . ."

"Get off the treadmill . . ."

"Enjoy life . . ."

"Let young, fresh thinking in . . ."

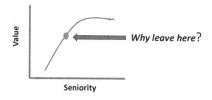

| **Why lose professionals near their best?** |

Figure 1.10 With the recent extension of humanity's average lifetime, traditional retirement ages may be too early. Many senior team members are at the peak of their ability. Often, standardizing a time for highly valuable talent to completely leave an enterprise results in a profound loss to both the organization and the team member.

What is wrong with the work environment that strongly motivates them to leave? Is there simply a natural tendency toward exhaustion in experienced professionals, or are they being repelled by under-appreciative leadership in the organization they are serving?

There are arguments that senior employees eventually reach compensation levels that are hard to justify. But if their compensation becomes so high, are not their contributions worth it? Is not their employer receiving experience-based value they cannot achieve with lower compensation?

Why can't highly experienced professionals be given the opportunity to continue to perform the work they love to do? Many senior professionals possess uniquely potent knowledge, derived from their long tenure. Can the sponsoring organizations, for example, regularly facilitate at least part-time work for these professionals, with compensation to fortify their retirement income?

But the question that remains is why do excellent senior professionals often become enthusiastic about ceasing involvement in work that they had loved all their lives? What has become missing in their professional environment? Not solving this problem is resulting in a major opportunity loss in our society.

While looking for what motivates human teams to perform their best, we should also look for ways to motivate highly experienced professionals to stay involved.

1.2.3 Program Use History

Some features of current programs are not obvious. These features should be understood when determining how to improve performance:

Original Structure Based on the Military

Our first human organizations that included standard reporting structures and rules were our military structures. The application of these structures started thousands of years BC. Although it may seem surprising, military organizations in the past had a more complete structure and were more consistent and complex than those organizations used to manage, say, the building of the Egyptian Pyramids, the Chinese Great Wall, and even the American Transcontinental Railroad.

The design of military leadership is based on a top-down flow of responsibility and authority. Orders are sent down from the top of the leadership pyramid, and leaders are solely responsible for determining the strategy and direction of the team. There is little planning feedback, trades of options, or other strategy development between the officers and their soldiers.

Because important commands and organizational decisions for the military are made in a threatening environment, they have to be generated and distributed quickly. Military leaders have little time for trading alternatives and fine-tuning the solution. Often decisions are approximate and suboptimal, knowing the alternative of a late decision will be much worse. Promotions of rank in the military are highly based on demonstrated strong, top-down leadership ability and the willingness to make decisions quickly.

Fighting a war is expensive. The first priority is given to protecting the troops and prevailing. Therefore, instigating ways of reducing cost is often a secondary priority when planning. Cost reductions are most often achieved via restrictions from a military's sponsor, usually a government.

As programs started to develop, they copied the organizations and processes used by the military. This approach remains to be of value for companies providing goods to the military. It allows the military customer to better understand the organization of the supplying company and how they planned their work. This approach also helps the program to identify its counterparts in the military organization.

But an important fact must be recognized. The missions of modern programs and the mission of military organizations are very different. The military must usually very quickly choose one of a number of reasonable plans. A civilian program, on the other hand, must take more time to evaluate the range of options, analyzing them with more in-depth techniques, to determine the most efficient and competitive plan forward. Overall strategy and next steps must be determined promptly, but usually not as quickly as needed for military action.

In addition, team-member motivations in a program must be appealed to, to induce high creativity and to convince individuals to do their best. This is much different from the motivation paths used in the military to follow orders.

Military leadership appreciates these functional differences and the need for a different organizational approach to develop new products. This is one of the reasons that the military turns to civilian program-based organizations to innovate and develop their new systems.

Figure 1.11 shows how the traditional top-down organization used for many programs copies what has been successfully used in the military. Figure 1.12 summarizes the differences in what drives civilian programs versus military organizations.

Application Is Only Recent

Most of the associated planning and management tools we use today were developed during or after World War II.

The designs of the organizations and the leadership processes applied to large public works before the 20th century were often ad hoc and inconsistent. For example,

Mimicking Military Organization Is Suboptimal

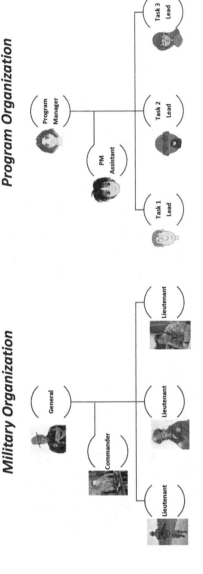

Military Organization

- Success organization for thousands of years.
- Decisions need to be made quickly.
- Speed valued over analytical depth.
- Talent assumed uniform at each level.
- Participants ordered to do what they may not want to.
- Orders may be given without rationale.
- Cost usually secondary.
- Defending homeland, fighting a war!

Program Organization

- Organizations recent and evolving.
- More time available to evaluate/decide.
- Poorly supported decisions discouraged.
- Members at one level each evaluated differently.
- Participants best motivated by "pull."
- Participants may debate direction.
- Cost is important.
- Building a new concept for the first time!

Figure 1.11 A program strictly mimicking the military-based organizational approach and processes will often result in acceptable work. But a modern program wanting to be in first place has different needs and benefits from a different approach.

Military Conduct Different from Programs

MILITARY	PROGRAM
Decisions made quickly to win and minimize human casualties.	Time taken for complete analysis before decision.
Decisions sometimes made with minimal data.	Premium placed on evaluating all accessible data before deciding.
Prompt decisions often valued over deep analysis.	Decisions without considering all supporting data are discouraged.
Strict enlisted person–officer distinction.	Hourly–salaried relationship less distinctive in successful organizations.
Standard organizational granularity and structure.	Organization structures more varied.
Assumed uniform capability in each level of organization.	Team members in each level of organization assumed different and unique.
Participants motivated by strict rules of conduct (orders).	Participants motivated by fulfilling developing self-actualization. Buy-in is needed for first-place performance.
Promotion based on seniority and leadership skills.	Promotion based on work capability and contributions and often less on leadership aptitude.
Promotion usually within officer or enlisted groups.	Promotion may bridge salaried–hourly divide.
Primary success measurements include full completion; cost is often secondary regard.	Success measured by high value from low cost, short schedule time, and small risk.
All physiological needs provided by the organization.	Participants provide their own physiological needs: shelter, food, transportation, safety at home.
Direction from superiors must be accepted (orders).	Participants may discuss and compromise direction from superiors.

Figure 1.12 Military conduct differs in many ways from modern programs.

pharaohs built the Great Pyramids of Egypt around 2500 BC, but records show that there were only four, mostly independent, managers responsible for its construction, one for each of its four faces.

In 2008 BC the Great Wall of China was constructed. Historical data reveals that the workforce was divided into three groups: soldiers, common people, and criminals. Otherwise, there were no further divisions of the work or the labor force. There was no master plan or work schedules. Millions of workers were simply ordered to complete their assigned work en masse until the wall was complete. In no case was a single manager assigned to lead the effort. There was no evidence of well-documented organization with rules of responsibility and authority, detailed planning, schedules, or systematic monitoring of progress.

In the 19th century, program planning and management started to emerge in the United States. Examples of large, complex programs include the Transcontinental Railroad and the rebuilding of the Southern states after the devastation of the American Civil War. But budgets were often open-ended, and schedules were seldom monitored or enforced. Methods to accurately predict the scope of the work and the resources needed to complete it had not yet been developed.

It was not until the 20th century that creation of programs and their management began to become a defined and repeatable discipline. In 1917, Henry Gantt created the first scheduling diagram. One of the first times the Gantt schedule was implemented was for the building of the Hoover Dam in 1931. Today, many programs use the Gantt Chart for planning and progress monitoring. Henry Gantt has been heralded as being one of the founding fathers of modern program management.

The Critical Path technique used to predict how long some work will take to complete was developed by DuPont in 1957 to help manage the complexities of shutting down chemical plants for routine maintenance. The development of the popular PERT (Program Evaluation Review Technique) planning depiction was sponsored by the US Navy to analyze the tasks needed to complete the Polaris submarine-launched missile program in the 1950s.

In 1962, the Department of Defense mandated that the WBS (Work Breakdown Structure) be used in all of its future programs.

In the 1980s, the focus was on the reduction of uncertainty for estimates of both the functions of completed products and the development resources needed to create them. Rigorous risk-management processes were also developed during this time.

In the 1990s, the program management emphasis was more on simultaneity—that is, performing multiple tasks at the same time to reduce time to market.

The development of today's program management techniques is generally focused in three areas. First, adaptation—that is, one program organization and management method does not fit all. Each program must adapt to achieve highest productivity. Second, strategic thinking—that is, the program management practices chosen must be highly connected with the business strategy. Third, globalization—more and more program content is being carried out by teams from different parts of the world.

It should be clear to the reader that program management techniques are still in a high rate of evolution and development and are not just being fine tuned. Many business management professionals, including the author, believe the evolution of these techniques is still in the early stages. The observation that the performance of first-place programs are so very far ahead of their other contenders is an example of this absence of process maturity.

Military program paradigms had been the starting point for many of today's program management techniques, partially because the military was the first customer for highly complex systems. Many of these systems were needed urgently, some recently to mitigate the Cold War. Cost was an important, but often secondary, factor to consider.

But, as has been stated, the missions of military programs and modern-day civilian programs are very different. To achieve high team performance, including lower cost, programs are starting to address the broad range of individual human needs in their teams.

1.3 Past Successful Program Elements

1.3.1 Program Success Elements

The author's greatest satisfaction is achieved from helping programs in the United States and the world perform their best. This is his self-actualization, a motivation category that will be defined and applied in following chapters.

The power of program teams first started inspiring the author at age 4. His mind was on fire, asking how a team of regular characters could create something as magnificent as, say, a moon rocket. Eventually, finding how to capture the creative magic from a team of people became his lifelong passion.

The author's working life started as a paperboy, then installing TVs, scooping ice cream, throwing luggage into airliners, assisting university scientists with research, and supporting a small medical startup before arriving at Lockheed Aircraft, now Lockheed Martin. He was motivated by finding how to assemble and manage high-performance development teams to end the Cold War.

After leaving his 37-year career at Lockheed, he wanted to chronicle the organizational elements and execution processes he had observed in highly successful programs during his professional experiences. He had implemented these success elements to successfully turn troubled programs around. The resulting manuscript was meant just for his own reference. But it turned into a book.

Figure 1.7 summarized what his primary task became later in his career.

Typically, a program would start with well-defined contracts and intentions. The desire to fulfill the needs and desires of the customer was always the first priority.

But sometimes a program would fall behind the plan in one or more of the four major performance areas—achieving the promised product performances, staying within planned cost limits, achieving schedule commitments, and managing risks/issues.

The author was assigned programs that were doing poorly. His early engineering expertise had been developing onboard computer systems to control missions and gather data. Developing these systems required understanding the design and operational concept of the system being developed. Many of the programs falling behind were doing so due to software development problems. Therefore, selecting the author to help given his background was an appropriate step. The author would often eventually be asked to manage system engineering, integration and test, and product support, and finally be assigned to be the program manager.

1.3.2 Elements When On-Step

As illustrated in Figure 1.13, when you are falling behind in a race, much of the pack is in front of you. If you want to move up to first place, you must travel faster than your competitors.

Figure 1.14 illustrates program performance falling behind and lists the options to remedy it. Falling behind can be due to any one or a combination of not adhering to the promised schedules, overrunning cost projections, not achieving product performance commitments, or being too risky.

As shown, there are three basic ways program performance can be remedied:

1. One is to allow the slipping to continue unsolved. The team will of course slip their final delivery date. The customer might forgive them for this delinquent outcome, but that is unlikely. It is possible that the original estimates of promised performances, delivery milestones, and estimated resources needed were in error.

2. A second option is to correct the program enough so that it will not fall further behind. The team can take pride in stopping further damage; however, this remedy is often still inadequate. The final delivery date remains delayed. Even if the customer accepts this solution, they will remember this deficiency, and, based on this disappointing performance, they may not be able to justify selecting this team for future business.

Three Levels of Performance

A. <u>Doing well</u>, with typical challenges

B. <u>Extraordinary</u>—On-Step
   A. **10%–20% ahead of 2nd place**
   B. **But makeup same as for A and C**

C. <u>Falling Into Trouble</u>

Figure 1.13 Much of the author's career was leading programs to be On-Step to get back on the original plan. This gave him a unique perspective to observe what was most effective and necessary.

Turnarounds Taught Success Elements

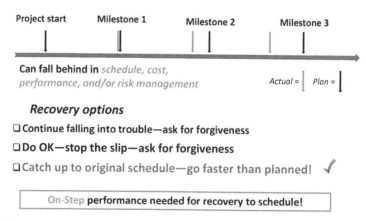

Figure 1.14 On-Step, first-place team performance is necessary to get back on the original plan.

3. However, if the intent is to bring the program performance back to where it was originally planned, work progress must proceed faster than originally planned. The program must be On-Step to achieve this needed high completion rate and catch up to the original plan.

For all the program saves the author has led, he asserted the commitment to catch up to the original plan. Therefore, it was necessary for the troubled program to get On-Step. Having to lead the turnaround of numerous programs, for both commercial and government customers, provided the author with a broad perspective of what is needed to be On-Step.

The major elements the author had observed that were used to achieve this are introduced in Figure 1.15. The implementation of proposed innovations and continuous improvement ideas were often essential ingredients to be successful. Successful program turnarounds inevitably left new and improved processes, tools, and products to be used by future programs in the enterprise. There have since been numerous actual examples of these improvements being applied again, greatly benefiting the enterprise business.

Figure 1.16 highlights the predicament of the team during intense portions of the development while staying On-Step. Team-member participation at this time is like being an occupant in a lifeboat. There is little time to worry about professional title, workplace elegance, or any other subject that provides no value.

Success Actions Were Repeatedly Found

- Identify essential work.
- Assign appropriate leaders.
- Derive independent team structure.
- Plan useful tracking.
- Apply collocated, in-person team interfaces.
- Review team member expectations.
- Create and manage successful contracts.
- Use metrics to avoid catastrophe.
- Avoid software development pitfalls.
- Create useful documents.

- Motivate innovations and process improvements
- Apply complete root-cause process
- Avoid configuration control mistakes
- ALL team forward risks and issues
- Build strong team ethic
- Leadership share early successes
- Leadership show success is special
- Forgive and mentor
- Grow team dedication with successes
- Open-minded enterprise supports On-Step performance

> *Is there something common to these?*

Figure 1.15 Highly successful organizational and process elements were repeatedly observed during program turnarounds. The mission of this book is to find what is common and to show how to apply it.

First-Place Teamwork Is Selfless

- "We must work as a team to survive."
- "We must assume any role that is needed."
- "Our most important task is the one we are working now."
- "No time to question the prestige of our role or workplace."
- "Sometimes our results will not be perfect, but it must be sufficient."
- "Meeting our commitments is necessary to survive."

Figure 1.16   Team members on a first-place team exhibit more altruism. With good leadership, they navigate a valuable work path between "inadequate" and "too perfect."

Team members must be willing to perform any task it takes to continue the team's first-place success. A large emphasis must be placed on developing improvements to shorten time to completion, including choosing effective tools. All team members must understand that highly cooperative teamwork is essential

Programs On-Step Remain a Paradox

#1 better than #2 and by large margin (10% to 20%)

- Noted in empirical studies by other authors
- *Performance*—promises achieved
- *Schedule*—commitments achieved
- *Cost*—commitments achieved
- *Risk*—identified and managed

Author applied #1 organizational and execution success elements he observed to programs in trouble.

Every program was saved and was completed successfully.

> *But what is common to make a first-place program?*

Figure 1.17   In most competitions, the first-place competitor is slightly ahead of second place. Why is this not true for many programs?

for the team to remain in first place. This work environment is an intense crucible of quickly trying and adopting improvements to stay On-Step.

As mentioned earlier, first-place programs are almost always ahead of the other contenders by a large margin (see Figure 1.17). What are these first-place programs doing that is special? What is the "secret sauce" that these programs are using?

1.4 Chapter Highlights

- This book refers to the special, high-performance level of some programs as being On-Step.
- First-place programs are usually On-Step.
- Success statistics of current programs are poor.
- Retiring professionals is often a source of great loss of enterprise capability.
- Programs have been in use for only about 100 years.
- Program structures and processes originally mimicked the military.
- Highly successful program organizational and execution elements have been recorded and validated.

Chapter Two

Why Motivation-Based Leadership

2.1 The "Secret Sauce"?

Motivation management is a different leadership approach that results in changing the way leaders interact with their reports. It establishes a very high level of team performance, putting the program On-Step (see Figure 2.1).

With motivation management, leadership is able to identify the developing motivation or self-actualization of each team member and align it with their task assignments. While exercising this approach, leadership knows that part of their work is to remove all obstructions preventing team members from completing their tasks quickly and successfully. In addition, good leadership looks for every opportunity to expand the scope of responsibility for each team member to grow in their profession as they perform what they do well.

For individual team members to receive, and watch others receive, targeted team-member support for growth from leadership creates high team enthusiasm. This enthusiasm, along with their self-confidence protected by leadership, provides the impetus for each team member to address and develop their interdependencies with the team. This results in a high level of aggregate teamwork in the program—a necessary ingredient for a first-place team.

As will be discussed later in detail, the use of motivation management results in new challenges for leadership. These are summarized in Figure 2.2.

A high level of teamwork creates a high level of trust among the team members. This trust motivates team members even more to complete their work on

Suspected Addressing Human Motivation Is Key

- Supercharges team enthusiasm.
- Increases team productivity by a large increment.
- Increases team and leadership happiness.
- Guides team-member selections.
- Guides efficient task-team mix.
- Puts a program On-Step to be first place.
- Leads with "pull," not "push."
- Model needed for early understanding and consistent results!

Figure 2.1   Evidence is that addressing human motivation is what puts a program into first place.

time and with the content they promised. High levels of teamwork also increase dedication to the enterprise and, in the long run, increase team-member retention.

The application of motivation management provides the additional performances that propel the team above their competitors and put it in first place. This is truly the "Secret Sauce" (see Figure 2.3).

Motivation-Based Leadership Has Favorable Consequences

Figure 2.2   Evaluating human motivation by team members and leaders in results in multiple advantages.

This Book Reveals the "Secret Sauce"

- Be the *first-place* program by large margin.
- Develop hidden talents in team members.
- Foster long-term team-member dedication.
- Increase the satisfaction of success in all team members.
- Develop outstanding sponsor and enterprise reputations.

Motivation management—The Secret Sauce

Figure 2.3 This book addresses how to use motivational management to put a program in first place and greatly increase team satisfaction.

2.2 Applies "Pull," not "Push"

Imagine a puppy in a small room that has just one small exit. Say you want the puppy to leave the room under its own power.

There are basically two ways you can do this. One, you can chase the puppy around the room until it finally leaves through the door. Or you can simply offer the puppy a treat at the door. Obviously, the latter method uses less energy, is faster, and leaves everyone with less stress.

The same is true for human beings. We complete work faster and are more creative and happy when we *want* to perform a task, rather than when we are threatened or intimidated to do so. This is motivation by "pull."

When professionals are motivated by pull, they take more ownership of their task and responsibility for complete closure. They acknowledge the work they must complete next. They feel freer to attempt to apply potentially valuable innovations and continuous improvement actions to achieve their commitments faster.

Team members motivated by pull are less coy about volunteering their concerns about what they believe might not be correct or the best way to proceed. They are less hampered by fear of reprimand from their superiors and embarrassment amongst their team members. As a result, they adapt to changing situations in the program work, or the team itself, faster and with more confidence.

Team members who are motivated by pull are usually more enthusiastic about their work. They have a higher level of morale and are usually more dedicated to their program and their home enterprise.

2.3 Frees Creativity

Motivation management leaders allow team members to be involved in program planning. They are free to impose on future plans their first-hand understanding of the challenges and constraints of what they are accomplishing, and they can identify and develop innovations and process improvements that leadership may not have known were needed or available. These highly targeted and effective improvements are necessary for a program to be in first place.

As mentioned, teamwork improves with motivation-based leadership. Team members have greater respect for their team-member interdependencies and pay more attention to them. Without hesitation, they delegate portions of their work to those specialists who will perform this work the best.

2.4 Distributes Vigilance

In many programs operating under traditional rules, only the program manager, members of their leadership team, or members of their risk-management team are empowered to identify risks and issues. This is an unfortunate mistake. Most often, the team members performing the essential work at the front line detect the real program risks and issues first. These team members can usually describe the current risks and issues most thoroughly and accurately.

Motivation-based management relies on all the members of the program team (including suppliers, the customer, and executive management) to bring to leadership and the risk-management team what they perceive as a risk or issue to the program. Experienced team members know that an unanticipated issue can terribly cripple the progress of a program and can even cause the program to fail. Motivation management facilitates the recognition of a greater span of sources of risks and issues, including those derived from the team members performing the frontline work. It results in early planning and avoidance and mitigation of all risks and issues, especially for those needing immediate attention.

2.5 Improves Known On-Step Elements

The successful On-Step program management elements discussed earlier actually achieve their success by addressing the motivation needs of the team members. A more detailed description will be provided later that describes what motivational needs are fulfilled by each success element. Using motivation-based management adds to the success of these elements and often facilitates the identification of new elements.

Managing motivation allows leadership to apply the On-Step success elements discussed earlier with greater productivity. Team members will know that leadership is attempting to fulfill their motivation needs and achieve success as directly and as soon as possible. In addition, they will understand that the known On-Step success elements were derived from the fulfillment of motivation needs. Knowing this, the team will support the implementation of these success elements with more conviction and enthusiasm.

A program team motivated by pull will validate or deny a proposed new On-Step element faster and with a thorough, fact-based argument.

2.6 Identifies and Guides Team-Member Development

Motivation management provides program leadership with a clearer understanding of the desired outcomes of their individual reports. In addition, it helps leadership avoid the mistake of trying to develop a talent in a team member who is not interested in pursuing it.

One of the important roles of leadership is to detect emerging new talents in team members—talents these individuals may be interested in developing. Leadership must give them the opportunity to try performing work associated with the potential new talent. The maturing of motivations in a team member often causes these potential additional talents to germinate. This insight gives leadership the guidance for making the best assignments for future growth.

2.7 Accelerates Learning What You Do Best

A necessary part of team members learning what they do best is for them to attempt to perform the different work assignments they are interested in. With this experience, team members learn if they can do the task well, and they enjoy the work. Leadership by pull and not intimidation gives team members the latitude to try new work assignments.

Because team members in a motivation-managed team are freer to assert their opinion, they can provide more feedback to fellow team members on the value of what they receive from them. This feedback is valuable to team members for guiding their growth.

2.8 Respects Personal Esteem

Team-member guidance based just on criticism without a plan will stymie their self-esteem and professional growth. Leadership feedback emphasizing only critique and making threats will damage the willingness of a professional to try to improve themself and engage and contribute to the team. Intimidation is humiliating to a proud professional individual.

The use of pull-based leadership, which includes objective critique with a plan to improve, will maintain a healthy self-image for the team member. A program with members with this kind of self-image is absolutely necessary for a team to have a strong and enduring "can-do" enthusiasm, which is necessary for the team to be in first place.

2.9 Provides a Fair, Positive, and Fulfilling Environment

As mentioned, team members who are motivated by pull naturally become more interdependent. As a result, the program will have a more supportive and pleasant attitude. With an optimistic outlook, the team will be much more tolerant to adversities. Individuals working with the other team members will improve their work processes faster and with less fear of reprisal.

Alumni of motivation-based leadership often reminisce about the growth and other opportunities they achieved in this leadership environment. This reminiscing may occur many years after their program is completed. This very favorable recall occurs despite the hardships and sacrifices they had to endure.

As will be discussed in the chapters that follow, when team members are able to achieve the needs of either their developing motivation level or their self-actualization, their high levels of participation and dedication to the team become extraordinary (see Figure 2.4).

2.10 Increases Customer Satisfaction

An important part of a program is keeping current customers pleased and engaged. In many cases, however, the work of assuring continued business requires searching for new customers. A team's high level of performance and their willingness to perform new, challenging work are major portions of establishing an outstanding reputation and finding new customers.

2.10.1 Satisfaction of Current Customer for Future Work

The need to preserve a team's current customer's enthusiasm in the work being done is very important. This is true even for nonprofit organizations, school districts, municipal works, and the like. But beyond the documented performances the team develops with the current customer is the reputation they develop in

Team Members Achieving Self-Actualization Make Sacrifices

- Forge intense team interdependencies.
- Strive for shortest path to completion.
- Ignores near-term professional gains.
- Incorporate innovations to expedite completion.
- Personal activities often secondary.
- Enthusiastically queries and learns to be successful.
- Adheres to team code of behavior.
- Does not accept defeat . . . invents solutions.
- Shares portions of their task with those best skilled.

Figure 2.4 When team members are allowed to achieve self-actualization, they work highly cooperatively, originating and implementing brilliant improvements and supporting teamwork-based success.

their industry. This reputation plays a major role in determining whether the team is selected for future work.

Of first importance is maintaining a high appreciation of the work being performed for all current customers. It has been documented in industry standards that finding new customers requires approximately five times the cost than that needed to maintain a current customer. The cost of finding new customers can be staggering—typically, 6% to 12% of gross revenues for an established company, 12% to 20% of gross revenues for a new company.

Impressing a current customer with a first-place team will benefit future business in many ways. Certainly, it allows the team to directly ask the customer for the opportunity to perform follow-up work. Indirectly, the current customer can become an excellent reference for enlisting future customers.

2.10.2 Providing Traits Customers Want

- **Integrity.** A first-place, motivation-managed team will make commitments (promises)—not just have goals—and achieve their commitments. For a customer, a history of providing all that is promised on time is highly appreciated.

  A motivation-managed team consists of members who are allowed to achieve part or all of their self-actualization. Members of these teams are generally allowed to participate in directly reporting work status and planning. In this kind of team, continued negotiations with the customer are performed primarily with the team members and team leadership, not some disengaged "new business" group. This direct rapport with the team provides a high level of trust for the customer.

  Of course, the customer will receive recognition from doing business with a team that has the reputation of being the best amongst contenders.

- **Team Consistency.** A motivation-managed team consists of dedicated, long-term team members. When working with the team, the customer will not instead be exposed to a consistent turnover of team personnel. Each turnover requires expensive overhead expenditures by the team and the customer for developing a new customer–team relationship and trust.

  Team members who are dedicated to the team through the life of its work establish a deeper understanding of the needs and wants of the customer because the details of customer desires are not lost due to frequent turnover of personnel. It allows customer–team counterparts to develop relationships that give team members the ability to "read between the lines" regarding customer desires, and it allows the customer to develop a deep trust in the team individuals.

  In a motivation-managed team, team leadership has developed an understanding of the motivational needs of each team member and the type of work they prefer. This allows a deliberate and much faster adjustment of team expertise and problem-versus-solution–based team member type mix when the customer needs change. This results in less total program cost and shorter time to program completion.

- **Technical Competence.** In a first-place, motivation-managed team, innovations and improvements to processes are encouraged at all levels. During any time in the program lifecycle, improvement proposals are appreciated and evaluated with thorough process.

  Team members feel content by being assigned to tasks that align well with their current self-actualization. With this contentment comes a desire to understand the customer's needs and challenges to great depth. There is less fear of reprisal due to customer interface protocols. Team leadership gives high recognition and praise to improvement ideas that benefit the customer.

- **Customer Focus.** In a modern, motivation-managed team, the customer will often be allowed to interact directly with the team developers, not just leadership. This allows the customer to develop a deeper trust in the team while allowing the team members to better understand customer needs with direct communication.

  In a motivation-managed team, team members appreciate that their work is serving their self-actualization, making them motivated to learn and serve all customer needs to maximize this benefit.

2.11 Chapter Highlights

- The "Secret Sauce" is management of team-member motivation.
- Applies pull not push.
- Frees creativity.
- Distributes vigilance.
- Improves historical success elements.
- Guides team-member development.
- Accelerates self-actualization.
- Respects individuals.
- Provides positive work environment.
- Improves customer appreciation.
- Helps acquire follow-on business with current customer as well as enlisting future customers.

Chapter Three

Motivation Model to Be First Place

3.1 Connecting Human Motivations with First-Place Performance

If you employ the elements described in the author's first book, entitled *Project and Program Turnaround*,[1] you will save your troubled program. The readers of this book might infer that these same success elements could be used to start and successfully complete a new program. But this extension of process was not discussed in the past book.

For this book, the author takes the next step of investigating, evaluating, and describing the human behavioral basis for the success elements described in his first book and uses this basis for creating a first-place program. A detailed description will be provided later in this book of how to incorporate motivation management and the success elements during program setup and execution.

Many of the current and proposed new constructs and processes used in programs are approximate. Some make sense and look appealing on paper but turn out not to be aligned with the needs of real human team members. Because of this, the actual improvements that result may not be as profound as predicted.

Like our fellow creatures on planet Earth, we humans have specific needs. Are there significant advantages to aligning these needs to the work we perform

---

[1] Pavelko, T. (2017). *Project and Program Turnaround*. Boca Raton, FL: CRC Press/ Taylor & Francis Group.

What Is the Foundation for On-Step Teamwork?

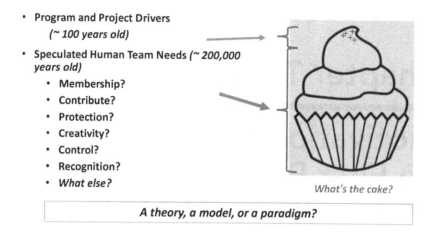

- **Program and Project Drivers**
  (~ 100 years old)
- **Speculated Human Team Needs** *(~ 200,000 years old)*
  - **Membership?**
  - **Contribute?**
  - **Protection?**
  - **Creativity?**
  - **Control?**
  - **Recognition?**
  - ***What else?***

What's the cake?

A theory, a model, or a paradigm?

Figure 3.1   When first researching the motivational basis for first-place program performance, it was thought that prehistoric human motivations might be the foundation.

in modern programs? If so, is there a theory and/or paradigm for identifying these needs?

Many leaders have suspected that this alignment with basic human needs is necessary for a team to perform its best. But what is the structure for the most fundamental human needs we must appeal to for a program to be its very best? Can we use these basic human needs to put a team On-Step? (See Figure 3.1.)

The search for these fundamental needs was started for this book by looking for the needs in prehistoric humans. Our humanoid species started about 200,000 years ago. So, the attempt was made to study ancient humans in hopes of finding common prehistoric social and individual behavioral traits and desires that are important to achieving team success today.

3.2 Prehistoric Humans

It is difficult to find a consolidated summary of the basic behavioral traits of humanoids during our prehistory (see Figure 3.2). Instead, most analysis is focused on the uniqueness and peculiarities of tribes and their migration in specific world regions such as Africa, Europe, Asia, and North America. Much is written about the size of the tribes in these regions, when and where they intermingled, how the local weather changed their culture over time, how geographic and resource constraints influenced where they resided, and more.

Prehistoric Motivations Are Premature

- **Modern root motivations starting 200,000 years ago?**
- **Reviewed historical analysis of Africa, Europe, Asia, North America.**
- **Regionalized behaviors chronicled but no *generalization*.**
- **Behavioral modernity noted, 50,000 years to present.**
- **Crops, livestock, art, abstractions 10,000 ago.**
- **Gradualist versus cognitive theory debate.**
- **Cognitive not yet specializing.**
- **Ancient motivations not relevant?**

> *Evolution recently chose cognitive specialty*

Figure 3.2 It was determined that prehistoric motivations could not be generalized and that these motivations have significantly evolved over recent millennia.

These societies started before the dawn of agriculture or the raising of livestock. Therefore, much is written about how these people hunted and gathered food.

What became clear during this review is that human behavior has in fact greatly evolved in just the last 50,000 years. That is to say, our species did not physically evolve our ability to understand and make predictions during this time, but that those humans with this inclination dominated by being the most fit to survive over multiple generations. In other words, human evolution accentuated some of our innate abilities: to reason, model, and predict. It can easily be argued that if we were to take members of our present-day human population of brilliant organizers, planners, and innovators and place them into a prehistoric environment with their ancestors of 150,000+ years ago, modern humans would perish quickly.

It became clear that modern human beings have evolved today to a distinct and specialized subset of what we were during prehistoric times. So, when trying to understand what the human species needs to be fulfilled in a program, we must evaluate what our human needs have more recently become—basic needs and abstractions that have become more acute over the last 10,000 to 50,000 years.

Much is being studied now about behavioral modernity, which is thought to have started in our species about 50,000 years ago. Many scientists believe this is about when humanoids began to specialize into today's version of a human being. There are even schools of study that believe the physiology of our central nervous system actually changed, if only slightly, during this evolution. Members of this school are referred to as *gradualists*.

There is another school of thought that believes that recent human behavior evolution results purely from the increased complexity and sophistication of the theories and paradigms we have developed in our minds. This school believes that our enriched development of abstract thought and art was purely due to accumulated observations and models we developed over generations to allow future predictions to be made. Members of this school believe that the physiology of our central nervous system has not changed. This is often referred to as *cognitive evolution.*

To what degree our recent human mental evolution has been based on physiological versus cognitive changes is fascinating, but not of much relevance to the purpose of this book. Our goal is to maximize the performance of modern-day teams. And it appears that our human motivational needs have recently been precisely refined in our history.

Study of our recent history indicates that there was a major introduction of more abstract thinking about 10,000 years ago. There is archaeological evidence that during this time there was a sudden increase in human planning depth; symbolic behavior, including art and ornamentation, music, and dance; the exploitation of large game for food; so-called "blade technology"; and more. The planting and cultivation of crops and raising of livestock also started during this time in different regions of the world.

What finally became evident is that any study that connects human needs and abilities to high-performance teams must examine present-day human beings. So, the author's attention was redirected toward analyzing our modern program teams—constructs only in existence since the dawn of the Industrial Revolution, a little over 100 years ago.

3.3 Modern Theories

In-depth academic studies of what motivates program teams to perform well have been conducted only recently, starting in the 20th century. Many of these studies are still in a preliminary stage and continue to mature.

The major modern theories of human motivation in program teams were reviewed for this book. The attempt was made to determine which single theory, or combination of theories, best mapped to the program success elements introduced earlier. Also, part of this evaluation was to look at each theory for the inclusion of some basic, common-sense characteristics to make it usable—characteristics that are believed to be a necessary part of any usable and effective human motivation model (see Figure 3.3).

A useful theory of human motivation must be simple, easy to understand, and easy to use. It should be able to be learned quickly. Seemingly artificial or

Process Should Not Counter Common Sense

- Is the proposed process simple?
- Is it learned quickly?
- Are any process components highly artificial or nonintuitive?
- Is motivation derived from *"carrots"* or *"sticks"*?
- Is there added headcount needed to implement its use?
- Is recurrent training necessary when using it?
- Is the value of the theory validated by multiple past successes?
- Does training and maintenance to apply this theory require a complex series of books, seminars, special classes, visiting experts, etc.?

> *Some modern processes may seem like a fad.*

Figure 3.3   A motivational-management process should be easy to understand and learn. It should be based on "pull"—inexpensive to apply and demonstrated to be successful.

nonintuitive components must be scrutinized. Also, any candidate theory must be examined to determine if it relies on "push" of the team members to do the work with penalties, threats, or intimidation, or "pull" them with positive motivation.

The cost needed to implement each paradigm reviewed was evaluated and compared. The complexity of the paradigms being proposed was also compared. Questions were considered, such as, are there added human resources needed to implement and maintain it? Is recurrent team training necessary? Should there be a small trial run done before applying it to the whole team? Is there a set of special books, seminars, classes, experts, or more needed to train and use it? Does this paradigm/process have a track record of success? These were important queries considered while evaluating the different motivation theories for this book.

The following presents a description of the theories that were evaluated (see Figure 3.4). Each one is evaluated for its ability to propel a team to be On-Step.

3.3.1 Herzberg Factor

This theory was developed by Frederick Herzberg in the 1950s. It is often referred to as the Two-Factor Theory of Motivation. Herzberg interviewed hundreds of engineers and accountants, asking them what the positive and negative feelings for their work were. He distilled two factors that he felt influenced employee motivation and satisfaction.

Contemporary Theories Are More Relevant

- Herzberg's Two-Factor Theory
- The Hawthorne Effect
- Expectancy Theory
- Three-Dimensional Theory of Attribution
- "X Versus Y" Management Theory
- Self-Determination Theory
- Maslow's Hierarchy of Motivations

Developed with application of programs and projects.

Figure 3.4   More recent human-motivational theories are found to be more valuable. They address the emerging use of programs.

The first was *motivation factors*. He believed that these made the team members feel satisfied and work harder. These included work enjoyment, being recognized, seeing their career progress, and more.

The second was *hygiene factors*. If these factors were absent, Herzberg thought this could result in lack of job satisfaction and motivation. These factors could include company policies, salary, benefits, relationships with managers, relationships with coworkers, and more.

Herzberg asserted that the absence of motivation factors did not necessarily cause work dissatisfaction. The presence of hygiene factors did not appear to increase satisfaction and motivation, but their absence did cause an increase in dissatisfaction.

This theory implies some obvious generalities. For leadership to motivate team members, they must make sure they feel appreciated and supported. For leadership to prevent job dissatisfaction, they must make team members feel they are being treated adequately—for example, by providing the best possible working conditions and fair pay.

This is a valuable introductory analysis of how to motivate a team but does not provide enough analytical granularity to customize achieving the motivational needs of each employee, nor does it provide guidance in how to populate the various task teams or select leadership.

3.3.2 Hawthorne Effect

This theory was first described by Henry Landsberger in 1950. It is named after a series of social experiments on the influence of physical conditions on team-member productivity at the Western Electrics factory in Hawthorne, Chicago. This investigative work was conducted in the 1920s and 1930s.

The researchers changed some of the physical conditions for the team, including lighting, working hours, breaks, and more. Of interest in all cases, team-member productivity increased when change was made in physical conditions. It was concluded that team members became motivated to work harder as a response to the attention being paid to them, and not the actual physical changes themselves.

These studies suggested that team members work harder if they know they are being observed. (As a teenage ice-cream scooper, the author recalls scooping with the most "finesse" when customers were watching.)

This phenomenon is both interesting and motivating. It seems to work as well when team-member attention is implied as when it is direct. For example, improving the workplace lighting has as much effect as directly telling the team members you like their work.

Knowledge of the Hawthorne Effect may have some tactical value when managing program execution. However, this theory has no value when trying to evaluate individual team-member motivations and populate the program teams with an effective mix of motivation types and leadership. It does not provide enough content to guide a program to be in first place.

3.3.3 Expectancy

This theory proposes that team members choose behaviors depending on their perceived outcomes. This choice includes how likely they perceive each outcome to be. This theory is based on three elements:

- **Expectancy.** The degree of belief by the team members that their efforts will result in the desired outcome. The degree of this value is determined by a large number of parameters, including past experiences of success, how difficult achieving the outcome is perceived to be, self-confidence, and more.
- **Instrumentality.** The degree of belief by the team member that the anticipated outcome will actually result from the contemplated activity.
- **Variance.** The value the team member places on the desired outcome.

According to Expectancy Theory, team members are most motivated if they believe they will achieve a desired outcome if they successfully complete an achievable commitment. They are not motivated if they do not want the predicted outcome or do not believe their efforts will lead to the desired outcome.

This theory may be helpful when trying to establish the most fundamental mechanics of motivation. It can be an important tool for analyzing the infrastructure of individual motivations in great detail. But it does not aid in evaluating, categorizing, and comparing individual team-member motivations at a higher level for guiding how to populate and lead program teams.

3.3.4 Three-Dimensional Attribution

This theory was developed by Bernard Weiner. He assumed that team members will select behaviors by what they attribute to failures in behaviors used in similar problem situations in the past. For example, if a student fails a test, the way they prepare for future tests will be different depending on whether they attribute the failure to lack of study versus illness on the day of the test.

This theory states there are three main characteristics of attributions that affect future motivation:

- **Stability.** A measure of how reliable and stable the attribution is.
- **Locus of Control.** The degree of influence or control the team member has on the attribution. Were past results caused by factors external to the team member?
- **Controllability.** Given that future outcomes can be controlled by the team member, how much control can be exercised?

This theory helps team members understand that they can improve their future work performance and the performance of the program team by analyzing what actions in the past can be improved. This theory brings additional detail and structure to this correlation.

But this theory does not offer the wide breadth of tools and guidance for team members and leadership to perform well. It does not give guidance on how to design a program organization or execute the needed work, other than providing some amount of structure for improving team processes from lessons derived from past mistakes.

3.3.5 "X" and "Y" Type Leadership

This theory was developed by Douglas McGregor, Professor of Management at the School of Industrial Management at MIT. He published his work in a book called *The Human Side of Enterprise*[2] in 1960. He divided the approach to program leadership (management) into two types:

---

[2] McGregor, D. (1960). *The Human Side of Enterprise.* New York, NY: McGraw-Hill Companies.

- **Theory X.** The assumptions upon which traditional, more military-modeled organizations are based, which to some appear adequate for the full utilization of the team members in a program. This includes strict, top-down leadership flow. Interpersonal relationships amongst the team members, and between team members and leadership, are kept formal. McGregor asserted that this method leads team members to be resistant to direction, to restrict their output, to be indifferent to organizational objectives, and to refuse to accept responsibility, and that it results in inadequate team-member growth and development.
- **Theory Y.** Selecting methods of managerial control appropriate to the conditions of modern industrial organizations: persuasion and professional help being as successful as the use of authority. More attention is devoted to the attitudes, needs, and other personal characteristics of the team members. Good leadership ability is asserted to be studied and learned, and not inherent.

At the time of its publication, this work was considered to be revolutionary. McGregor asserted that Theory Y management is a critically needed first step toward bringing the best from team members. For example, it emphasizes how valuable the team members' perspective is when determining the program status and direction.

Theory Y management is a necessary starting point for a program to be On-Step. It does not, however, give guidance on how individual team-member motivations are identified and categorized or on how to use the knowledge of these motivations to populate the various task teams and choose leadership. In addition, it does not show how to capitalize on the knowledge of individual motivations to lead a team to be in first place.

3.3.6 Self-Determination

This is a recent theory developed by Edward Deci and Richard Ryan, psychologists at the University of Rochester in New York. It states that people have three innate psychological needs:

- **Competence.** The need to control outcome and experience mastery.
- **Relatedness.** The universal desire to interact, be connected to, and experience caring for others.
- **Autonomy.** The universal urge in people to be causal agents of their own life and act in harmony with their integrated self. However, the authors make it clear that this is not a need to be independent of other people.

In addition, the authors define two types of motivation:

- **Extrinsic Motivation.** A person performs a task because doing so will yield some kind of reward or benefit upon completion.
- **Intrinsic Motivation.** A person performs a task purely because of enjoyment or fun.

These conceptual elements are still being developed to learn how to bring about commitment, engagement, and high innovative productivity in teams. Work is being performed to clarify the definitions.

Work remains to mature this theory to where it can be used to guide program management. Strategies for leading team individuals and companies—including designing compensation, approaching education, and more—are being formulated using this theory. However, the author believes this theory is not yet mature enough to be practically applied.

3.3.7 Maslow's Human Motivation

Abraham Maslow was an American psychologist educated at the University of Wisconsin. He published a paper entitled *A Theory of Human Motivation*[3] in 1943. The content of this paper has been a starting point and/or a reference for most theories of human motivation that have been developed since.

Maslow's theory states that, in regard to any human activity, there are five layers of motivation. When involved with an activity, an individual proceeds up the hierarchy of these five layers, starting at the bottom—physiological needs. Maslow assumes that an individual achieves most or all of the motivational needs of a given layer before ascending to the next layer.

Maslow identified the top and final layer as self-actualization—the desire to become everything that one is capable of becoming. His theory states that this is the pinnacle of the hierarchy of human motivation (see Figures 3.5 and 3.6).

Maslow's theory has been chosen to be the best one for determining and organizing individual team-member motivation in this book. It is an excellent starting paradigm for organizing and populating the program and executing the work in a way that allows it to achieve first-place status. Here are the reasons:

- The Maslow paradigm applies well to the team behaviors observed by managers leading and authors writing about successful modern programs. Maslow's hierarchy follows the typical development steps for professionals, starting at their need for basic subsistence and income and ascending to

---

[3] Maslow, A. H. (1943). A theory of human motivation. *Psychological Review, 50*(4), 370–396. https://doi.org/10.1037/h0054346.

Maslow—Cornerstone of Modern Motivation Theory

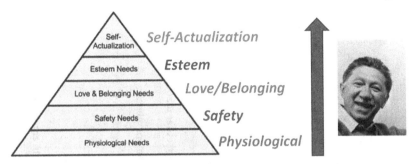

- **Motivation maturity is bottom up.**
- **Partial to complete fulfillment before next level.**
- **Self-actualization = "what you're meant to be."**
- **Starting point for other motivation theories.**
- **Starting point for process described in this book.**

Figure 3.5   This classic theory was found to be the best foundation for the processes developed in this book. It maps well to basic program dynamics and the author's experiences.

Maslow Maps to Real Experience

Self-Actualization

Esteem

Love

Safety Physiological

- **Partial to complete fulfillment before higher.**
- **Continual trial, error, rejection.**
- **Journey through life.**
- **Self-actualization may not be what we thought it would be.**

- **Maps to observed team motivations.**
- **Maps to typical professional development steps.**
- **Focus on "pull" motivators, not intimidation and fear.**
- **Identifies the value of "passion" in first-place teams.**
- **Ascendance follows human evolution.**
- **Foundation for other motivation theories.**
- **Applied and verified for over 70 years.**

Figure 3.6   In many cases, this theory is the starting point for the development of later motivational theories. It has been highly validated and is well known.

Each Motivation Level Has Special Desires

MOTIVATION/ SELF-ACTUALIZATION LEVEL	CHARACTERISTICS AND NEEDS TO FEEL UNENCUMBERED
Level I: Physiological	Assurance of fair compensation.
	Allowed to perform work completely as agreed.
	Appreciation of transactional agreement.
	Assurances that someone is looking out for you.
Level II: Safety	Closely connected to Level I.
	Assurance of continued income for good work provided.
	Visibility provided of long-term plan that ensures consistency.
	Feedback provided that work performed meets or exceeds expectations.
Level III: Love	Provide a cordial and friendly work relationship with leadership.
	Value the insight of these individuals regarding the feelings and preferences of other team members.
	Have them coordinate casual social events for the team.
	Ask them to help facilitate face-to-face, in person communication among team members.
	Establish optimistic team environment.
Level IV: Esteem	Provide advancement opportunities with specific requirements.
	Highlight possible routes to promotion to higher levels.
	Promotion only after complete accomplishment of requirements.
	Make their professional level visible to team and enterprise.
	Demonstrate that leadership is looking for future promotional opportunities in enterprise.
	Accept promotion may be higher priority for them than product purpose.

MOTIVATION/ SELF-ACTUALIZATION LEVEL	CHARACTERISTICS AND NEEDS TO FEEL UNENCUMBERED
Level V – Professional	Leadership examine work history to verify this self-actualization. (Leadership appreciate this level seldom clarified for Junior professionals.) One on one discussion with leadership to clarify professional self vision. Acknowledge their innovations to achieve self-actualization ideal. Assign growth assignments that freely challenge the abilities of their expertise. Publicly value achievement of professional accomplishments during execution. Adapt to changes, growth of individual self-actualization ideals. Establish job title that describes their special role.
Level VI – Altruistic	(Leadership appreciate this level seldom clarified for Junior professionals.) One on one discussion with leadership to clarify Altruistic vision. Provide assignments, responsibilities that connect with Altruistic vision. Commend with written and spoken words their achievements of vision. Provide routes for benefactors to express their appreciation. Adapt to changes, growth, evolution of individual's vision. Allow time for leadership to understand and support this complicated self-actualization.

Figure 3.7 A primary goal of modern program management is to allow each level of self-actualization to contribute as freely and with as much substance as possible. [Explanation of this figure is on the following page.]

their need to be in a team, gain personal recognition, and eventually to achieve their special purpose.

- Maslow's theory focuses on "pulling" team members to be their best, as opposed to relying on intimidation or threats.
- Maslow's theory is constantly used as a starting point and/or major ingredient for the other theories on human motivation and behavior that have been developed since. It has been verified with study and successful application for more than 70 years.
- By identifying self-actualization, Maslow has justified the essential need for the abstraction of "passion" for some team members to do their best. This recognition is needed for organizing and managing a program that is On-Step!

Interestingly, the ascending hierarchy of Maslow's motivations in many ways follows the history of human evolution. Humanoids started with assuring they fulfill their physiological needs 200,000 years ago. Over the millennia, we humans have developed our needs for being safe, belonging, being loved, achieving social stature, and finally learning and achieving our unique concept of what we should do—our self-actualization.

It is important to note that Maslow's theory maps well to the author's leadership experiences. In a slightly modified form, it clearly describes why the organizational and process elements he has observed and successfully applied to turn around large programs in trouble has worked well. As you will read, the author has slightly extended Maslow's hierarchy and has observed that an individual's self-actualization in the workplace can settle at any one of these motivation levels.

3.4 Motivations in Modern Teams

Motivations differ amongst the members of any program team. Individuals just starting their career focus mostly on establishing themselves, including having ample shelter and food. Later, they pay attention to worrying about team relationships and job title (see Figure 3.7 on previous pages).

Self-actualization is at the pinnacle of the hierarchy of human motivations, according to Maslow. It describes what our individual purpose is.

Usually, resolving our self-actualization takes experience. Sometimes it ends up being something we had not imagined we were good at or even wanted to be associated with. Many times, its manifestation is as simple as fulfilling one of the lower levels of motivation in Maslow's hierarchy. Examples will be provided throughout this book.

3.5 Chapter Highlights

- Prehistoric human motivations are discovered to be premature to be used to model and evaluate motivations in modern-day programs.
- Human functional specialty has evolved over last 10–50,000 years.
- Modern motivation theories evaluated:
  - Herzberg Factor
  - Hawthorne Effect
  - Expectancy Theory
  - Three-Dimensional Attribution
  - "X" and "Y" Leadership Theory
  - Self-Determination Theory
  - Maslow Human Motivation Theory
- Maslow maps best to industry experience.
- A team member's self-actualization may settle on any one of Maslow's motivation levels for programs.
- Maslow's five-level motivational hierarchy is slightly augmented by the author, as described in the following chapter.

Chapter Four

Changes in Program Leadership Indicated

4.1 Traditional versus On-Step

In Chapter One, we discussed the programs of the pre-Industrial Revolution adopting the military top-down structure, in which authority was given high priority, quick decisions were valued, and orders were obeyed without suggestions or challenges.

Today, however, teams that are in first place are there not necessarily by making *prompt* decisions but by making the *optimal* decisions (see Figure 4.1). Well-thought-out decisions that are accurate and effective, based on all the relevant data that can be practically acquired, are the cornerstone of first-place programs.

The time to determine the next direction of modern program teams typically needs to be made in hours or days, and not the critical short responses needed on the battlefield. Situational data and proposals for future program steps must be collected from all available sources. Often the most valuable source of this information is from the team members performing the frontline work.

The new breed of leadership must understand that the execution of modern programs is often represented by an organizational chart shaped like an upside-down pyramid. Modern leadership must place a high value on understanding the status of the program derived from the front-line team members. They must highly value improvement suggestions and innovations from these team members. It is essential that these sources are used for program planning to remain in first place. Again, the frontline team members many times have the most in-depth

Military Compared to Modern Programs—Very Different

MILITARY	PROGRAM
Decisions made quickly to win and minimize human casualties.	Time taken for complete analysis before decision.
Decisions sometimes made with minimal data.	Premium placed on evaluating all accessible data before deciding.
Prompt decisions often valued over deep analysis.	Decisions without considering all supporting data are discouraged.
Strict enlisted person–officer distinction.	Hourly–salaried relationship less distinctive in successful organizations.
Standard organizational granularity and structure.	Organization structures more varied.
Assumed uniform capability in each level of organization.	Team members in each level of organization assumed different and unique.
Participants motivated by strict rules of conduct (orders).	Participants motivated by fulfilling developing self-actualization. Buy-in is needed for first-place performance.
Promotion based on seniority and leadership skills.	Promotion based on work capability and contributions and often less on leadership aptitude.
Promotion usually within officer or enlisted groups.	Promotion may bridge salaried–hourly divide.
Primary success measurements include full completion; cost is often secondary regard.	Success measured by high value from low cost, short schedule time, and small risk.
All physiological needs provided by the organization.	Participants provide their own physiological needs: shelter, food, transportation, safety at home.
Direction from superiors must be accepted (orders).	Participants may discuss and compromise direction from superiors.

Figure 4.1 The needs of a military organization and the needs of a modern program are quite different. This is why more effective ways to organize and lead modern are being pursued.

and thorough understanding of work status. They often have highly inventive ways to solve a problem, beyond the obvious or traditional leadership responses.

In addition, new leadership must lead by understanding and managing team-member motivations while removing barriers to progress. They must participate in developing the growth path of team members to achieve their self-actualization. The characteristics of modern leadership are markedly different from those of traditional leaders.

4.2 Old versus Modern Leadership

Figure 4.2 summarizes the comparison of the characteristics of a traditional leader versus the modern On-Step leader. As can be seen, the difference in outcomes is *excellent* results, not just *good* results.

The modern leader knows that the best understanding of the task at hand and of the ways of efficiently completing it are derived from the guidance of all the members of the team. The new leader cultivates a team appreciation of guidance inputs from all members, emphasizing the value of what the team individuals are doing and showing gratitude. They are patient when mistakes are made. They understand that for a team member to intentionally make an error is unusual.

Modern leaders understand that the most valuable contributions come from team members when they are provided a minimally burdened path to achieve what motivates them. They understand that often the most brilliant and effective contributions come from those team members achieving part or all of their self-actualization.

Modern leaders understand that no single individual, including the program manager, can have all the insight and best solutions to make a program be its very best—to be the first-place contender.

Figure 4.3 lists how team-member motivation deteriorates when traditional leadership traits are applied, squelching the highly valuable insights and brilliant innovations developing in their minds.

4.3 Lessons for New Leaders

Figure 4.4 highlights important lessons that a modern leader should know when applying motivational management.

We individually have an ultimate capability and passion—something that we are exceptionally good at.

The implications of self-actualization are mysterious (see Figure 4.5). Many wonder, how can a free and competent mind with the ability to do many things

On-Step Leaders Need Courage

TRADITIONAL LEADER	ON-STEP LEADER
Solely determines direction and organization.	Guides maximum planning and organization from team.
Garners attention; harsh, abrupt.	Establishes high self-worth for each team member; listens, integrates.
Highly enforces pyramid organization.	Upside-down pyramid leadership.
Team members guess what the boss wants.	Team members apply their own thinking.
Little attention to individual development.	Gives opportunities for development and nurtures.
New ideas often considered a hindrance.	Cherishes innovation, continuous improvement.
Low tolerance for personal issues in team.	Provides team members room and support to mitigate personal issues.
Quick to reassign after big mistake.	Gives a second chance.
Always punitive response to poor performance.	Forgives poor performance when appropriate.
Asserts authority once via organization chart.	Constantly demonstrates authority with leadership.
Track record of good results.	Track record of excellent results.

Figure 4.2 On-Step leadership must give team members more freedom to identify risks and issues, help with future planning, and create new solutions while leading the team to maintain strict adherence to schedule promises and efficient use of resources. Some will consider this to be unconventional.

have some kind of predetermined capability? We have been told from our youth that we can be whatever we want to be.

But when we boil off what may often be our cultural accoutrements, we find a passionate essence that will motivate us to do extraordinary things. Sometimes the contents of our self-actualization are a surprise even to us. The good leader will help each team member identify their specialty and open the door to allow it to flourish. The good leader understands that self-actualization may change as it is clarified or as a result of other circumstances.

Rarely, the program cannot provide a role for a valued team member that completely addresses this member's self-actualization. The good leader realizes that, for some team members, this partial fulfillment will not be acceptable to them. This impasse is infrequent, but when it occurs, leadership should make the effort to find a suitable role for this team member. A special effort should be made by leadership to detect this incompatibility while interviewing a potential new team member. The resentment a team member may express when the program is not appealing to their basic needs can be demoralizing to the rest of the team.

Most team members, however, will appreciate the opportunity to fulfill their motivational needs, even if only partially, and will enthusiastically support the team effort. They understand that this experience will help them achieve their self-actualization needs and may even further clarify and open new personal/career development paths they were not aware of.

4.4 Business Culture Realignment

The introduction of modern leadership can be disruptive. Figure 1.2 summarized the misconceptions and fears of an attempt to be a first-place program. Often new PMs perceive that the changes needed are too big or unconventional for their leadership to invest in. Figure 4.6 shows some of the changes needed to be a first-place program. New PMs may fear that executive leadership will consider these new features to be too risky to accept. They fear these changes may cause traditional executives to be suspicious about intent.

Leaders using more traditional organizational and leadership methods may then be resentful of the outstanding progress the new leadership approach achieves. Some may not accept that it is impossible for one leader to anticipate all problems and know the best answers for a program.

Often, enterprise executives expect immediate impact from the new leaders they assign. Some may have limited patience to accept that, to be highly effective, the new PM needs the time to establish the organization, the team mixes, the leadership assignments, and the planning—and that these changes are needed to be the best.

Effect of Ignoring Motivation

TRADITIONAL LEADERSHIP TRAIT	MOTIVATION IMPEDED AND PROGRAM OR PROJECT LOSS	Self-Actual most effected
Solely determines direction and organization.	Removes valuable planning support of task completion, resource estimations, and issue/risk analysis from team members. Arbitrary guidelines are used to populate task teams with professionals of undetermined motivations. Team members receive little recognition for their contribution.	Physiological Safety Professional Altruistic
Garners attention; harsh, abrupt.	Team members are motivated by fear of losing income, team involvement, and more. Team members are not allowed to achieve their motivation needs. Team members are fearful of communicating information to leadership and between fellow team members.	Physiological Safety Love Esteem
Highly enforces pyramid organization.	Adds labor to conduct internal communication, discourages valuable upward communication. Team members feel their motivational needs are overwhelmed by structural protocol. Team members may surmise some leadership are hidden behind their organizational authority. There may be some reluctance to communicate among team members because of rigorously enforced structure.	Professional Altruistic
Team members guess what the boss wants.	Team members may waste precious resources attempting to please the boss. Valuable effort is diverted from team individuals' analyzing and developing solutions for urgent program or project problems. Leadership may fall into the trap of evaluating reporting personnel by the degree of attention they receive from them.	Physiological Safety Love Esteem Professional Altruistic
Little attention to individual development.	Valuable emerging capabilities in team members are not developed. Team members are demoralized because they feel that they are only being used to accomplish the current task. Team members do not perform their best because they surmise there is no interest from leadership to help them develop.	Physiological Safety Love Esteem Professional
New ideas often considered a hindrance.	Highly valuable innovations and continuous improvement proposals that could improve team and product performance are ignored. The satisfaction of finding and capitalizing on a more efficient path for the team is denied to all motivation levels. Leadership implies that the value of any innovation or improvement idea from the team is low.	Physiological Safety Professional Altruistic

Behavior	Description	Needs
Low tolerance for personal issues in team.	Dilutes team perception of leadership worrying about their motivations and other needs. Leadership example desensitizes team members from empathizing with and supporting other team members. Substantiates fear by some that team members are only valued by the volume of work they complete.	Physiological Safety Love Professional Altruistic
Quick to reassign after mistake.	Team members are reluctant to try improvements by observing others because not given a second chance if their attempt fails. Team members are primarily motivated by intimidation, fear of losing their current role. Team members see no avenue from leadership to allow them to take risks to improve themselves or the team.	Physiological Safety Professional Altruistic
Always punitive response to poor performance.	Team members are always motivated by the fear of leadership ignoring their physiological needs instead of fulfilling their innate motivations. Team members are reluctant to offer suggestions to improve design or processes due to fear of a resulting mistake. Team members fear trying to personally grow because of intolerance of mistakes.	Physiological Safety Love Professional Altruistic
Asserts authority via org chart.	Respect for managers is low because suspicion some may be hiding behind the authority bestowed by the organizational structure. Some team members may isolate important details of their work because of their lack of trust in the organization design. Team members lose motivation by having to abide by what they may feel is an arbitrary and regimented organizational process.	Physiological Safety Love Professional Altruistic
Track record of good results.	Most professionals are NOT motivated by "good" results. They instead want to do their very best! Good team members are not excited and motivated by team performance that is only acceptable.	Physiological Safety Love Esteem Professional Altruistic

Figure 4.3 Ignoring team-member motivations and issuing all program direction from leadership destroys the team's creativity and enthusiasm, which is needed to propel them to first place. Leadership that ignores motivation often relies on intimidation and fear to get work done.

There Are Important Factors When Managing Motivation

- The new professional transitions between the motivation classifications before they achieve their self-actualization.
- An individual's self-actualization will be their primary motivation but may still be influenced by other levels.
- An individual's self-actualization may subsequently change up or down the six-level hierarchy.
- Leaders must detect, nurture, and facilitate transitions.
- Still all team members are commonly bonded with code of conduct, colocated office layout, team commitments, and more.
- Team mixes may be refined by leadership after team has demonstrated performance.

Figure 4.4   Leadership must appreciate that team-member self-actualization may change either during a program or when moving to another one. Sometimes an individual's self-actualization is a compound of motivations but is dominated by one of them.

Some Lessons Are Counterintuitive

- We all have a valuable, but mysterious, self-actualization.
    - "God given," "our destiny," "meant to be"?
    - Subconscious psychology, intrigue?
- Often our self-actualization is different from what we imagined.
- Each hierarchy level need not be 100% fulfilled before moving to next level.
- One's self-actualization may change or clarify.
- Some work tasks provide only partial self-actualization needs—stay with it!
- Some bosses are afraid of leaders who appear subordinate to their team.
- Team plan on long planning step back before first place steps forward.
- Some senior team members are fearful of new approach—be trustworthy.
- Motivation based leadership is never "plug & play." Constant attention needed for changes.
- Rarely someone has no self-actualization and not looking—*avoid!*

Figure 4.5   Some clarification of self-actualization and what is encountered when applying motivational management is needed. For example, the concept of self-actualization does counter our belief that one can do well in choosing whatever they want to do.

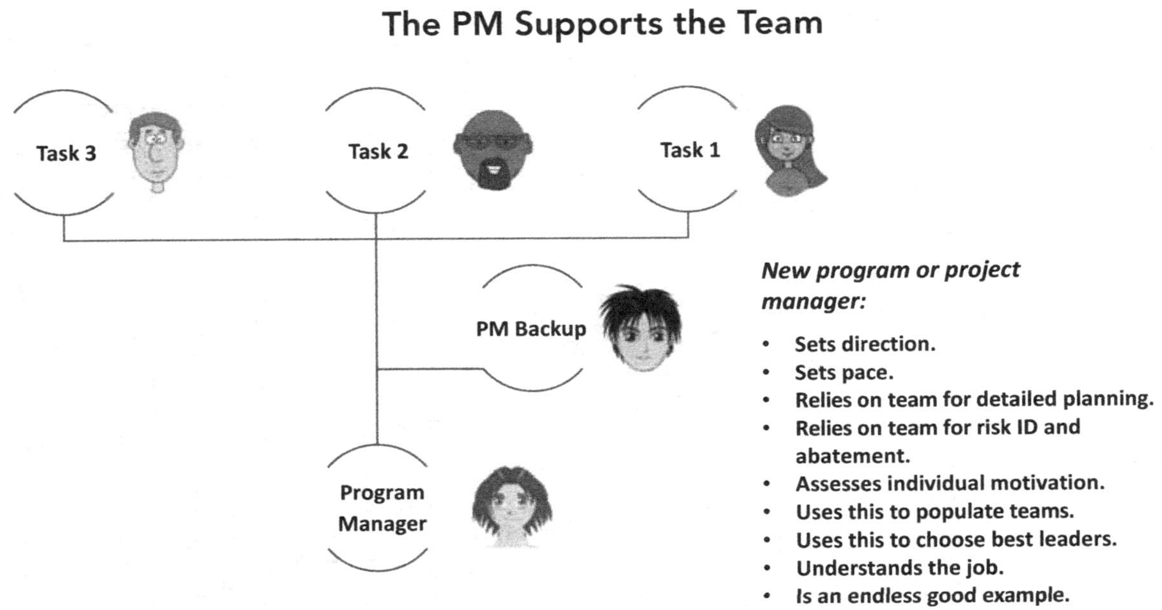

The PM Supports the Team

Task 3 Task 2 Task 1

PM Backup

Program Manager

New program or project manager:

- Sets direction.
- Sets pace.
- Relies on team for detailed planning.
- Relies on team for risk ID and abatement.
- Assesses individual motivation.
- Uses this to populate teams.
- Uses this to choose best leaders.
- Understands the job.
- Is an endless good example.

Figure 4.6 Part of the challenge of applying motivation leadership is to assume the role of removing barriers and supporting the team. This begs the depiction of an upside-down organization chart, which is often how it works. This support must be constantly provided while strongly leading the direction and pace of the team and maintaining final approval authority.

Furthermore, some higher-level managers may even be uncomfortable to see a PM that is subordinate to the insights and recommended direction from their team. Their lack of comfort can be exacerbated when they see that this approach is successful. The modern program manager will appreciate the cause of this angst and not respond with arrogance. It may take time for high-level individuals who have a more traditional leadership background to observe and appreciate the benefits of the modern leadership approach.

Some senior-level team members may be suspicious about this modern leadership approach. They may surmise that it is a fad and will pass. Some senior team members may be used to being told what to solve, then providing solutions that were successful in past applications, despite these solutions' having been superseded by superior designs or by advancements in the supporting technologies. The good program manager must be aware of this potential and patiently give these valuable senior participants tasks that motivate them to stay up to date.

Usually, senior team members will see the high value of the motivation-based leadership approach and comply with it. They will become more receptive to new ways of solving common problems. They will observe that frequently the solutions that result are more resource efficient and achieve higher performances.

In some cases, senior team members may not want to change the way they service the program but do want to continue to offer some insights and solutions that are highly valuable. In this case, leadership should attempt to provide these professionals the traditional leadership interface they prefer. Unfortunately, their contributions may become less valuable with time.

In rare cases, a senior team member may be insistent on strictly adhering to and applying old and obsolete solutions. These stubborn objections may be visible to the team and demoralizing. They tend to contradict leadership emphasis on the value of innovation and process improvements. In this case, the program leadership should consider the impact of removing this individual from the team. Sometimes the disruption to the team can result in a higher penalty than the loss of this person's expertise.

The leaders of first-place programs understand that leadership never becomes automatic. To them, leadership is not simply the act of setting up a process and program organization and then monitoring its performance as it is allowed to execute on its own. The best leadership requires constant attention to developing the motivations of their team members. Yes, this task is in addition to the myriad attentions and tasks needed to lead any program. But this ongoing attention to fulfilling individual motivations is needed for the program to be the best amongst competitors.

Keep in mind, the modern leader delegates more situational awareness and planning responsibilities to the other team members. So, modern leadership is not so much about increasing workload but rather about redistributing the substance and priorities of the work being done.

4.5 Evaluate and Engage with Added Human Factors

Modern program leaders must evaluate the self-actualization of their individual reports on the enhanced Maslow list of motivations developed for this book (see Figure 4.7, in which the level of Self-Actualization is replaced with Professional and Altruistic motivations), especially when it comes time to make assignments. For newer team members who haven't yet discovered their self-actualization type, leaders are there to help them in this process of self-discovery. While leading the team, they also must detect any changing or new motivations—often leading to a change in self-actualization in the team individuals—and provide opportunities to grow them.

The modern leader must establish a free and open interface with all team members so that team-member insight may be included in planning future work. Also, leadership must have a wide-open door to listen and evaluate risks or issues that any team member (including suppliers, executive management, and customer representatives) brings forward.

As will be discussed later, the modern leader must keep each team member sold on the attributes of the program throughout the lifetime of the work.

4.6 Leaders Must Constantly Adjust

As discussed, On-Step leaders must monitor and adapt to changes in the growth of their team members. They cannot simply institute a fixed process or plan for

Self-Actualization—Developing or One of Six Destinations

Self-Actualization

- *Altruistic*
- *Professional*
- *Esteem*
- *Love*
- *Safety*
- *Physiological*

Figure 4.7   The author has modified the classic Maslow motivation hierarchy in two ways. First, after maturing as a professional, a team member may settle at any of the maturity levels as their self-actualization. Second, the author has added two levels of self-actualization—the Professional and Altruistic levels. A team member's motivation may change levels during the support of a program or when they move to a new program.

Modern Leader's Role Is Constantly Supportive

- Identify hidden talents in reports.
- On-Step pace can make emerging talents apparent.
- Give assignments that develop talents:
  - Achievable steps
  - With employee concurrence
- Mentor development.
- Share new talents with enterprise.
- May be a *"Win, Win, Win."*

Figure 4.8 A tenet of applying motivational leadership is to identify and develop hidden or developing talents in the team's individuals. This includes providing assignments that grow these new areas and then being available for mentoring. This attempt highly benefits the team member, the team, and the enterprise.

each team member, then apply it without adapting or refining it for the team member responsible (see Figure 4.8).

Leaders must pay attention to the changing and maturing motives of their team's individuals. They must consider the talents and self-actualization of each team member when assigning them. They must constantly be on the lookout for clues that improve their understanding of each team member's motivations.

Furthermore, first-place leaders must plan and administer achievable growth assignments for team members who are exhibiting new interests and talents.

4.7 Chapter Highlights

- On-Step leadership is very different from traditional.
- Modern leadership is establishing a new direction.
- There are specific changes in leadership culture needed.
- Modern leadership places more emphasis on human factors.
- Modern leaders are constantly adjusting.

Chapter Five

The Impact of Motivation-Based Leadership

5.1 Improves Existing On-Step Elements

The application of motivation-based leadership results in significant changes and improvements in the way leadership is performed (see Figure 5.1). As mentioned, past program management success elements were derived by trial and error. These elements were applied by many past leaders and were observed to

Valuing Individual Motivation Is Key

- Supercharges team enthusiasm.
- Guides member and leadership selections.
- Guides achieving effective team member mix.
- Increases team productivity.
- Increases team contentment and pride.
- Emphasizes using "pull," not "push."
- Puts program On-Step!

Figure 5.1 Determining and including consideration of individual motivations while leading is essential to be a first-place team. It helps establish a higher level of team integration, vitality, and progress rate than can be achieved with many past leadership methods.

result in highly successful outcomes (see Figure 5.2). We will discuss in the following sections that these success elements actually facilitate achieving the needs for the individual motivations of the team members. Achieving these needs is probably why these elements were observed to be so successful.

With leadership addressing and appealing to team-member motivations during program execution, not only are the beneficial impacts of these success elements

On-Step Elements—Learned from Past

- Select program manager per criteria.
- Plan from current status to next needed accomplishment.
- Determine minimal organization structure using highly independent pieces.
- Select task leads with product familiarity.
- Document leadership and team-member responsibilities.
- Implement integration and test flow to find faults early.
- Team review all contracts.
- Establish colocated work area.
- Book special facilities early.
- Emphasize in-person communication.
- Assign a *schedular*.
- Create the master schedule.
- Establish effective configuration control.
- Choose predictive metrics.
- Enforce complete root-cause process.
- Set up complete supplier management organizations.
- Establish risk management process and team.

- Establish common tracking and margin management processes.
- Schedule periodic and special meetings.
- Adhere to program plan process when meeting.
- Keep program plan current and strictly followed.
- Solicit and manage innovations and process improvements.
- Develop team ethics—a business imperative.
- Record all software development details in SDP (if software being developed).
- Avoid known configuration-control mistakes.
- Assign one person per responsibility.
- Apply reuse, knowledgeably.
- Use team members' guidance for planning and risks/issues identification.
- Consider multiple books.
- Document only important info.
- Follow recommended recruiting guidelines.
- Offer mentoring to all enterprise team members.
- Encourage enterprise dedication.

> *These elements successfully saved past failing programs.*

Figure 5.2 This is an introduction of the successful organizational and process actions the author applied and led when turning troubled programs around. A more detailed discussion will be provided later on how motivation management supports these and additional success elements. Also, recommendations will be made on how to apply them.

increased, but also team members may identify additional success elements—new elements that can even further improve the performance of the program.

5.2 Guides Team Mix

Classification of team-member motivation can be used to distinguish team members who are associated with what the author refers to as "problem-oriented" versus "solution-oriented" individuals (see Figure 5.3).

Teams Need Mix of Two Types

- **Problem-Oriented** Team Members
    - **Thoroughly analyzes problem tasks.**
    - **Usually most patient.**
    - **Takes pride in work constancy and achieving realistic commitments.**
    - **Recognized as providing necessary expertise.**
    - **Primary originator of process improvements.**
    - **Creates most of the product.**

- **Solution-Oriented** Team Members
    - **Motivated by completion vision.**
    - **Always looking for shorter paths.**
    - **Often optimistic, "can do."**
    - **High energy.**
    - **Often impatient.**
    - **Source of potent/risky innovations.**
    - **Too many can muddle progress!**

Needed mix depends on task.

Figure 5.3 The author has observed two distinctly different types of team members: problem oriented and solution oriented. He observed that sometimes a team member will transition from one type to the other during the program work or when moving from one program to another. A mix of both team-member types, with relative amounts appropriate to the work being performed, is essential.

- Those whose stable self-actualizations of fulfilling Physiological, Safety, Love/Belonging, or Professional needs tend to be problem-oriented individuals—sometimes respectfully referred to as "steady eddies."
- Those individuals whose self-actualization goal at the time is to increase their Esteem or to achieve an Altruistic goal are usually solution-oriented individuals. (These team members are usually the best candidates for leadership roles.)

5.3 Introduces Two-Step Execution

To use team-member motivation to highly incentivize the team and make the program first place requires establishing the understanding amongst the team members that the program will partially or completely fulfill their motivation needs, and that the outcome of the effort has high value not only for them individually but also for society. This rationale is to establish team members' buy-in to the importance of the task they will be asked to accomplish. Then leadership must create a work environment that allows these team members to directly fulfill these needs.

However, leadership must revisit and at times augment the buy-in rationale during the entire life of the program to remind the team members of their value and what they are deriving from their experience. These two program leadership steps will be distinguished in more detail in following chapters (but see Figure 5.4).

The information content and emphasis used to implement each of these two steps vary for each team member, depending on their specific self-actualization. In addition, these two steps include incorporating team-member participation by providing inputs to determine the direction and achieve the successes of the program (including program planning, innovations, and risk and issue assessment).

Establishing team-member buy-in during Step 1 and then leading motivation-based team commitment achievement while removing barriers in Step 2 requires constant attention by leadership. Throughout the life of the program, leadership must readdress the high value of the work they are accomplishing and its special value for each team member. That is, leadership must consistently return to Step 1 and repeat portions of it.

5.4 Suggests Inverted Pyramid Organization Function

Illustrating a program team organization this way is a dramatic departure from the traditional pyramid shape chart. But many of us who have managed large

Two Steps to Create First-Place Program

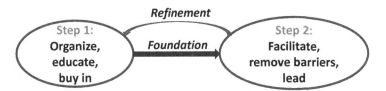

Refinement

Step 1:
Organize,
educate,
buy in

Foundation

Step 2:
Facilitate,
remove barriers,
lead

- Canvas motivations (preliminary).
- Determine team mix.
- Pick leads.
- Simple, draft organization.
- Draft operational guidelines.
- Draft or refine program or project plan.
- Review expectations of team roles.
- Normalize values; create and refine code of conduct.

- Refine planning from team input.
- Address individual motivations.
- Encourage efficient effort.
- Leadership eliminate obstacles.
- Highlight progress.
- Honor accomplishments.
- Provide allowable transparency.
- Develop member potentials.
- Encourage early warning.
- Address threats.
- Galvanize team code (ethics).

Figure 5.4   This is an introduction of the two steps required to set up and complete a first-place program. The first step includes organizing and introducing new team members, developing the program plan, and developing buy-in from the team members. The second step includes executing the plan while developing individual team-member abilities.

programs realize that the best programs are to a large extent managed this way (see Figure 5.5).

This depiction emphasizes that while being responsible for the direction and performances of the program team, the PM and the leadership team also have the role of detecting early and removing obstructions to progress for the team members. In this capacity, the program management is truly subordinate to the team members doing the work.

This inverted depiction also points out a critically needed feature of modern program management that is not found in the traditional, top-down, command-based structure. It emphasizes the need for the front-line individual contributors to provide recommendations for future program direction, observed risks, predicted future issues, proposed innovations, suggested process improvements, and more.

The following is a very simple example of applying the inverted pyramid organization with favorable results:

A large program was maintaining a program office in one building, with hundreds of team members. The customer would frequently visit for status.

The PM Works for the Teams

- **PM integrates commitments, sets direction, facilitates work, approves changes.**
- **PM sets pace, removes barriers, provides the most profound example.**
- **But . . . *The Team is part of Developing Completion Plan, Identifying Risk/Issues and Does The Work!***
- **PM must maintain fragile balance between prescription and permissiveness.**

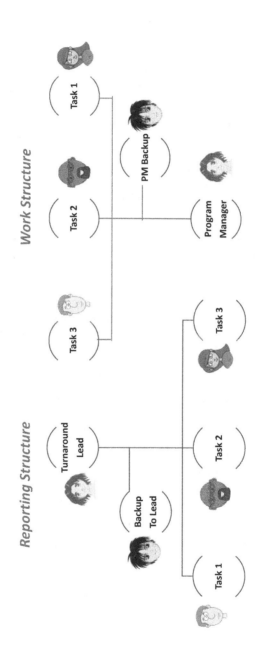

Reporting Structure

Work Structure

Figure 5.5 As discussed earlier, the actual work structure for the team is the upside-down pyramid. The PM sets the work pace, establishes direction, approves decisions, and removes barriers to progress but does not try to direct how to accomplish the details of every task. Usually, the individuals performing the work have a more comprehensive insight and offer superior solutions. Using the best ideas from their team members is necessary for a program to be in first place.

Unfortunately, the bathrooms, although clean, did not look their best. The program manager wanted to impress the customer but felt it was hard with bathrooms in this condition.

Traditionally, a PM would contact maintenance management and complain. Maintenance leads would look into the situation, possibly reprimand the existing building maintenance team, change priorities, and likely provide additional costly resources to improve cleaning.

Unfortunately, as a consequence, the building maintenance team would likely feel abused and would believe they looked deficient in the eyes of this important program they were serving. They probably would feel deflated because no one had brought this problem directly to them. However, the PM would likely take pride in taking immediate action and making the "tough" decision.

The PM on this program, however, took a more modern approach. He decided to visit the maintenance technician in person and ask how they could make the bathrooms look better. He especially asked if it was possible to remove the discoloration in the grout around the sinks.

He learned that the technician felt they could remove the discoloration but did not have enough time because they were spending so much time emptying wastebaskets that were situated deep in the cubicles and offices. The technician went on to suggest that the program team members could keep their wastebasket by the entrance to their work area instead of close to their desk. This would allow the maintenance technician to simply reach into each area, grab the wastebasket, empty it without entering the area, then move on. Plus, this would not interrupt ongoing work in these areas.

So, the PM asked all the team members to this—and the results were outstanding and immediate! The bathrooms now appeared immaculate. The frontline maintenance personnel had suggested an efficient and innovative process improvement that successfully helped the program in multiple ways. In fact, the maintenance personnel felt like they were now more a part of the program team and its success!

Their dedication to maintaining the building and the enterprise was increased. Just one example of how leadership working for those in the front line (inverted pyramid) can bring many benefits while increasing teamwork and worker dedication.

5.5 Updates Leadership Roles

The work of modern motivation-based program leadership is more arduous than that of the leadership performed with a traditional approach. These leaders must consistently refine their understanding of the level of motivation maturity or self-actualization of their individual reports. In addition, they must detect and facilitate the development of emerging new motivations and talents in the reports.

These leaders must receive, evaluate, and thoughtfully incorporate inputs from all program team members. These include primarily work-planning guidance, perceived risks, observed issues, recommended innovations, recommended process improvements, and more. These leaders must constantly maintain the balance between appropriately applying the most knowledgeable team inputs while maintaining leadership authority and establishing top-level program direction (see Figure 5.6).

5.6 Provides Leadership Selection Guidance

One of the requirements of modern program leadership is their willingness and ability to evaluate individual team-member motivations and use this to tailor their guidance for these individuals.

Many acceptable leaders have a mature self-actualization level of Esteem. Fulfilling the needs of their boss is one of their high priorities. They often carefully design the next steps they believe are needed to be promoted. These individuals often make fastidiously complying to the wishes of their superiors a first priority.

Modern Role of Leadership Expanded

- **Leaders must detect, facilitate, and nurture transitions in self-actualizations of team individuals:**
  - **Up or down six-level list**
  - **May indicate a previously unappreciated talent (different self-actualization)**
- **May refine team mixes with team experience.**
- **Bond team with common code of conduct, colocated work area(s), team commitments, etc.**
- **Detect and predict subtle barriers to progress and remove them.**
- **Constantly verify shortest path planned to completion planned while incorporating recommendations from team members.**

Figure 5.6 Modern leaders must determine team-member motivations to make assignments and establish effective team mix. They must constantly look ahead of current activities to predict future barriers to team progress, then remove them. In addition, they must constantly evaluate improvement suggestions that may shorten the path to completion while detecting and nurturing new talents and changing motivations in the individual team members.

Other PM candidates have an Altruistic self-actualization. Their usually passionate need to help individuals and the world do better give them the fortitude to work the many complex and multidimensional problems a leader must solve. Team members rarely question the motives of a lead with this self-actualization.

The preference of one of these two sources for selecting leadership depends mainly on the code of conduct of the enterprise and the needs of the leadership role. Of course, there will be exceptions to looking just amongst one of these two kinds of self-actualization for leaders.

Program leadership must understand that, while having ultimate decision authority, they must not assert highly prescriptive direction without a rational basis. Some team members may not agree with the direction they are finally given, but they should have access to the argument used to justify it.

In addition, leadership must incorporate any higher-level perspective they may have, their personal contacts, and any other influences at their disposal to knock down barriers to the team for the direction the program is taking.

5.7 Provides Guidance for Team-Member Development

Program leadership must assess the maturing or self-actualization level of motivation in the individual team members as well as detecting emerging motivations. They must determine if newly detected motivations are a prelude to an emerging talent or possibly a change of self-actualization type. These new motivations must then be checked for durability when team members are subsequently given a growth assignment.

5.8 Chapter Highlights

- Motivation management has multiple benefits.
- Improves On-Step.
- Guides team mix.
- Suggests two-step program execution.
- Requires changes to leadership roles.
- Provides guidance for leadership selection and team-member development.

Chapter Six

Motivation Management Details

6.1 Benefits of Maslow Paradigm

The use of Maslow's theory of human motivations as a starting point, with the refinements developed in this book, is the best foundation to prepare a program team to achieve a high level of execution—one that puts it in first place (refer to Figure 2.1 on page 26). The following sections describe the major benefits of this approach.

6.1.1 Applies Common Sense

Our developed six-level, Maslow-based paradigm satisfies basic common sense (see Figure 6.1). It relies on the positive values of motivating people to do their best rather than using threats or intimidation. Intimidation may have a more immediate result but creates long-term resentment, dysfunction, and low performance. Threats and intimidation can never be used to convince a modern professional to perform their best and bring forth highly valued improvements and innovations.

Our Maslow-based paradigm is simple and can be learned quickly. The only novel element it contains is the concept of self-actualization.

No complex or recurrent training is necessary to learn this approach. No special paraphernalia or additional personnel are needed to implement and maintain its benefits.

Good Motivation Management Process
Appeals to Common Sense

- **Are the proposed paradigm and process simple?**
- **Are contents derived from proven and accepted past work?**
- **Is the approach proven by successful prior application?**
- **Is the approach easy to learn?**
- **Do any theory components seem artificial?**
- **Does the approach rely heavily on penalties and guardrails?**
- **Are sizable added resources and cost required?**
- **Is frequent recurrent training necessary?**
- **Does training and maintenance require an expensive series of proprietary books, seminars, special classes, experts?**

> *Be on guard for the fad processes.*

Figure 6.1 When using a human motivation process, its application should be simple and easy to learn and use. Its principles should concur with common human experiences. Often new processes that seem esoteric or arbitrary are of low value. Beware of those laden with extensive retraining and expensive instructional aids. A good motivation-management process should have demonstrated value in past applications.

6.1.2 Conforms to Real Human Examples

Self-actualization, according to Maslow's theory and this book's extension of it, is the final form of human motivation maturity in every individual—"what you are meant to do." Understandably, this concept challenges strict analysis and for some may even sounds "corny." Our grandparents may have talked about our special talent and what we were meant to be, but in our free society, it is hard to accept that we each actually have some kind of individual destiny.

Some self-test questions regarding your self-actualization: What do others value in you, sometimes to your surprise? What do others consistently associate with you? What talent do you have for which your response is, "Not that special"? Is there something that others repeatedly celebrate in you and/or associate with you but you evaluate as not important or worthy of consideration?

Often a person's self-actualization changes with time and maturity. But many times, what an individual believes they want to be is not what their self-actualization is.

One example is a gentleman, let's call him Mr. D, who worked for the author and who was a highly capable leader of software developers (see Figure 6.2).

Many would refer to him as a "natural" in this role. He totally understood the status of all current software and system development issues, worked well in identifying all options, was very fair with all team members, and was very patient. He was loved by all his reports. He was reliably successful, leading teams of up to 30 people to develop high-quality, embedded real-time software for critical applications. I envied his consistency and the high respect he garnered.

Yet, this person insisted that what he really wanted to do was write children's books. Eventually, he left the company and pursued this calling—this was clearly what he imagined himself to be.

Many months later, one of the company employees bumped into him selling hardware at a local warehouse store. He admitted he was barely making ends meet and had not sold any of the books he had written. Eventually, he returned to the company, prospering at doing what he really does well. He recognized this as his self-actualization and that this was the work he loved and enjoyed the most.

As mentioned previously, as a young boy the author dreamt of being an astronaut and a musician. His mother frequently had to wake him up from his "daydreams" of being on the moon. Also, for hours he would play a favorite record and pretend he was performing it, imagining impressing people at his performance.

Motivations Differ and Evolve

- **Junior team members—trial and discovery**
- **Sometimes, self-actualization not what you imagined**
- **One of final self-actualization levels**
  - **Physiological & Safety—***"P's" family, "L's" compensation*
  - **Love—***"H's" and "D's" love of team and leads*
  - **Esteem—***"A's" planning promotion, addresses specific needs of role*
  - **Professional—***"M's" respected subject-matter expert, innovator*
  - **Altruistic—***"T's" protect US and improve world with best teams*

> **How can leadership use this?**

Figure 6.2 About five years is needed for a starting professional to determine their self-actualization. It will often consist of a combination of some of the six types, with one being predominant. Many times, an individual's self-actualization is not what they imagined it would be when younger.

During his life he become a flight instructor and other advanced pilot ratings. He played guitar and did vocals. He wrote dozens of songs and has even been encouraged by professionals to stay at it.

He has loved these experiences, which have allowed him to live out activities he imagined in the past. But the reality is that analyzing how programs can be their best is the author's self-actualization. This work and the book you're reading are more important to him than anything else. He has come to realize that this is what he is meant to do.

Most new professionals do not immediately learn what their self-actualization is—trial and error are required. Recall that the self-actualization of a professional ends up being one of the six motivational levels the author has identified. Figure 6.2 and below are a few more examples of how a professional's self-actualization can end up on any motivation level.

- Mr. P is an excellent controls analyst with great academic credentials and a consistent track record of high-quality results. He also has a sizable number of young children. Very cheerfully, he makes it clear that his family is his first priority.

  Ms. L has stated a number of times, "I work for money." It appears that her career work is purely transactional. She consistently provides high-quality work results on time and receives fair compensation for it, and she apparently expects nothing more.

  Both Mr. P and Ms. L are motivated by fulfilling their Physiological and Safety needs. These are, of course, the first two levels of our six-level hierarchy. These professionals are not very interested in team bonding, their title, or some professional or altruistic abstraction. They simply want to provide income, food, shelter, and basic necessities in a dependable way—this is their self-actualization.

- Ms. H is motivated differently. She has had decades of experience in the same industry, and when she talks about her past experiences, her emphasis is always on the joy she has received from the comaraderie with her fellow team members and her leaders. She often comments on the high quality and congeniality of her fellow team members. She is quick to contribute to the planning and conduct of social events. She always displays above-average empathy for both the work and personal matters of her fellow team members.

  Ms. H's self-actualization is fostering and maintaining the belonging and love in her team. She has performed her work long enough to feel secure about her Physiological and Safety needs, and she is interested in elevating her professional title. She has done a consistently fine job, always providing good-quality work on time, and it is very important to her to maintain a preeminent interpersonal stature within her team and in the eyes of her boss—this is what brings her the most satisfaction. Her self-actualization is Love/Belonging.

- Mr. A, on the other hand, is consistently and carefully plotting the requirements and actions he needs to achieve the next higher level of professional title. He has carefully planned the steps needed to be promoted, or at least to increase his extent of responsibility in his current role.

  He seems to pay more attention to the value of his performance, as perceived by his leadership, than in the impact of his work on his team members or society at large. He often sets firm milestones for achieving certain professional titles that he feels he must gain to reach his full potential.

  Mr. A is candid and open about his detailed plans for future promotion. He shares the professional titles he believes he should have at specific times in the future, and he implies that not achieving these titles on time would be his failure. His self-actualization is increasing his level of Esteem.

The author has worked in teams in which employees stated that just staying employed was a measure of continued Esteem! This included tenure at a medical startup and at a renowned advance development organization for aerospace. Many of these team members felt that just being kept as a member of these organizations garnered a high degree of Esteem. One team member of the medical startup, with extraordinary academic credentials from a highly accredited school, told me, "I'm just proud to be working here and not having been fired yet!"

But some individuals have a more long-term ideal—an enduring idealization they crave to achieve. Sometimes it takes a professional a long time, even decades, to realize they are motivated by the self-actualization types of Professional or Altruistic.

A Professional self-actualization is to be the best at some specialty—being well respected in some engineering specialty, being an exceptionally accomplished and sought-after musician, being a highly effective teacher, being someone who can accurately record courtroom proceedings, and many more. These professionals may not be that interested in changing the world, but rather in being recognized for performing some job or function resulting in singularly valued and respected results.

An Altruistic self-actualization has the need of doing something that is perceived to benefit society. This is more than just benefiting large groups of people. Those with Altruistic self-actualization instead may have a motivational need to cure a disease, reduce global warming, make the world safe from war, and more. They're often motivated to develop a new product or process that will change and improve human living conditions, even if just a little bit.

Leadership of a first-place program must attempt to identify the level and need of self-actualization in each team member. Junior team members may still be transitioning through the six levels of motivation until they discover their self-actualization.

Leadership must use their knowledge of the maturing motivations and level of self-actualization in each team member when assigning them to a task team and choosing leadership. They must then check that their self-actualization needs are being fulfilled with their assignment. They must check for any emerging new talents from the team member resulting from a change of their self-actualization, then nurture its growth.

Fulfilling the needs of maturing motivations or changing self-actualization for each team member will bring great value to the program—it is essential for the effort to be in first place.

The reader should again note that the definition of self-actualization used in this book is slightly extended beyond the definition in Maslow's writings. Maslow has defined self-actualization as the final, highest step of human motivation that can be achieved. He defined the other motivational steps, including Love and Esteem, as interim steps to self-actualization. This book, however, acknowledges that these interim motivation steps are for some people their ultimate self-actualization step, doing what they are "meant to do."

For example, Mr. P, the team member I mentioned earlier, is a highly talented and professional controls engineer. Yet, his self-actualization is to build his career to support his family. He believes he was meant to be an excellent father—that is his purpose.

Mr. P is very friendly and has integrated well with the team but has little impetus to further develop team belonging or love. He has little interest in plotting his next promotion. He is interested in listening to philosophical discussions of the social impacts of the product he is working on, but he does not ponder over this subject on his own. He only wants to make sure he is being fairly compensated, and he provides highly professional results to justify this compensation. But he is not striving to be a noted specialist in his work.

As for all professionals, Mr. P's self-actualization may evolve and change in the future. But at the time, his self-actualization is stable. He simply wants to provide for the Physiological and Safety needs of his family.

6.1.3 Guides Problem-Oriented/ Solution-Oriented Classification

In all programs, the members of the team can be divided into one of two categories: *problem* oriented or *solution* oriented (see Figures 6.3 and 6.4). Team members are not locked into one category—a member in one of these categories may move into the other category at any time for a wide range of reasons. More details regarding these categories are:

- **Problem-oriented team members.** These individuals focus on working the current problem. They make sure the solution that is derived is complete.

  They usually create most of the product content. They are the "pistons" of the team. They take pride in the work they accomplish being consistently

Team Types Have Valuable Attributes

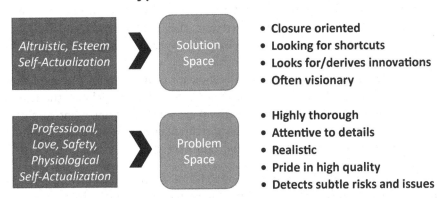

Figure 6.3 Problem-oriented professionals make sure all work is thoroughly completed and all details have been addressed, and they are often the first to detect subtle risks and issues. Solution-oriented professionals strive for closure—they are on the lookout for the shortest path to completion.

Team Types Have Weaknesses

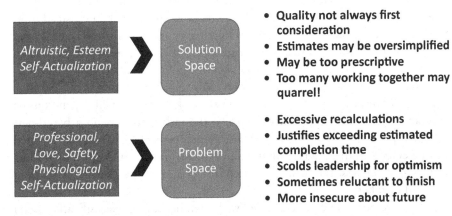

Figure 6.4 Problem-oriented professionals are very protective of a complete solution, which can result in exceeding cost targets and completion time. Solution-oriented professionals occasionally cut corners and may be too prescriptive if they are a team leader.

and highly thorough while achieving their commitments. They tend to be more patient and methodical than solution-oriented people. They are usually the originators of detailed improvements in process and product design.

Problem-oriented people are usually careful about making promises—they want to make sure they have evaluated all the details. Many are most realistic about the evaluation of a given situation and conservative about their estimates.

- **Solution-oriented team members.** Members of this group are motivated more by the vision of a completed task. They tend to have a "can do," "will do" attitude that is optimistic. They usually exhibit high enthusiasm and energy to bring their task to closure.

  Members of this group usually look for a shorter path to completion. They tend to be the source of major innovations to achieve the team's commitment. Members of this group are sometimes impatient, and care must be taken to make sure the shortcuts they use do not reduce product quality or otherwise bypass important issues.

Problem-oriented team members tend to be most secure when there are remaining problems to solve. Solution-oriented team members tend to be most secure when all known problems are solved and the team can move on to a new task.

Deriving the right mix of problem-oriented and solution-oriented team members in the various teams is essential for a program to be On-Step—to be and stay in first place. The six-level hierarchy of human motivation that we have developed is an important tool for establishing this mix.

The basic application of these motivation assessments is simple. Team members who are motivated by levels of Esteem or Altruistic self-actualization goals tend to work in the solution space. Those team members who are instead motivated by Professional, Love, Safety, or Physiology self-actualization needs tend to work in the problem space (see Figure 6.5). Of course, there will be a small number of team members in transition between motivation types and new professionals in the process of learning what their self-actualization is.

The needed ratio of these two types in the task team mix will depend on the substance of the program. For example, if the task is to develop a brand-new design or process, the mix should contain a larger percentage of solution-oriented team members. If the task is to improve an existing manufacturing line or product distribution process, the team should consist of a larger percentage of problem-oriented members.

There are pros and cons associated with members of each classification (refer again to Figures 6.3 and 6.4).

Solution-oriented team members tend to be more visionary. They are constantly looking for the shortest path to complete the work at hand. They crave

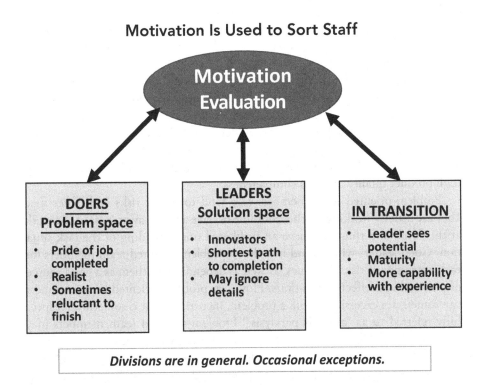

Motivation Is Used to Sort Staff

Motivation Evaluation

DOERS
Problem space

- Pride of job completed
- Realist
- Sometimes reluctant to finish

LEADERS
Solution space

- Innovators
- Shortest path to completion
- May ignore details

IN TRANSITION

- Leader sees potential
- Maturity
- More capability with experience

Divisions are in general. Occasional exceptions.

Figure 6.5 Knowing a professional's self-actualization can be used to determine if they are more problem oriented or solution oriented. Leaders tend to be more from the latter group. Some professionals may be in the process of changing their self-actualization or maturing their motivation to discover their self-actualization.

and appreciate innovations that will allow them to shorten the completion duration. They tend to scan the resources in their team to find the most efficient combination to get the work done. As mentioned, they are most comfortable when the task is complete. Unfortunately, some solution-oriented team members may underestimate or oversimplify the details of the work needed. As a result, when executing the work, the quality of their results may suffer. With their tendency to be impatient, solution-oriented members may become overly prescriptive and even overbearing.

Unfortunately, some solution-oriented members may believe that only they know the best way to complete the work. They may not devote enough time to listen to all other team members so they can balance a proposed fast completion plan with achieving adequate product quality. In addition, if a leader populates a team with too many solution-oriented members, they will find these team members may often disagree and quarrel. The resulting disruption can be seriously detrimental to team progress. Solution-oriented professionals who patiently balance task completion speed with maintaining product quality should be highly valued.

Problem-oriented team members place a high emphasis on making sure each task is completely solved to fine detail. They often do not compromise their standard of achieving a high-quality product or process level just to meet a milestone. Problem-oriented team members tend to be more realistic, often based on past experiences evaluating the work to be done and estimating the time and resources needed to complete it. They place ultimate emphasis on achieving high product quality and full completeness.

Problem-oriented team members also tend to detect risks and issues first. They are usually working on the front line or have a better awareness of the work at this level, and thus they have an unfiltered understanding of the task situation. Good leaders will depend heavily on problem-oriented team members for early warnings of risk and issues, as well as depending on them as a good source of practical and effective solutions. However, problem-oriented team members can sometimes excessively work a problem, incurring what is sometimes respectfully referred to as "analysis paralysis." Problem-oriented team members may strive to add detail and accuracy to a solution that may not be needed.

In the name of achieving a high degree of thoroughness, quality, and accuracy, problem-oriented team members may sometimes feel totally justified to slip a promised delivery time. This, of course, is at odds with the basic need discussed earlier of finishing a task by the committed time. Problem-oriented team members have been known to scold both their leadership and solution-oriented team members for being too optimistic about the feasibility of performing some tasks or predicting when they will get done. Problem-oriented team members may even be reluctant to stop working a task, even though it is adequately completed.

Still, leadership must be careful about making sure they incorporate all concerns from all members of the program team. They must adequately evaluate these concerns and determine their risk and impact while maintaining a high rate of program progress.

The distinction of problem-oriented and solution-oriented team members is a general one. Each team member is unique and may contain traits representing both classifications (see Figure 6.6). A team member may be a member of one classification for a given task and the other classification for another task. In addition, this team member's self-actualization may be transitioning up or down our six-level motivation hierarchy.

Leadership must detect and facilitate team members transitioning between problem-oriented and solution-oriented classifications. They must provide work opportunities to support the transition and be available for counseling. The mix of problem-oriented and solution-oriented team members may need adjustment

Factors Pertain to All Team Members
During Evaluation

- Classifications of development level or self-actualization type are general; each team member mixes with secondary needs.

- Team members may be in transition up or down six-level motivation hierarchy.

- Leaders must detect, facilitate, and nurture transitions of self-actualization content.

- All team members are bonded with common code of conduct, colocated office, team commitments, ethics, etc.

- Team mixes may need refinement with team experience and developing product maturity.

Figure 6.6   These are general guidelines that apply to the evaluation of the motivation of the team members.

with actual program execution experience and a better understanding of the abilities and inclinations of each team member.

Regardless of the individual team member's developing motivation, self-actualization, or problem-versus-solution classification, all team members must be united by a common code of conduct, ethics, a colocated work environment, and common completion commitments.

6.1.4 Lessons

First, the role of leadership to lead a first-place program, a program On-Step, is not traditional (see Figure 6.7). Successful PMs must walk a fine line between the extremes of being too prescriptive and too permissive. They must allow all suggestions to be freely heard. These include suggestions from the bottom up of organizing how best to perform the work, estimates of how long it should take to complete the tasks, and what the current risks and issues are. Still, the leader is the individual who ultimately decides what direction the team finally takes.

The PM and the leadership team must be fully accountable for the successes and failures of the team. They must encourage and exemplify developing innovations and process improvements for the daily work. They must be at the forefront of progress, knocking down barriers for the team. They must always be approachable by any team member and treat each one with a high degree of respect, patience, and fairness. The good PM must show very little "moodiness," regardless of their personal situation.

Lead to Empower Team Members

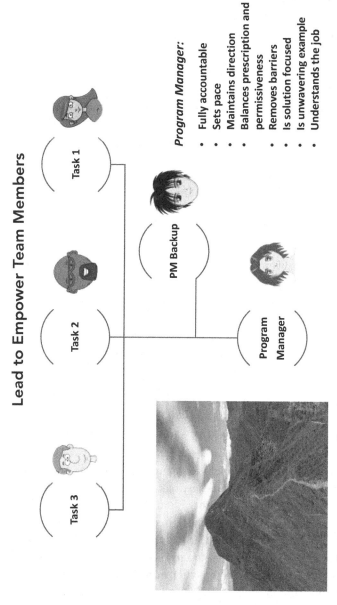

Program manager walks narrow path!

Figure 6.7 The PM must define the direction of and establish the development pace of the program. They must focus on leading the development of solutions while being an unwavering example of good ethics. They must anticipate and remove barriers to the team so the team can establish as much of the planning and risk identification as possible.

The leadership of a first-place program must be an unwavering example of the team's work ethic and professional code of conduct. Often, they will be the first to arrive to work and the last to leave.

It is essential that leadership of a first-place program understands, at least at a top level, all the elements of what is being developed and the job needed to create it. These elements include customer needs, business details, business profitability, product and process design, supporting technologies, their enterprise capabilities, and subcontractor and supplier capabilities. They must be good at listening and communicating work information to all stakeholders.

In addition to all this, they must of course maintain a useful understanding of the developing motivations and self-actualizations of the members of their team, with the knowledge that the leadership team is ultimately responsible for mutually designing the teams, determining the work plan, and assigning tasks.

Good leadership skills by themselves are not enough for the modern PM. Leaders may not comprehend the in-depth details of the work being performed, but they should understand the basics and be able to be conversant with it. Otherwise, they will only be aware of the symptoms of sub-par performance without understanding its origins. This is not adequate for a first-place program.

All that the author has just described again implies the classic, upside-down organization chart for team-member interdependencies. First-place PMs use all the inputs and recommendations from the team to finalize direction, then eliminate the barriers that develop during execution. In addition, they directly listen to the frontline workers to identify both the immediate risks and issues and a potentially better plan to completion. Much of the time, good program leadership takes a supporting role.

Here the two-step process outlined in Chapter 5 comes into play, first organizing the team and establishing buy-in then executing the program.

6.2 More About Self-Actualization

6.2.1 A Paradox

Application of our Maslow-based motivational hierarchy can be used to organize and provide direction to lead to be in first place by addressing the different levels of human motivation we have defined. Self-actualization is the most mature motivation state, and an individual's self-actualization is represented by one of the six levels of motivation in our hierarchy (see Figure 6.8).

Addressing the levels of motivation that are present in the different team members results in a team that works up to its potential and is content. Team

Book Supplements Maslow with Six Levels of Self-Actualization

- Physiological—*Adequate and fair compensation.*
- Safety—*Work environment free of fear. Long-term work outlook.*
- Love—*Enjoy and support personal relationships with team members and leads.*
- Esteem—*Tactical planning for promotion, title emphasis, acceptance by a renowned organization.*
- Professional—Internal: *Be best/expert capability; sought-after engineer, consultant, pilot, musician.*
- Altruistic—External: *Improve society; stop global warming, cure disease, build best programs, government leadership, clergy, etc.*

Figure 6.8　As mentioned in earlier chapters, the author has replaced the traditional Maslow level of Self-Actualization with Professional and Altruistic motivation levels. In addition, the author has observed that a professional will adopt one of these six levels as their primary self-actualization at a given time in their career.

members whose needs have matured to a motivation level of self-actualization are necessary for the program to be On-Step. Team members whose self-actualization is at the Professional or Altruistic level are usually most passionate about achieving the purpose of their work and therefore are often more selfless. Individuals with an Esteem-based or Altruistic-based self-actualization are usually the best leaders.

Team members motivated by a Professional or Altruistic self-actualization have a passion to achieve their ideals, and this desire is most often very enduring.

The concept of self-actualization echoes concepts that we might evaluate as old fashioned. Imagine your parents or grandparents referring to "what you're meant to be," your "destiny." Don't we all have a free will to do whatever we want?

However, there are a number of scientific rationalizations that lead to this concept of inherent purpose. Perhaps self-actualization is simply addressing an interest that for some reason occupied our minds during our early years. Perhaps this self-actualization self-image has always been in the back of our minds as a subconscious and fundamental intrigue.

But the fact persists that virtually all of us have something we are especially capable of doing well. As mentioned earlier, we are often surprised when others point out some capability we have as "special." Finding this self-actualization takes trial and error and thus time. There are some people who discover what they are "meant to do" early in their lives, but they are few.

6.2.2 Source of High Fulfillment

Team members are happiest and most content when they are either seeking or fulfilling their self-actualization (see Figure 2.4 on page 31 and Figure 6.9). Those who realize their self-actualization may make extraordinary personal sacrifices with persistent dedication when they perform their work. Their near-term personal needs often become secondary when an imminent work milestone must be accomplished.

Team members who fulfill the needs of their self-actualization often spontaneously devote extra effort. Their current job title or the accoutrements of their work area may not be the most important measure to them. Instead, they will be highly motivated by completely achieving the commitments of the task, even if it requires doing so in a way never before attempted.

Team members fulfilling their self-actualization are usually looking for a shorter path to success, particularly if they are more solution based, with tendencies toward leadership. But this can be true for problem-based professionals as well. They absorb additional knowledge and proficiency quickly and successfully incorporate it. They will ask someone who has the special expertise they need to become involved, if they believe this person is better qualified.

Facilitating Individual Motivation Allows Members to Be Their Best

- **High initiative, less leadership needed**
- **High commitment to success**
- **High productivity**
- **Vigorous pride of accomplishment**
- **Intense member cooperation**
- **Enthusiasm to plan ahead**
- **Lower turnover**
- **Team cheerfulness and optimism**

Figure 6.9 Recognizing and facilitating each professional's self-actualization results in numerous favorable team-member attributes that are necessary for the team to be in first place.

These professionals are constantly looking for innovations or process improvements to complete the work faster and with higher quality. They cherish others who offer helpful innovations, and they inherently distribute the portions of their task to those who are most skilled for the subject needing attention. There is little controversy over the resulting task assignments agreed upon by the team members involved.

Team members fulfilling their self-actualization possess a high level of initiative, requiring less direction regarding what to do next. It is often very hard for them to accept defeat. The productivity per capita is high in these teams, and there exists a high degree of cheerfulness and optimism. Team members in this environment tend to adhere to a strong code of team ethics. Complaints from their team members tend to be less frequent and are well substantiated, and there is less employee turnover in these teams. Members of these teams form close bonds with fellow team members.

Team members who fulfill their self-actualization needs make the program and the enterprise the best amongst competitors. Their work becomes the standard by which others judge their own performance, and their enterprise name is the first that comes to mind when customers think of who is best in their business genre. They have found the "Secret Sauce."

6.3 Guidance for Identifying Team-Member Motivation

Program leadership must never assume that they are performing any kind of psychoanalysis! There is no proposal in this book to probe deep into the minds of team members! But a cursory understanding of the motivation maturity or self-actualization of each team member is essential.

Important factors that allow team members at each level of motivation to feel unencumbered should be reviewed (see Figure 6.10). A summary description of actual examples of professionals at each motivation level is included.

Each team member's motivation needs and the way they manifest them is unique. For example, one individual may find their self-actualization is achieving their Physiological/Safety needs so they can be a responsible parent, while another person may be striving for these same needs so they can fulfill their dream of buying their first home.

As we have discussed, an individual's motivation needs may change during execution of the program or when moving to a different program. This change can be up or even down our motivation hierarchy. It is a high priority for leadership to detect and facilitate these changes.

For example, a team member whose self-actualization was their personal need to be the best in their field (Professional self-actualization) may now be more interested in achieving a higher job title, such as enterprise consultant. Esteem may become their motivation level, their new self-actualization. Leadership should mentor and facilitate any change in the motivation level for anyone on the team. Of course, this must be done within the needs and restraints of the program they are servicing.

As mentioned before, despite the differences and changes in self-actualization for each team member, there are still factors common amongst team members. For example, team members are bonded with a common code of conduct—a common set of ethics. The team members share the same team commitments. Most share their work in a colocated area with common provisions.

Each team member in a first-place program must feel that the facilities, work tools, and other considerations allocated to them by leadership are equal to those allocated to others at their professional level. In addition, leadership must make a conscious effort not to show or imply favoritism when communicating with any of the team members.

6.3.1 Identifying Motivation Level

When setting up and selling the program (in Step 1) and executing it (in Step 2), leadership must evaluate and accommodate individual motivations. This must be performed while removing barriers for the team so they can easily achieve their team commitments.

Figure 6.10 lists what is needed for team members at each level of motivation to be unencumbered. This book has simply added Professional and Altruistic self-actualization levels to the traditional Maslow hierarchy. In addition, this book acknowledges that self-actualization can rest at any one of the original levels that Maslow would have said is an interim step.

For example, a team member may simply have a passion to achieve the highest professional title they can. Sometimes this need is more important to them than the social effect of what they are working on, how socially integrated they are with their team, or even how important the income they receive is to their home and safety. The self-actualization of this team member would be to achieve high professional Esteem.

The leadership process of identifying individual motivations should be mutually performed with the team member, who will understand that this analysis is not secret and is designed to help them define a professional path. In addition, it will help them to progress along this path at a high rate, with a high degree of satisfaction. It will help them to determine what they do best.

The first step for leadership to help a team member, especially a new member, to identify their professional goals and aspirations should be one or more direct, uninterrupted discussions, during which the leader should realize that the first

Each Level Has Real Examples

BOOK MOTIVATION LEVEL	ACTUAL EXAMPLES	NEEDS TO FEEL UNENCUMBERED
Level I—Physiological Self-Actualization	Mr. P1—Six children primary responsibility, excellent analyst, very pleasant with work time constraints. Ms. L—"I work for money"	Assurance of fair compensation. Allowed to perform work completely as agreed. Appreciation of transactional agreement. Assurances that someone is looking out for them.
Level II—Safety Self-Actualization	Mr. P2—Fastidious about completion requirements being mutually understood and agreed to.	Closely connected to Level I. Assurance of continued income for good work provided. Visibility provided of long-term plan that ensures consistency. Feedback provided that work performed meets or exceeds expectations.
Level III—Love Self-Actualization	Ms. H—Solely referred to coworkers and leaders relations when discussing past experience. Valued for deep insight into coworker needs.	Provide a cordial and friendly work relationship with leadership. Value the insight of these individuals regarding the feelings and preferences of other team members. Have them coordinate casual social events for the team. Ask them to help facilitate face-to-face, in-person communication amongst team members. Establish optimistic team environment.
Level IV—Esteem Self-Actualization	Mr. A, Mr. C—Gauge of self is highly professional title. Have thoroughly thought-out strategy for promotion to next level.	Provide advancement opportunities with specific requirements. Highlight possible routes to promotion to higher levels. Promotion only after complete accomplishment of requirements. Make their professional level visible to team and enterprise. Demonstrate leadership is looking for future promotional opportunities in enterprise. Accept promotion may be higher priority for them than product purpose.

BOOK MOTIVATION LEVEL	ACTUAL EXAMPLES	NEEDS TO FEEL UNENCUMBERED
Level V — Professional Self-Actualization	Mr. R—Configuration control expert Mr. M1—Accurate complex simulations Mr. G—Consult simple answers to critical mechanics problems	Leadership examines work history to verify this self-actualization. (Leadership appreciates that this level seldom clarified for junior professionals.) One-on-one discussion with leadership to clarify professional self-vision. Acknowledge their innovations to achieve self-actualization ideal. Provide growth assignments that freely challenge the abilities of their expertise. Publicly value achievement of professional accomplishments during execution. Adapt to changes, growth of individual's self-actualization ideals. Establish job title that describes their special role.
Level VI - Altruistic Self-Actualization	Mr. M2—Better the world leading developing of first of kind high tech Mr. T—Improve the world with high-performance teams Mr. W—Care for all humans with medicine Mr. B—Make the world better by understanding materials	(Leadership appreciates this level seldom clarified for junior professionals.) One-on-one discussion with leadership to clarify Altruistic vision. Provide assignments, responsibilities that connect with Altruistic vision. Commend with written and spoken words their achievements of vision. Provide routes for benefactors to express their appreciation. Adapt to changes, growth, evolution of individual's vision. Allow time for leadership to understand and support this complicated self-actualization.

Figure 6.10 The basic needs of a professional at each of the six levels of self-actualization are shown. In addition, examples of real professionals at each of these levels and their specific characteristics are listed.

answers may not reveal the person's deepest, most basic motivating passion. Follow-up sessions should help the team member to this greater understanding.

Leadership should be reminded that the answer they receive to the question of goals and aspirations from low-seniority team members may often be less certain and may vary rapidly in the future. This is partially because this employee may not have had enough experience to precisely describe what they do well—only after working a number of assignments will this become clearer to them.

As the program gets underway, leadership should observe the work habits of each team member to clarify and verify what their (suspected) most important motivation is. This can include examining the questions they ask of leadership, the degree and kind of enthusiasm they show in their work, their willingness to make personal sacrifices for the work to stay on schedule, and more.

Any following resolution of a team member's motivational needs by leadership must be shared with the team member, and together they should reach a consensus on what these motivations currently are. This analysis must not be perceived to be performed behind their back. At this time, the goal is to "corral" this team member's general area of motivation, not to define it explicitly. As mentioned before, a determination of the self-actualization details of an individual requires trial, error, and time.

These discussions on motivations must be frank. Sometimes the team member's apparent motivations point in a different direction from the professional route they thought they would take. It also must be made clear that no one type or level of motivation is considered to be superior to another. Each is equally important and can be used to drive a successful career and a first-place program.

Leadership must follow up their analysis by providing work assignments appropriate to the observed motivation of the team member—assignments that may help the team member further understand and develop their motivation. This will both verify that the motivation identified is accurate and help the team member further grow their specialty.

Please keep in mind that often when less experienced professionals are developing, they may eventually find their self-actualization to be something they were not aware of. For example, the author became good at recruiting, organizing, and leading teams that specialized in developing onboard embedded computer systems. To do this job well, he had to thoroughly understand all the functions of the system being controlled. With a physics education, he had a rudimentary understanding of a wide range of sciences and technologies.

An experienced PM saw a potential in him and gave him the opportunity to lead a systems engineering team for a satellite program. He was surprised by this assignment, but he thrived in this new environment and enjoyed the work immensely. This step led to him to become a program manager making valuable contributions by applying modern team leadership principles. He eventually discovered that his real self-actualization was making the world better by learning how to assemble and lead the most effective teams.

6.3.2 When Is Self-Actualization Found?

For most professionals, discovering their true self-actualization is a long-term and sometimes awkward process. Through a series of professional trials and in other ways, it can take as long as decades, usually requiring serious frankness and honesty that ignores social pressures and pre-existing self-images.

However, finding one's self-actualization does follow a well-known series of maturing steps first proposed by Maslow. These steps are presented below to give some review of the challenges and growths experienced by new professionals. This division of steps is also needed to compute a minimum duration for professionals to achieve their self-actualization.

The basic motivation maturing steps for a developing professional are:

1. **Physiological.** When a new professional starts a job, their first concern is usually assembling a simple domestic expenditure budget that provides them basic shelter, food, and transportation. They may have to share living quarters with others, cook simple recipes at home, and drive or share a used automobile. Many new professionals have accrued debt for their education and, as they get underway in their professional life, may accrue more. They usually appreciate that, with sensible planning and restraint, they can save and build a reserve that will allow their condition to improve. For some, adequate healthcare is also of primary importance, particularly if they are closer to middle age, are responsible for a family, or have a pre-existing medical condition.

2. **Safety.** Many employers have a probationary period of one to six months, during which the new professional is evaluated for adequate job performance. Beyond this point, the new employee will often feel an added sense of safety. Additional safety is derived from becoming acclimated to the personal relationships and code of conduct in the work environment, as well as proving to themselves they are providing value. Often during this time, the new professional begins considering benefits details, 401(k), requirements for promotion, and what their strengths and weaknesses are. The author has observed that completing these Physiological and Safety levels takes a minimum of six months.

3. **Love/Acceptance.** At this point, the new professional begins socializing more with coworkers and friends. Some new professionals pay high attention to the personal needs and personalities of the people they work with. They may partially judge their professional performance by how much they help their coworkers achieve their needs. On the other hand, some new professionals may pay little attention to the personal desires of their coworkers. (In fact, it has been documented by some authors, including Maslow, that some new professionals jump ahead to the Esteem development level rather than remaining at the Love level to garner the love and acceptance of their coworkers.) Completing the Love/Acceptance level takes up to one year.

4. **Esteem.** Eventually, the developing team member focuses their interests on their professional title, making sure their monetary compensation is in accordance with their professional level and the opportunities they may wish to pursue for leadership. Some professionals develop a highly detailed plan with shrewd progress metrics to track their achievement of these desires. They may pay high attention to fulfilling the job requirements of advanced roles or new opportunities and may even leverage personal relationships to achieve a higher-level responsibility or leadership. (As mentioned above, some professionals may consider their job title, the documented extent of their responsibilities, or the number of people they lead as a way of achieving their Love/Acceptance needs.)

   During this time, the professional typically is developing a reputation in the enterprise they work for and even in the industry they are a part of. Completing the level of Esteem takes about four years.

5. **Self-Actualization.** The idea that we all have something we are "meant to do" heavily grates against the ideal that we have a free will and can do whatever we want to do. Of course, the ideal of free will is an inherent part of Western culture. Yet, many, if not most, professionals eventually discover what they were meant to do. And often it is not what they thought they were going to be or even wanted to be.

   Friends and work peers may be consistently conveying to the professional that they are really good at doing something. Some observers may say they have a special talent in this area. The professional may even enjoy performing the work in this area because it is easier and "fun" for them. The basis for this phenomenon is open to much investigation.

   For some professionals, self-actualization rests on one of the four steps of professional development listed above (and refer to Figure 6.8 on page 86). For example, a professional's self-actualization may be to simply provide for the physiological needs and safety of their family. Or they may achieve exceptional pleasure in monitoring and developing the social interactions in the team they are working with. Some professionals pay their highest attention to their job title, even more than the substance of what they are working on.

Still, a professional may ascribe one of two levels of self-actualization that are more abstract. These are either a *Professional* type, such as "being the best controls analyst," "being a highly knowledgeable and effective car mechanic," "being an outstanding portrait artist," and more. Or an *Altruistic* type, such as "helping eliminate global warming," "finding a remedy for Alzheimer's disease," "preventing nuclear war," and more.

After summing up the above development durations, it may be concluded that it takes a minimum of five years—even decades in some cases—for a professional to determine their self-actualization.

6.3.3 Making Team Assignments

We now have a means of determining when team members are eligible to be leaders in the program. Potential team leaders most often have an Esteem or Altruistic self-actualization. But with their enthusiasm to complete the work, there is the risk that they may bypass important details. Work peers and upper management must look out for the possibility that, sometimes, a leader may entertain shortcuts to complete their task faster, and care must be taken that these shortcuts do not reduce work quality.

As mentioned, an overabundance of leadership-type professionals in a task team may result in arguing and excessive competition in the team, which can cause progress to be stymied.

Problem-oriented team professionals tend to be more realistic about the work to be done. They are shrewd about identifying all the necessary elements of the work needed to complete a task. They take the most pride in performing the work thoroughly and bringing it to complete closure. Occasionally, however, they insist on performing work details or iterations that require valuable resources and time and end up providing little additional value. Leadership must be on guard for problem-oriented individuals attempting to further refine their solution but providing no needed added value.

There are unfortunately the unusual instances of a team member who does not exhibit any motivation. Perhaps, for personal reasons, this individual may not wish to be associated with the program or its leadership. Maybe they are highly distracted by other issues in their life. It is best for leadership to meet in person with these individuals and attempt to mutually identify the problem. Sometimes the issue can be rectified with the help of leadership. But if not, leadership must show good faith by helping to find another spot in the enterprise or in the industry where this professional would rather be.

6.3.4 Traditional Leadership Misses Out

Figure 4.3 (on page 57) showed the motivations that are impeded and the losses to the program that result from traditional top-down, direction-based leadership. As can be seen, some of the immense potentials of a team are lost by the traditional leadership approach. These teams will not be in first place in today's world.

Highly experienced senior professionals, when their self-actualization is recognized and addressed, usually offer the most valuable innovations and practical process improvements, providing the greatest amount of high-quality work for the program and the enterprise. They will not be motivated to "leave the rat race" when they reach retirement age.

6.3.5 New Tools Review

So far (see Figure 6.11), we have developed a structure of categorizing motivations to make programs highly successful—to be in first place. We may use this structure to determine if individual team members are oriented toward carefully working problem details versus developing solutions and quickly moving on. We use this as guidance to populate the program teams for maximum development speed, while using resources efficiently.

Let's Summarize

1. **Modern program success is poor.**
2. **Best programs are ahead of competitors by large amount.**
3. **Good paradigm developed to categorize team-member motivations.**
4. **Team-member motivation should be used to populate the teams, choose leadership, and lead teams to be most effective.**
5. **Detecting and fulfilling team-member motivation is primary to being in *first place*.**
6. **It is time to take a modern approach to organization and leadership!**

Figure 6.11 There have been a number of important motivation-management lessons presented so far in this book. These are some of the major ones.

In addition, we can use the content of individual self-actualization to choose leaders and to guide selecting the substance for instructing and leading the teams.

The following chapters will examine in depth the two-step process outlined in Chapter 5 for setting up and executing a program using our understanding of team-member motivations.

6.4 Chapter Highlights

- Additional Maslow starting points discussed.
- Approach adheres to common sense.
- Approach confirmed by real examples.
- Problem-oriented–solution-oriented team mix guidance.
- Self-actualization—unique and profound.
- Guidance for identifying team-member motivation.
- Old-fashioned leadership missed opportunities.

Chapter Seven

More on the Two Steps to Success

7.1 Details Introduction

In the previous chapters, we developed a motivation model for programs. We showed how to use it to identify the level of motivation maturity or self-actualization of each team member. We showed how we can use this model to determine whether each team member is more problem or solution oriented. Leadership can use this information when selecting leads and establishing the best mixture of these two team-member orientations in the task teams.

The two steps needed to create and execute a program to be in first place will now be described in detail (refer to Figure 5.4 on page 67).

The first role of Step 1 is to organize the team, provide them a clear view of what is to come, and establish initial leadership commitments of the guidelines and expected results. This is the time to establish buy-in of the work to be done from team members. Step 1 will be revisited throughout the life of the program to maintain a current understanding of the needs of the program and how each team member is necessary to get the work done.

By this time, the PM will have been selected and will execute the first tasks of Step 1, which include selecting and assigning the leadership team. Subsequently, the entire leadership team must execute more of the details of Steps 1 and 2 (see Figures 7.1 and 7.2).

Step 1—Set Up: Organize, Educate, Buy In

- Determine program and task leads.
- Highlight never before technologies, schedule, customer value, etc.
- Review value of work enterprise.
- Cultivate high team buy-in.
- Determine and start appealing to individual motivations.
- Use motivations to derive effective team mixes.
- Evaluate ability and experience of each team member.
- Detect emerging motivations/talents.
- Leadership must be credible and optimistic.
- Open door is a high priority.

Figure 7.1 This reveals more details required during program setup. Part of this work is to link individual team-member motivations to their assigned work.

Step 2—Execution: Leadership Executes

- Allow team to organize and plan as much as possible.
- Impower team with issue and risk management.
- Navigate between too prescriptive and too permissive leadership.
- Eliminate barriers to progress.
- Share program status (within sensitive data constraints).
- Keep program commitment statement current.
- Appeal to current and emerging motivations in individual team members.
- Maintain open door to discuss clarification, risks and issues.
- Encourage innovations and process improvements.
- Refine team mix and adapt mix to changes.
- Immediately resolve excessive internal conflicts.
- Never imply defeat.
- Give second chances.
- Protect the team from criticism and adverse developments.
- Follow detailed leadership elements and processes presented later (further detailed in *Project and Program Turnaround*).

Figure 7.2 This reveals more of the details performed during the program execution phase. Highlights include leadership's keeping the team informed of commitments and status, encouraging innovations and improvement ideas, maintaining a positive team attitude, managing emerging and changing motivations in the individual team members, and foreseeing and removing barriers to completion.

After their selection, leadership must start evaluating the self-actualization of both the candidates being evaluated and those already selected. As mentioned, leadership must use the results of this evaluation as guidance with other factors for team-member placement. The status of the motivation maturity or current self-actualization of each team member may not be the only factor considered, but the evaluation of team-member motivation and appropriate placement is a necessary part of a program achieving first place.

Leadership's first cut of the understanding of each individual's self-actualization is initially used to populate the task teams. This evaluation may change with experience working with the team members. Plus, as discussed earlier, a team member may transition from one self-actualization level to another at any time in their career. Members of leadership must not be alarmed by a sudden change in motivation that may seemingly appear without warning. Often this change has been developing in the team member, but they were afraid or embarrassed to share it. Other times, the team member simply was not aware their self-actualization was changing, or they were reluctant to accept the change.

Again, Step 1 is the time to garner buy-in from the team individuals, to build team enthusiasm, and initiate the concept of complete and open team communication. Subjects covered by leadership should include:

- Product description
- Top-level program requirements and description of solution
- Program organization, including suppliers
- Introduction of individual leaders
- Drafting of master schedule
- Showing how leadership will rely on the team members' assisting with:
  - Guidance on planning and resource distribution
  - Developing the program risk and issue identification
  - Choosing the one individual accountable for each responsibility
  - Achieving organizational simplicity
  - Taking advantage of leadership's open door
  - Providing a draft code of team conduct
  - More

Step 2 comprises leadership's providing an environment to fulfill the promises made in Step 1. During this time, leadership is navigating the fine line between being too prescriptive and too permissive. The team members participate in determining the shortest path to complete the work without diminishing product quality.

During this time, leadership must detect and eliminate present and future obstructions to progress. They must make sure the team is following guidelines and is incorporating the proven, motivation-based execution success elements to be presented in more detail later in this chapter. Using these elements is necessary for a program to be in first place. Leadership makes the final decision on all subjects and is responsible for the outcome.

During Step 2, leadership must consistently highlight good progress to the team and the enterprise, using their evaluation of team-member self-actualization to tailor the substance of these highlights.

For example, if the team requires many members who are problem oriented and who are looking to fulfill their Physiological and Safety needs, then leadership might specifically emphasize the likelihood of work follow-up and the need for maintenance support for the current product once delivered.

Of course, only facts must be provided, not vague optimism. But the emphasis on positive shared accomplishments should be tailored to the motivational needs of all team members.

Program leadership must revisit the importance of the work being performed and the success of the actions to date when revisiting Step 1 throughout the execution of the program. The volume of work performed during these Step-1 revisits will lessen as the program is executing, but revisiting Step 1 should never be completely eliminated during the life of the program.

There may be times when a team member's motivations or self-actualization are totally incompatible with the needs of the program, and this individual may decide to leave the effort. This outcome is far better than discovering that a team member is not a good fit by their poor performance. The savings resulting from finding a better fit for a team member who is not interested in the program is necessary to be a first-place effort.

7.2 Step 1: Organize, Educate, Buy In

At this time, the PM must inform the new team of the expected program outcomes and any constraints. Most of this content will originate from the customer and the sponsoring enterprise. Coverage should include deliveries, promised work products, specified performances, schedules, cost restraints, required product reliability, and more. At this time, the PM and their team must clarify and acknowledge these requirements with the customer and the enterprise (see Figure 7.3).

The PM must provide a clear, simple description of the tasks to be executed. Some top-level requirements will be flowed down to detailed requirements, depending on the size and complexity of the work. Examples of simple requirements statements include, "Reduce overhead by 2%," "Vehicle shall travel 250 km or more on one eight-hour charge," "Total program costs shall be less than $2.2 million," or "Delivery of Phase 1 shall be completed by August 3." To achieve a high degree of team-member focus and accomplishment, the team commitment must be simple to state and easy to remember.

Determine Status and Destination

- B (Program Commitment)
  - Must be simply worded.
  - May be first of multiple steps to complete.
  - Provides focus and measure of success.
  - Describe B first so content not to be prejudiced by current status.
- A (Current Status)
  - Benefits from independent review.
  - Necessary to access size of task.
- Plans shortest path from A to B.
- Provides guidance for the *program plan.*

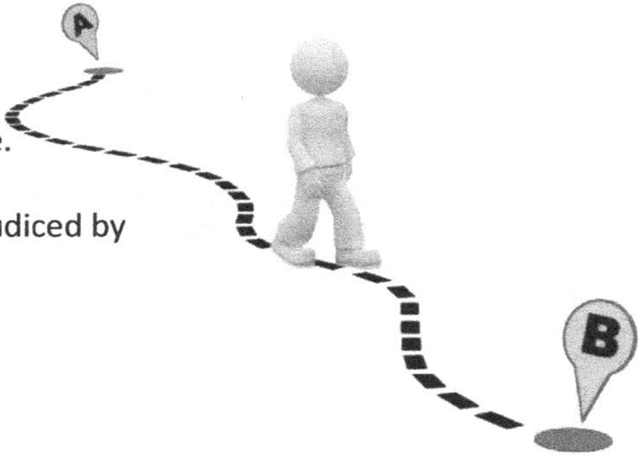

Lack of this analysis is frequent source of failure.

Figure 7.3 High importance must be given to determining the work commitments using simple wording and the complete current status of the program. This status should be described after the commitment is determined to avoid its definition being prejudiced. The shortest path with acceptable risk must be planned to get to the commitment (point B). This plan must be part of the program plan.

Next, the PM must develop a draft design of the organization. At this time, they should select the leader for each team or specify the need for one if one is not available. It is then advisable that the PM work with the new team leads to select team members, requiring their approval of all team-member selections.

At this time, leadership should start evaluating the motivation maturity or self-actualization needs of the new team members. This will also be used to guide team-member assignments.

In the past, the PM's "wisdom" was often relied upon to select team leads and team members. At other times, there may have been an independent board approval process to review the credentials of the favored candidates. Unfortunately, sometimes this resulted in only academic performance and experience level being used as the criteria for team-member selections, but these criteria do not address the ability of candidates to work together or their desire (motivation) to do the work.

This step of selecting team members was often considered to be one of a series of routine steps needed to organize and start a program. However, the results of this step are especially important for establishing a team that will be in first place. It unfortunately has not always been granted the high emphasis and analytical time it deserves when a new program is getting started.

A major message repeated in this book is that team-member motivation and self-actualization must be considered when assembling a first-place team. As has been repeatedly stated, this book provides a process for determining team-member motivations and applying this knowledge so the program will be the first-place competitor.

The processes in this book emphasize decomposing the program teams into *task* teams rather than *functional* teams. It has been observed that first-place industries excel using this approach. The author's experience is that task teams, not functional teams, provide the necessary work focus and individual account-ability to achieve the planned team commitments.

Support organizations with titles, such as "product centers," "center of excellence," or "job shops," comprise members with the same specific professional expertise. These organizations often deploy their expertise into program teams devoted to creating a product. If a functional expert is placed in a program team from one of these organizations, they must report to the program leadership for program-related direction during their service. Occasionally, a functional organization will be part of a first-place program if their technology highly dominates the product being created. Examples of technology areas that might be subject to this organization are mechanical assemblies, electronic systems, and software systems.

The importance of having no more than one layer of intermediate leadership between the PM and the individual contributors must be repeatedly emphasized. Additional layers seriously isolate the team members from the top leader.

The experience of the author and his colleagues is that most program task teams have a minimum of approximately 10 team members, in which case the PM usually should be the single leader. For programs consisting of 20 or more team members, a minimum of two task leads would be acceptable.

Many team members consider the PM to be the ultimate evaluator of their work performance and their interests. For most, this person is the "top boss." Too many layers of leadership will leave the individual team members feeling isolated and diluting the awareness to address their progress, motivations, and development.

For example, the author has led development programs with over 500 team members and only one layer of leadership—task-team leaders—between him and the individual contributors. His door was open to all team members for any comment, concern, or question. This shallow reporting depth allowed him to more completely evaluate work status and team-member sentiment by using what author Tom Peters refers to as MBWA (Management by Wandering Around[1]). The reporting of team status by task-team leaders is usually thorough and accurate, but sitting next to an individual contributor in their work environment brings additional, and often critical, insight. It is often the best way to learn where the perceived and real challenge areas and roadblocks are in the work.

The first wave of leadership selection may be incomplete—there may be leadership positions that require weeks more to fill due to the uniqueness of their requirements or the lack of available candidates.

But as soon as the first-draft task-team leadership has been selected, the PM should conduct a series of meetings with them to refine and document team structures and general program guidelines. This content should include detailed task guidelines, expectations for team members and leadership, and a draft code of conduct. In addition, this new leadership team should discuss the best way to convey to the new team members the team structure, team tasks, plans, and rules in a way that will achieve their enthusiasm and buy-in for the work ahead.

It is unfortunate that often team members join a new program without learning about its high value and how it will appeal to their developing motivations or self-actualization. The purpose of the early buy-in here is to establish genuine team enthusiasm as soon as possible. High team enthusiasm and high team-member subscription to success are key for the team to be in first place.

---

[1] Peters, T. J., Waterman, R. H. (2004). *In Search of Excellence: Lessons from America's Best-Run Companies.* Harper Collins.

7.3 Step 2: Facilitate, Remove Barriers, Lead

Step 2 is the execution phase of the program. It demands that leadership success-fully navigate the thin pathway between being overly permissive and being too prescriptive with their directions (refer again to Figure 7.2 above and Figure 5.6 on page 70).

Leadership must allow the team members to perform as much of the continued program planning as possible. This includes jointly determining with leadership the shortest work path to completion and the estimation resources needed to do so.

Leaders must not just relegate their leadership to an automatic process and then step away. They must appreciate that the team members performing the work almost always have a more complete knowledge of the current develop-ment status of the program. Team members usually have a better ability to originate highly effective, detailed planning, with guidance and overview from leadership. In addition, team members can precisely target valuable innovations and process improvement concepts.

Obstacles and constraints will occur during execution of the work. They can take many forms, including laborious bureaucratic intricacies, supplier delays, design or parts obsolescence, inadequate available resources, and many more. Leadership must promptly detect these barriers, both current and future, and take immediate action to mitigate them. They must perform this detection and avoidance as much ahead of the team's current work as possible so as not to delay progress, while involving all team members as much as practical in developing the detailed descriptions of the present and potential barriers, as well as with the process of generating avoidance and abatement plans.

In addition, leadership must be transparent to the team regarding the status of the program work. This status data should include work accomplished per plan, adherence to schedules, current risks and issues, planned future events, and more.

Leadership must highlight and give credit for all accomplishments by all team members, even if minor. This not only praises completed work but reminds the team of the high value of thoroughly completing every task, big or small. Leadership must remind the team that those big accomplishments are usually achieved by fully completing many little ones.

Leadership must constantly encourage team members to promptly and openly report what they perceive as a risk or issue. Most programs will include a risk-management team responsible for detecting risks and issues and managing asso-ciated avoidance and abatement plans, but this team may miss some potential risks and issues. As mentioned, team members working on the front line often find these risks and issues first. Leadership must pay high attention to their reports and take immediate action to validate and process the concerns they bring forward.

Leadership must completely support and help mature the team's ethics. They must be spotless examples of these ethics, even at casual off-campus events; their excellent example must even be maintained after the program is completed. The high ethics that accompanied this program must never be demoted by a leader later on to have been arbitrary or temporary.

Unfortunately, some leaders have taken pride in keeping two sets of behavioral rules or ethics, choosing to break the team's ethical rules in some settings. This behavior sends team members mixed messages, dilutes the importance of ethics, and must not be done.

Despite the wide range of items they are responsible for, leadership must consistently be on the lookout for emerging motivations and capabilities in their individual team members. They must nurture these by discussing with the team members what potentials they see in them and giving them work assignments that verify and develop these new areas.

Team leadership must always encourage and promptly evaluate, apply, and award innovation and process improvement proposals from the team. Team members should be complemented for bringing new ideas forward, even if they are not implemented. This emphasizes the high value leadership places on all innovation and improvement proposals.

If a team member is trying to accomplish an assigned task with the best of intentions and fails, every effort should be made to give this person a second chance. If this task is critical to the progress of the program, this second attempt may be supplemented with the support of other team members with more knowledge or experience with the task. But the team member who failed should not be dismissed from completing this work and being responsible for the outcome. If it is determined that additional training or experience is required for this team member, a path to achieve it should be provided. Harsh demotion, removal, or firing of a team member who has demonstrated genuine intentions but fell short is inappropriate and will deflate the morale and progress of the entire program.

Leadership must incorporate the program's organizational and execution elements that have been proven to put their program in first place. These elements are derived from their success in appealing to the motivational needs of the team members and leadership. Many were discovered by trial and error in programs and projects throughout the 20th century. These elements will be discussed later in detail.

7.4 Two Steps Through Program Life

The major purpose of Step 1 is to set up the program, and, as mentioned, it must be revisited with updates to contents creating buy-in throughout the life of the program. These updates to Step 1 content will be derived primarily from experiences in Step 2 (see Figure 7.4).

As discussed before, part of Step 1 is the activity of selling potential and new team members on the high value of the work they're doing. This must be revisited to keep the team aware of their purpose. It is necessary to keep the team at the high level of vitality to be first place. Accomplishments, successes, and lessons learned occurring in Step 2 are part of the feedback to Step 1 (see Figure 7.5).

During a Step 1 revisit, the team must be reminded of the benefits they are providing to their enterprise, their municipality, their country, and the world. The unique and special contributions that individual team members are making should be pointed out. Team members must be reassured that they are not only a member of a winning team, but that they are a necessary part of it.

Part of complimenting their unique contributions is thanking them for any personal sacrifices, including loss of time with family, postponing vacation plans, working swing and graveyard shifts, and more.

Knowledge of individual team-member motivations is usually increased and refined by the work in Step 2. These are the program's specific commitments, the expectations of leadership and team members, and the team code of conduct— all derived and first provided in Step 1—may be refined. This is important information to revisit, share, and discuss when revisiting Step 1.

Re-addressing the Step-1 team buy-in points by leadership should be laced into their daily conversations with team members during Step 2 throughout the life of the program. Reviewing the progress of the team on the master schedule with a clear description of the path to the next major milestone should be provided to all team members at the task- or program-meeting levels, ideally at least weekly. This maintains the positive team feeling of making concrete progress and gives team members another opportunity to offer ideas to improve efficiencies.

7.5 Fulfilling Motivation Needs for Success

Figure 6.10 (on page 91) summarized what team members, whose self-actualization is one of the six levels of our self-actualization hierarchy, need to appeal to their motivations and feel unencumbered. Included were examples of real individuals motivated at these levels.

Facilitating each team member's level of motivation during their motivational development or self-actualization plays a major part in establishing a first-place program. It codifies their commitment to success and enhances their pride of accomplishment when assignments are completed. When leadership seeks to

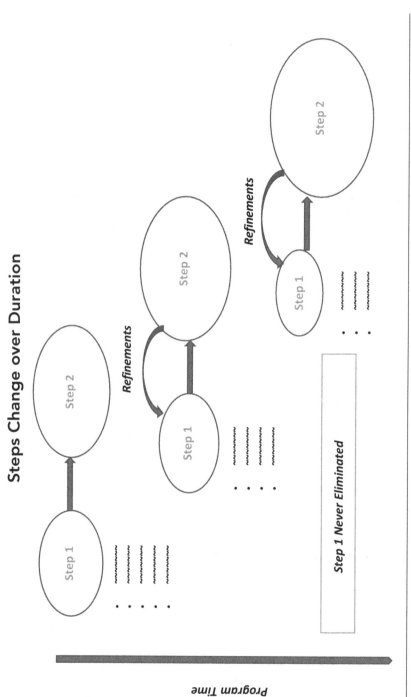

Figure 7.4 As the program is executed, Step 1 is revisited with refinements from Step 2. This is partly to ensure continued team-member buy-in and maintenance of the most efficient and effective work completion plan. This iteration may occur multiple times during the performance of the work.

Feedback Throughout Life of the Work

Step 1 Setup

- Select leadership.
- Task planning.
- Staff mix for success.
- Commitments—requirements and constraints.
- Effective organization.
- Tracking for success.
- Successful supplier contracts and management.
- Best use of metrics.
- Software development planning if applicable.
- More . . .

Refinement

- "Successes!"
- "How our team is special."
- Grow team dedication.
- Maintain tempo and team pride.
- Fine tune mix, assignments, processes for success.
- Highlight progress.
- Maintain enthusiasm.
- More . . .

Step 2 Execution

- Perform work.
- Refine commitments.
- Develop innovations and Improvements.
- Root causes for product or process failures.
- Avoid configuration control mistakes.
- All team vigilant.
- Team code of conduct awareness.
- More . . .

Figure 7.5 Some additional details of Steps 1 and 2 and feedback contents are listed. This constant feedback helps minimize time to completion, maintains high product quality, ensures the best team mix, and maintains high team morale and enthusiasm.

make it possible for each team member's motivation needs to be fulfilled, these team members take more initiative and need less direction.

As mentioned, team members must be allowed to integrate with program planning. The frontline team members often know best what is important to do next. Productivity per team member in this integrated planning environment becomes very high.

Facilitating individual motivations intensifies cooperation amongst the team members. Because their developing motivations and self-actualization are being fulfilled, they become more compromising and more focused on teamwork to maintain this rewarding environment. Together, the program team and leadership plan further ahead, identifying risks further in the future and mitigating them before they become expensive issues. When individual motivations are facilitated, the team members' moods are cheerful and optimistic, and turnover is low.

Sometimes a program team that is in first place can seem to develop a sense that they can conquer any problem. Leadership must watch that this self-confidence does not turn into arrogance, which can lead to unrealistic expectations, disappointment, and resentment from outside organizations. Leadership must always emphasize and exemplify team humility.

Often the greatest benefits to a team come from those members motivated by a Professional or Altruistic self-actualization. These members have a vision and a passion for high professional excellence and for benefits to society beyond the stated purpose of the program, and they often make big personal sacrifices to be closer to achieving their vision.

Team members motivated by Esteem or Altruistic self-actualization are usually looking out for feasible and effective innovations to expedite work completion, striving for the shortest path to complete the work. Many of them develop intense team interdependencies to achieve a faster outcome and completion. While doing so, they may ignore their near-term personal desires or opportunities for professional gains. If they do not have the ability to perform a portion of their task, they will usually enlist someone who has this ability or learn how to do it themselves.

Team members motivated by Esteem or Altruistic self-actualization usually take the team's code of behavior very seriously and follow it, despite often considering unconventional shortcuts. They tend to be the most passionate about achieving the commitments of the program.

A good program leadership team comprises members who are somewhat or very much like this. They often portray examples of sacrifice that the other team members follow, and they have some of the highest energy in the team.

However, be cautious about too many team members like this working together, as they can become competitive; although this can bring forth accelerated and innovative improvements, with too much internal competition, they can become combative and seriously disrupt the progress of the team.

7.6 Past Successful Leadership Elements— The Natural Consequence

As a result of applying motivation techniques and adopting a two-step process, a natural set of essential leadership elements will become apparent. Interestingly, via a separate route, many of these success elements have arisen by trial and error when organizing and executing programs throughout the 20th century. These success elements are applied during Steps 1 and 2 to put the program into first place (refer to Figure 5.2 on page 64). These elements are discussed in detail in the chapters to follow.

As mentioned, these program success elements are supported by decades of trial and error within the wide range of business genres in teams big and small. The author has successfully applied these elements many times while assuming leadership of big and important programs, usually in serious trouble. By incorporating these elements, he was 100% successful in leading these programs back on track to achieve their originally promised performances.

What needs to be done during Steps 1 and 2 will be discussed for each success element presented in the following chapters. The reader will see that these elements fulfill the developing motivational needs and eventual self-actualization of all team members.

These essential organizational and process elements will be discussed in approximately the chronological order that will be needed when organizing, planning, and executing a new program. The reader, of course, has the option to the study these elements in detail, starting at the place at which their own program is now.

7.7 Chapter Highlights

- Two-Step execution details:
  - Step 1—Organize, Educate, and Buy In.
  - Step 2—Facilitate, Remove Barriers, and Lead.
- Step 1 revisited for program lifetime.
- Addressing individual motivations result in On-Step performance.
- Proven success elements, natural result.

Chapter Eight

Step 1 (Setup, Buy In): How to Do It

8.1 Starting a Program

This chapter presents in detail the steps to start a program. It also presents the team-member buy-in elements that should be discussed and revisited throughout the life of the program.

It should be emphasized again that the guidance in this book applies to all programs, regardless of whether the team is creating a process or product, if the customer is a private company or a government, or if the program is big or small.

Also, this guidance applies to all generations of team members and levels of professional seniorities, as opposed to some published leadership approaches that strive to identify what their authors consider the specific peculiarities and needs of the various team-member age groups and generations.

The guidance provided in this book is derived from our basic human motivations. This fundamental starting point applies to all humans, regardless of age, generation, professional level, cultural orientation, etc. These variables may sometimes influence which level of motivation in our hierarchy applies to a given individual, but not the definition and function of these levels.

8.2 Finding a Great Program Manager

The best PMs are motivated by knowing that this job is what they do well and that this work largely or completely meets the needs of their self-actualization.

They should have had experience with, and thus appreciate all the challenges associated with, being such a leader and manager. This experience and appreciation are usually achieved via prior entry-level assignments. The PM candidate must thoroughly understand the intent, the business argument, and even the social impact of what they're going to lead. These items should be part of achieving the needs of their self-actualization (see Figure 8.1).

The PM must empathize with the wide breadth of team-member personalities and strive to fluently communicate with them and develop them. The PM must be enthusiastic about candidly and honestly communicating with each team member, team leadership, executive management, the customer, subcontract management, vendor management, and the other team interfaces. Each of these interfaces may require a different communication style, plus a keen awareness of what data is sensitive/proprietary and therefore must be avoided. The PM must desire to communicate often with these interfaces and develop trust.

Look in Enterprise for PM

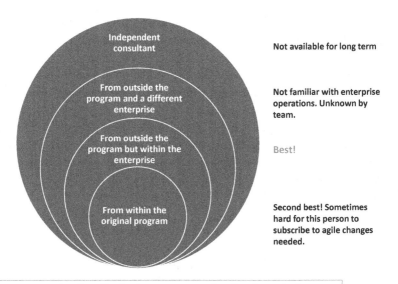

Enterprise familiarity improves motivation knowledge.

Figure 8.1   The best source of a program manager (PM) is usually from outside the program but within the enterprise. Sometimes it is difficult for a leader who has been managing the program from its start to adjust to the quick, "clean-sheet" changes that might be necessary during full program implementation. It is of high value that this individual has worked with the unique operations of the enterprise and is known by enterprise executives.

The PM must have an overall knowledge of what they are about to lead, from both a technical and a business perspective. They must have sufficient breadth of knowledge and experience to verify the competency and credibility of the specialists on their team.

In addition, the PM must have the knowledge of how to achieve acceptable profitability for the enterprise while achieving customer needs. They must be conversant with the basic business concepts relevant to their program. Their depth of knowledge and management skills will likely include cost, revenue, cash flow, supply chain, sales, orders, required deliverables, earnings before interest and taxes (EBIT), and more.

The self-actualization of the PM should drive them to make special sacrifices as the leader. They should be present as much as practical when their team is working extra hours. They frequently should be one of the first to arrive at the workplace and one of the last to leave, and they must be accessible during and after normal work hours (see Figure 8.2).

The PM must understand and accept that they are ultimately responsible for all outcomes of the program. They will be the point of contact for all those external to the team, including customer, enterprise executives, suppliers, managers of other programs, and more.

There Are Important Attributes
the PM Must Have

Step 1
• Self actualization = solving rigors of implementation.
• Believes in intent of effort.
• Develops trust with all team members.
• Knowledge of business and technical elements.
• Balances profitability with customer needs.
• Understands work volume needed based on experience.
• Can anticipate issues and detect them early.
• High allegiance to completing work and team success.
• Always present and accessible with one backup person.

Figure 8.2 These are some of the major characteristics a PM should have. They must enjoy the challenge of responding to simultaneous social, economic, technical, and customer-appreciation needs.

The PM must maintain a high level of enthusiasm in the team. They may acknowledge inconveniences but never appear to be defeated. They must always be an example of following the team code of conduct, including the team ethics policy, and they must do so when they are off campus in a casual setting, and even years after the program is completed.

The best source for this PM is someone who has worked for the enterprise as a manager in the past—ideally, someone who has helped with acquiring the new business to be performed by the team but is not a charter member of the program team. It is a valuable advantage to have a thorough familiarity with the subject matter of the new program. In addition, having a high familiarity with the enterprise interface processes, with all the team members external to the enterprise, and with the customer representatives is of high value.

There are examples of experienced leaders, "quick studies," not familiar with the subject of the program they may join and still be acceptable performers. There are experienced leaders from outside the enterprise who can eventually come up to speed; they can eventually learn the enterprise culture, team-member biographies, customer organization, customer points of contact, and more details of the content of what is being developed. But it will take time for this person to develop both trusting relationships with all stakeholders and the intuition to anticipate issues in the work to be accomplished. In addition, it takes time to learn who in the organization and enterprise are the best sources of expert advice when development problems occur. The learning delays and mistakes made by the quick study may allow the program to perform acceptably, but not to be in first place.

The new PM must have the courage and experience to allow the team members to plan and schedule as much of the work as possible. Team members who are accomplishing the actual tasks usually have the best insight into the details of the issues and will often create a plan with the highest probability of success. They also have the most recent and realistic understanding of what resources are needed to complete each development step. In parallel, the PM and leadership must still verify the relevance and accuracy of these inputs.

The good PM will appreciate that the estimates that leadership receives from the team members while the program is underway often represent a worst-case assessment. The PM and leadership must carefully challenge these estimates so that the teams devote the rigor to perform their tasks better than their worst-case estimates. This requires that the leadership and the PM have detailed knowledge of and past experience with the subject of the program—this gives them the credibility to argue that the initial estimates may be pessimistic. It should be noted that challenging the team to perform better will, in addition, encourage them to develop innovations and improve their work processes.

This PM must continually emphasize the importance of innovations and continuous process improvements to enhance the performance of their work. These improvements can be manifested in many ways, including reducing time to completion, reducing cost, improving the performances of the product being developed, and creating high reliability that final results will be achieved and will continue to perform as predicted.

The PM must constantly pay attention to identifying and satisfying the motivations of each team member. Candidates for this role must have experience managing motivation and self-actualization to bring forth the most valuable work results from each team member. In addition, they should motivate the team members to develop a high level of dedication to the team and the enterprise.

The PM should pay special attention to those team members motivated by some Esteem, Professional, or Altruistic self-actualization concept. They should appreciate that the greatest effort and sacrifices usually come from these team members. In addition, they must look out for new abilities in every team member, and they must share the potential value of these new capabilities with their leadership and help the team member to further develop it.

The new PM candidate should have had experience having been on, and ideally performing leadership functions on, a previous first-place program. They should have developed the intuition to detect if a program is On-Step. If they encounter a program that is not On-Step, they should have the experience to quickly identify what is missing and develop a plan to rectify it.

There will be occasions when the motivations of a new team member do not align at all with the needs of the program. For example, this team member may require that they work with individuals they have worked with before (Love/Belonging), but these individuals are not members of the program team they are being considered for. In these rare cases, the PM must realistically identify the incompatibility and must have the fortitude and patience to assist this individual with finding a position in another program that meets their needs.

Table 8.1 Finding a Great Program Manager
SELF-ACTUALIZATIONS FULFILLED

Self-Actualization Level	How Fulfilled by This Success Element
Physiological	Appreciates the PM understands work to be done and how to complete it.
Safety	Takes satisfaction in observing the PM understands the work and what must be done to complete it. Believes forecasts under this leadership will be honest.

Love/Belonging	Desires a personal relationship with a competent leader they admire. A great PM has the credentials and interpersonal talent to provide this with discretion.
Esteem	If the PM demonstrates understanding of the needs of these team members to competently represent their title and eventually be promoted, they will be supportive.
Professional	Highly appreciates that the PM understands the work to be done and that they place a high value for team members with in-depth expertise.
Altruistic	Observes that a good PM understands their altruistic goals and will consider them when determining work priorities. They appreciate this can result in faster progress to achieve their goals.

8.3 Creating a Highly Effective Organization

8.3.1 One Lead Per Task Team

The first draft of the organization for the program is initiated by the PM after consultation with enterprise management and the charter task leadership. There should be additional consultation with the customer, supplier management, other team members, and other supporters of the effort to refine this draft, if it is determined this will bring value.

The PM must establish a policy of having only one leader for every task or task team. Task leadership by committee must not be allowed. Accountability by one individual for a task is the only way to ensure its completed execution. Single accountability is necessary for a first-place program.

The newly assigned task leads must develop, integrate, and approve the work plan for their task. They must be fully knowledgeable about the current status, issues, plans forward, and more for the task they are responsible for. The task leader must be solely accountable for the success of their task.

Understandably, the task leader may not have the answer to every detailed question at a specific time, but they must be capable of obtaining the answer from their team quickly. Like the PM, they will not solely determine the direction of the work of their task team but must understand and approve the direction they mutually derive with their team members.

This principle of having only one lead per task may be foreign and uncomfortable for some new team members—managers they had reported to in the past may have assigned a team of professionals to lead the task work. This team approach may have been a way for some task managers or PMs to ensure a thorough evaluation of the work plan and consensus on decisions. However, this same high degree of thoroughness and consensus can be achieved with one lead, with the bonus of having a single point of accountability. This avoids dangerous ambiguities and delays resulting from the vague accountability derived from a leadership team.

There may be a lingering issue in the minds of some readers about the apparent dichotomy in the leadership role proposed in this book.

On one hand, this book highly endorses the principle of having one responsible lead for each task, and on the other hand, it promotes the "upside-down pyramid" organization.

The reader may therefore ask, "Do the team members work for the PM, or does the PM and their leadership team work for the team members?" The answer to this question is *both*.

The PM is singularly responsible for the entire conduct a success of their team. It makes sense that they have full authority over all the actions of their team. One may assume that, if they have this authority, they naturally must consistently exercise it.

But this is where leadership must exercise restraint to allow critical status information and new ideas to be brought forward and processed from all team members. The PM and their leadership team derive first-hand performance status and suggestions for forward planning from their reports. In this way, there is a consistent back and forth between 1) the authority of the PM and leadership for establishing the direction of the program and preserving the well-being of the team members, and 2) the solicitation and application of information from all team members to establish planning details, identify risks and issues, and identify valuable process improvements and innovations.

8.3.2 Leading the Task Leads

Higher-level management must have patience with new task leads. Some leads may be temporarily awkward and make mistakes while adapting to the role of being the single point of task accountability. Higher-level leadership should support these leads with discussions regarding mistakes they may have made and how they can prevent them in the future. Then, these task leads should be allowed to continue to lead their team. It is rare that a developing task lead maliciously counters the program plan. Of course, if this repeatedly occurs, it is grounds for immediately replacing this task lead.

A draconian policy of giving each task lead only one chance to do their job, then replacing them if their outcome is below par, will be perceived as unfair by the task lead and the program team and will damage the morale of the program. Any kind of simple, metrics-based dismissals without thorough consideration of the professional's work performance or forgiveness for mistakes will prevent a team from being first place.

In the rare case of repeated serious mistakes by a new task lead, either due to inability or lack of interest, a new lead must be found. However, if the existing task lead is genuinely enthusiastic about learning how to lead their team, the PM must consider letting them keep their assignment while they receive remedial training and mentoring. Sometimes, a trial period can be applied to determine if this person should remain in their leadership role.

8.3.3 Complete Task-Team Participation

In addition to having one leader per task or team—and if of value—representatives from the customer and suppliers should participate in the task-team work as much as practical and allowable, although this may be limited by restrictions of proprietary data or other sensitive information. Task-team members from outside the program organization, such as subcontractors and suppliers, may suggest alternative successful ways of solving a problem. In addition, they can be very helpful by keeping their home enterprise apprised of progress and issues so as not to confuse or alarm them. Their involvement can improve the quality and efficiency of their organization's contribution to the program. These representatives may even volunteer to assist with accomplishing the needed work as a contributing member of the task team.

The policies of assigning one leader for each task and implementing team involvement from representatives from the customer, suppliers, and other parts of the home enterprise adds greatly to the buy-in by the team members. It shows that clear decisions will always come from a single accountable source and that input from all stakeholders will be accepted to develop the most effective plan. It assures team members that they can achieve the needs of their self-actualization more directly and at a higher speed.

8.3.4 Well-Partitioned Task Teams

The program organization must be divided into pieces (mostly task teams) that are as independent from each other as possible. This cannot be overemphasized. All program stakeholders must be able to quickly pinpoint the accountable team for any work effort immediately.

To help support this, each piece or task team must have a clear name that describes its function, not just the subject matter it is associated with. For example, "Delivery Cost Estimation" has a clearer meaning than "Distribution Overheads." This clarity of organization and naming will greatly reduce recurring errors by internal and external stakeholders trying to find where to provide or receive information. This clarity will also assist the program leadership in verifying that the organization has adequate coverage for all the needs of the work.

There Is a Method to Establish Independent Pieces

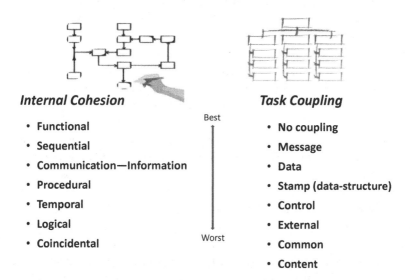

Internal Cohesion

Best

- Functional
- Sequential
- Communication—Information
- Procedural
- Temporal
- Logical
- Coincidental

Worst

Task Coupling

- No coupling
- Message
- Data
- Stamp (data-structure)
- Control
- External
- Common
- Content

Figure 8.3 A qualitative method has been developed to determine the independence of the various pieces in a whole system. Examples include individual software programs in an integrated software delivery and task and functional teams in a program organization. This degree of independence is determined by how related the subfunctions are in the system—*cohesion*—and how minimal the communication/interdependency is amongst these pieces—*coupling*.

A successful approach toward dividing a system into pieces that are as independent as possible was developed in the 1970s by Yourdon and Constantine.[1] This approach was first conceived as a way to divide team efforts into pieces and was then used as a way to divide large amounts of software into independent and manageable parts.

It merits the independence of each division in a system by assessing the closeness of the interactions of the functions in each part, called "cohesion," and the amount/type of communication between parts, called "coupling." Figure 8.3 shows the hierarchy of bad-to-good evaluations of these two parameters. As can be seen, the most independent pieces are those in which all the activities in the piece are functionally highly interdependent and where only top-level results

---

[1] Yourdon, E., Constantine, L. L. (1979). *Structured Design: Fundamentals of a Discipline of Computer Program and Systems Design*. Raleigh, NC: Yourdon Press. Out of print.

are communicated between it and the other pieces in the system, or there is no communication at all.

The PM, existing leadership, and, when possible, representatives from the customer, the enterprise, and the suppliers should draft a set of potential designs for the organization, then the total cohesion and coupling scores for each one should be evaluated and ranked. The importance of dividing a program into pieces that are independent and directly labeled cannot be overemphasized.

Highly experienced professionals tend to assume that they can comprehend or adapt to any organizational design. One highly respected technical manager was heard to say (by the author), "This program is just one big pie. You can cut it up anyway you want, but it's still a pie!" But being unclear about what portion of a program to go to to exchange information will result in recurring confusion, erroneous communication, and wasted time for even the most experienced team members.

There was, for example, a PM who had the task of leading the redesign of a large software development team. The original team organization was represented as a dataflow diagram! It contained over 20 functions interfacing in a complex manner. After careful trades incorporating coupling and cohesion, the PM was able to distill this team into five major functions. They were given simple, direct titles based on their functions, and each functional division had one task lead. The software being developed for this program was a major part of its success. Millions of lines of critical source code, designed to execute in a real-time, embedded physical environment, were involved. After this reorganization, software development schedules no longer hampered the progress of this program, and program team members knew exactly where to go regarding any software question or issue, because it was clear which task leader was responsible for specific inquiries. Software development no longer paced the schedule of this program, which was achieved by simply dividing the work into highly independent pieces.

A program team can perform acceptably, even if saddled with wasteful, recurring team-member communication errors caused by poorly designed task partitions. This team can even be a profitable venture in the enterprise portfolio—but they will not be a first-place performer.

An additional feature of the new organization that may need to be considered is how well it interfaces with or even mimics the customer's organization. In some cases, organizing the program in a way similar to the customer's organization may allow the customer to communicate progress and issues in their terms, allowing them to conduct business from the familiar framework of the design of their home organization. Sometimes, the program should even compromise what they derive to be the most ideal organizational design and mimic their customer's organization. By doing so, they may achieve greater customer confidence and satisfaction.

Figure 8.4 shows a simple example of a poorly partitioned organization versus one that is better organized. Please note that the infraction is splitting up the manufacturing function, which is typically highly cohesive.

Figure 8.5 shows a typical organizational structure that may result from proper partitioning. It consists of a PM, their backup/assistant, a layer of task leads, and the various task teams. The simplicity of this design must be maintained regardless of program size. As mentioned, this must be accompanied by simple task-team titles that directly describe what each task team does. These directly titled, independent task divisions make it much easier for all team members to know who is accountable for what.

It is also important to repeat that, with few exceptions, there should only be one layer of leadership between the PM and the team members doing the work. As covered in Chapter 4, leadership in many ways services the individual contributors performing the work, and from a functional perspective, the organizational diagram is inverted.

8.3.5 General Operation

In addition, the role of the PM is to detect and try to fulfill the needs of the developing motivations or self-actualization of each team member. They use their more strategic view of the enterprise, their experience, and the potency of their role to remove any impediment to the program team's achieving their commitments before they are encountered.

As the team matures, the team members, the enterprise, and the customer must be solicited to comment on the design of the organization. For example, someone may offer a name for a task team that is more explicit than the original one. Someone may even recommend a change of design of functions and responsibilities of a task team to better correspond to the specific backgrounds or personalities of the team participants. It is not unusual or unacceptable for the design of the program organization to be influenced by the specific backgrounds, connections, and/or strong preferences of the available team members. Of course, the PM must ultimately determine if implementing these unique preferences will cause future confusion or otherwise jeopardize the success of the work.

Another reason for changing the design of the organization can be the change in program work substance as the work progresses. For example, the customer may change the requirements and/or required delivery dates. Also, for some products, the type of organizational design required changes as the product transitions from trades and design, to build, test, integration, support, etc.

Given a well-organized program with highly independent and well-named task teams, team members will know exactly where to go for information or to

Physically Separated Teams Must Be Highly Independent

Poorly Partitioned Work

Better Partitioned Work

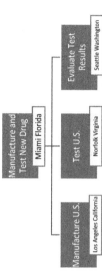

- **Manufacturing should not be separated.**
- **Communication is delayed.**
- **Prone to errors.**

- **Team functions are highly cohesive.**
- **Only finished content between teams.**
- **Less expensive and error prone.**

Figure 8.4   Here is an example of how a single function may be arbitrarily divided into two teams that are separated by long distances. Note that manufacturing work is highly cohesive, with much communication (coupling) amongst its sub-pieces. Conducting product manufacturing in two locations will usually hamper development speed, increase errors, and prevent the effort from being in first place.

Important Features When Organizing

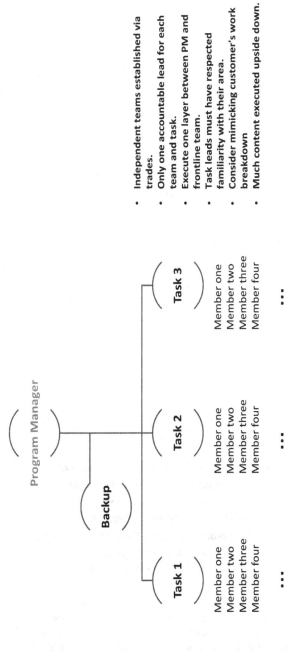

- **Independent teams established via trades.**
- **Only one accountable lead for each team and task.**
- **Execute one layer between PM and frontline team.**
- **Task leads must have respected familiarity with their area.**
- **Consider mimicking customer's work breakdown**
- **Much content executed upside down.**

Figure 8.5   There are important features needed to be a first-place team. For example, there must be only one individual ultimately responsible for each task. The PM should not be separated from frontline, independent contributors by more than one layer of leadership. Occasionally, to gain more customer satisfaction, the program's organization should mimic that of the customer's to provide them familiarity and to easily identify counterparts.

provide their results. In addition, as mentioned above, this division of work and responsibility will make it much clearer for connecting organizations, such as the customer, suppliers, executive management, other enterprise programs, and others to know who to communicate with, saving a great amount of time resulting from reduced communication confusion and mistakes.

During Step 1, new team members will be pleased there will only be one level of management between them and the PM (see Figure 8.6). They appreciate that fewer layers in the organization result in less cost and time adhering to organizational protocols, as well as fewer errors communicating between the team members and leadership. All team members will observe that the program leadership is placing a high priority on assembling a simple and easy-to-use organization structure with an emphasis on supporting the team members.

Also, during Step 1, team members will participate in identifying and naming task teams that are highly independent. This will result in a simple and clear organizational structure that is of value to all the team. With fewer tightly coupled interfaces, team members will incur fewer overheads communicating between themselves and other task teams, as well as suppliers and subcontractors. Because of a clear and well-partitioned organization, there will be less search time or errors due to team members wrongly assuming the functions and responsibilities of a particular team. Individuals and agencies servicing the program are immediately guided to the area they need to interface with, due to the organization's simple and intuitively clear divisions and labels.

Organizational Attributes for First-Place Program

Step 1
• One responsible leader per task.
• Only one layer of leadership between PM and worker.
• Division into independent parts, directly named.
• Work plan and risk/issues solicited from workers.
• Teams are product, not functional, oriented.
• Leaders facilitate teams achieving their commitments.
• Suppliers, customer, and other enterprise organizations are team members when practical.

Figure 8.6   These are additional attributes of a first-place program. They appeal to the needs of all six types of self-actualization identified in this book. These attributes are mainly established during Step 1 in the design and setup of the program.

Table 8.2 Creating a Highly Effective Organization
SELF-ACTUALIZATIONS FULFILLED

Self-Actualization Level	How Fulfilled by This Success Element
Physiological	Appreciates that having a clear and simple organization protects high productivity and completion of their promised work.
Safety	Having one leader per task clarifies points of accountability, resulting in fewer mistakes. Simple organization helps leadership adapt to changing program needs.
Love/Belonging	Experiences more teamwork in the organization resulting from high clarity of roles and well-defined individual accountability.
Esteem	A simple and clear organization clarifies potential promotion paths and needed performances to be promoted.
Professional	Appreciates assigning one leader per task precisely defines task accountability. In addition, appreciates that highly independent organizations reduce team mistakes.
Altruistic	Appreciates that a simple, intuitive organization helps programs achieve complete closure and faster progress, which helps achieve their altruistic vision sooner.

8.4 Organize for Managing Suppliers

The term "suppliers" includes vendors who provide existing off-the-shelf items, usually purchased via a purchase order, and subcontractors who provide one-of-a-kind items, usually via a contract. Subcontracted deliverables are made and delivered per the requirements established in a contract.

Three roles must be executed in the program to manage purchases from suppliers (see Figure 8.7).

For vendors, procurement is relatively simple. The purchasing organization usually has an expert who wants to buy an existing, off-the-shelf process, device, or part. This person is usually the de facto procurement manager and the technical lead. They rely on a buyer who is a member of the procurement organization to initiate the procurement, negotiate price, establish a delivery schedule, and verify that required purchasing milestones are adhered to as defined in the enterprise's operational standards. The requesting expert verifies that the items are delivered per the request. This verification is usually completed before final payment is given to the vendor. Again, this type of purchase is used for products that have been completed and often exist in inventory. Sometimes there is a range of options offered with a product, but nothing new or original is requested by the buyer.

Supplier Management Team
Must Have Checks and Balances

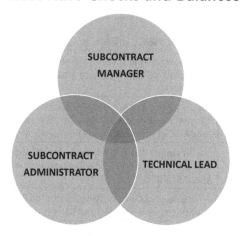

Figure 8.7   A typical and very successful approach to managing suppliers, especially subcontractors, is to divide the management task into three independent roles. The subcontract administrator is the legal point of contact and makes sure that all deliverables, dates, support, and more are provided to and from the program, as documented in the purchasing contract. The technical lead maintains a detailed understanding of the product being provided and verifies that it meets the needs of the program. The subcontract manager integrates the work of the administrator and the technical lead and is responsible for the success of the product(s) being provided.

These three procurement roles become more distinct for subcontracts and are often referred to as subcontract manager, subcontract administrator, and technical lead. These roles are usually held by different individuals to avoid a conflict of interest. But each individual performing a role may have multiple subcontracts to service. For example, a technical lead might perform this role for a number of items being developed under different subcontracts.

Because most subcontracts involve developing something new, they are usually more costly and entail more risk than the simple procurement of an off-the-shelf item. Therefore, the program devotes more overhead costs to managing subcontract procurements to monitor the development closely and minimize risks.

The subcontract manager leads the entire subcontract procurement and is the point of contact in the program for what is being purchased. This manager is totally accountable for the success of the procurement process and the resulting deliverables. They lead the subcontract procurement and approve the development plans and work products they receive from the subcontractor with the subcontract administrator and the technical lead.

The subcontract administrator works with the subcontract manager to make sure all government statute, enterprise, and supplier contract standards are fulfilled. This administrator oversees the evaluation of the subcontractor candidates and ensures adherence to the enterprise selection process. They make sure all required documents in the contract have been created and provided on time by the program and the subcontractor. They assist in verifying that all contract deliverables from the program and the subcontractor are received with promised content. They usually represent the enterprise as the official signator for all subcontractor interfaces, including letters and approvals.

The technical lead also reports to the subcontract manager. This person thoroughly understands all the technical requirements in the subcontract, the product design, and the team organization the subcontractor provides in response to these requirements.

This technical lead is the technical expert in the program for understanding and explaining the product that the supplier is providing. Along with the subcontract administrator, they are responsible for making sure that planned design reviews and testing by the supplier provide adequate content. They must verify that the subcontractor has proven that all specified technical requirements are in the product they are providing. Verification evidence may be provided by development testing, acceptance testing, analysis, similar past work, and/or other means.

Simple procurement organizations with three highly independent parts to manage the suppliers fulfills the needs of all levels of team-member self-actualization. During Step 1, new team members will appreciate having one lead for each procurement task. They appreciate that this makes status reporting and problem resolution simple, direct, and faster (see Figure 8.8).

It is additionally appealing to each team member that, when possible, supplier and subcontractor representatives will be members of the task teams. New members will appreciate that this feature facilitates procurement of goods and services with higher speed and that there is a greater probability that what is provided is exactly what is required.

Table 8.3 Organizing for Managing Suppliers
SELF-ACTUALIZATIONS FULFILLED

Self-Actualization Level	How Fulfilled by This Success Element
Physiological	Provides stability to work execution by increasing assurances of supplier achieving their commitments due to good supplier management.
Safety	Reduces fear of disruption to workflow due to poor supplier work execution.

Love/Belonging	Appreciates how thorough management of suppliers and sub-contractors make them more a member of the program team and accountable for its successes.
Esteem	Appreciates and abides by official leadership titles and functions used for supplier management. Thorough supplier management improves probability of the success of their work and eligibility for promotion.
Professional	Thorough supplier management assures that their work quality and adherence to milestones will not be jeopardized by supplier issues.
Altruistic	Reduces probability that supplier issues will jeopardize the team's achieving committed dates, product quality, and closure. This provides steady progress toward achieving their altruistic vision.

Communicate the Supplier Management Process

Step 1

- Present management processes used for subcontractors and vendors to team.
- Supplier management and tracking process must be described in program plan.
- Rationale for supplier selections and interface protocol for each supplier must be provided.
- Attempt (within propriety or competition date restrictions) to integrate supplier representatives as team members.

Figure 8.8   The process used to manage the various suppliers with a cursory rationale for choosing them must be presented in a team communiqué and the program plan. Ideally, supplier representatives are able to be treated as members of the program team.

8.5 Selecting Excellent Task Leads

The PM must select good task-team leaders, ones who not only must have the rudimentary ability to organize work, but also must lead the work on schedule with well-matched assignments to the members of their team. They must have an experience-based, in-depth understanding of the task to be done.

The task lead's self-actualization needs should be partially or completely fulfilled by the work of leading their assigned task. This imparts a passion in them to make sure the work is done well. For example, their self-actualization might be, "incorporating state-of-the-art solutions and minimizing build cost for the development and delivery of new subsystems." This would likely be in the category of Professional self-actualization.

Sometimes, the need for the task leader to understand the details of the task they are leading is overlooked when PMs look for task leaders with outstanding organizational and leadership skills only. But at the task level, the best results will only be achieved if the task leader has a detailed knowledge and appreciation of the work to be done, including knowledge of the typical mistakes made when performing this work.

Figure 8.9 shows that many times good candidates for the task leadership role are current individual contributors in a task team working on a product similar to the one they would be leading in the new team. Good candidates may appear to be shy of leadership experience, but they are often the "go-to person" for in-depth knowledge of the product being worked on. These candidates usually take a high degree of pride in achieving their task commitments thoroughly and on time. They are highly respected by the teams they work in for their in-depth knowledge and their consistently fair ethics. They highly value the insight they receive from the other team members when determining the status of the task and when planning their next steps. This is the kind of task leader needed for the program to be in first place.

One example of choosing the best task lead occurred when the author was asked to evaluate a very large and important program in trouble to get it on a solid schedule track. The core of this program employed more than 500 people. The author started by developing a new assortment and organization of task teams for this effort. He made a point of assigning task leads to these new teams who were well indoctrinated with the technical issues of their area. These new leads were well respected by their team peers for their high degree of knowledge and their objectivity.

In one instance, the author asked a mild-mannered team member, who was respected for their expert understanding of all the development issues at hand, to lead one of the new task teams. This individual responded with surprise and a great amount of uncertainty, as they had never led a team before.

Yet, this person had a better knowledge than anyone else of the problems and associated risks this new task team would encounter, and, fundamentally, this individual was passionate about seeing this subsystem perform correctly. Their commitment to completing this first-of-a-kind subsystem on time and with high quality was part of their self-actualization.

With a degree of caution and trepidation, this person took the role. Team members were actually relieved and excited that someone with credible knowledge was

Best Task Leaders May Not Be Obvious

Enterprise-Sponsored Leader

- Received leadership training.
- Leadership experience.
- On the "fast track."
- Has demonstrated acumen.
- "Safe choice."

Knowledgeable Leader

- "Go to" knowledge of product and work.
- Consistently achieves commitments
- Respected by team.
- Necessary for first-place program.
- Maybe future leader.

Figure 8.9 Often, PMs look for polished and experienced leaders, many of whom have had special leadership training. But usually, managing a development task is best serviced by someone who thoroughly understands all its details of the particular product being developed—someone who has had experience with the past successes and failures of the product being developed (or similar) and has a passion to deliver it successfully and completely. Sometimes they are coy about being a lead but are usually a better choice for a program to be in first place.

leading them. This product area, which had traditionally been troublesome, was now completing milestones in record short durations, with very high quality.

This new team was highly proud of the work they accomplished and of each other.

An outside general-purpose leader, well endowed with leadership training, can often lead the development of an acceptable development solution, but usually, this will not be a solution suitable for a first-place program.

Table 8.4 Selecting Excellent Task Leads
SELF-ACTUALIZATIONS FULFILLED

Self-Actualization Level	How Fulfilled by This Success Element
Physiological	Takes comfort in knowing the task lead is thoroughly knowledgeable about the task.
Safety	Takes comfort in knowing the task lead is aware of all associated risks, issues and highest priorities delivering promised work on time.
Love/Belonging	May be of benefit to the task lead by providing insight into the personal needs of some team members. Appreciates higher team comfort resulting from members having confidence the task leader understands the work.
Esteem	Appreciates and participates in exhibiting high respect for each task lead being the single point of responsibility for their task. Simplifies their ability to quickly complete their assigned work.
Professional	Provides a single individual to whom to offer their expert insight and capabilities.
Altruistic	Addresses important organizational needs in a simple way to assure the completed task is high quality and delivered on time. This assures a fast and steady program pace toward achieving their altruistic vision.

8.6 Interviewing Prospective Team Members

The distinction of team members who are problem oriented versus those who are solution oriented has been discussed—how those in the first group tend to immerse themselves in analyzing and solving problems the best they can, whereas those in the second group tend to be most satisfied when the problem is solved.

Also discussed was that those motivated by Physiological, Safety, Love/Belonging, or Professional self-actualization needs are usually problem oriented, while those motivated by Esteem or Altruistic self-actualization tend to be solution oriented.

Asking a candidate what their priorities were when they had delivered a previous product will help determine which category they fall into. For example, if the person has a Professional self-actualization of always providing a complete and high-quality product, the thoroughness of their work may be more important to them than driving to complete on time (problem oriented). However, the same person may include timely and complete closure as part of their self-actualization and will emphasize the closure mechanics and the importance of delivering on time to support the team (solution oriented).

All task teams will have some combination of problem-oriented and solution-oriented members. This needed mixture will depend on the work at hand. For example, if the task involves thorough analysis with widely accepted processes and complete documentation of findings, the need will be greater for problem-oriented team members. If, on the other hand, the task involves providing an acceptable solution as quickly as possible, the need will be greater for solution-oriented team members.

As discussed before, too many solution-oriented team members can result in strong differences of opinion on how to proceed. The competitive bickering that might result can actually defeat the value of the task team. So, if you are leading a team with a large number of solution-oriented members, make sure they listen with fairness and objectivity and participate cooperatively.

Although, as we said earlier, whether a team member is likely problem oriented versus solution oriented can be determined by assessing their motivation. There a simple question the author has asked applicants, whose answer provides a great deal of additional insight.

The question is, "Tell me about something you did in your work or scholastic history where you think you just 'hit it out of the park'—something that was truly special." When listening to the answer, the interviewer should not focus so much on what they say they did but instead what they emphasize. Some prospects will talk about an activity that was appealing to them because the work content was enjoyable or they liked their team members; they may add that they really liked their boss or lead. They might emphasize that it was a harmonious work environment and very satisfying to them. These people tend to be problem oriented.

As mentioned, problem-oriented team members take pride in providing complete and high-quality work products in the time they promised. Their performance is usually consistent and dependable. They are careful about clarifying the details of the commitments they make and take pride in adhering to their commitment. Problem-oriented team members usually perform most of the program work.

Some job prospects, however, will answer this question differently. They may refer to a "wild" idea they had that they decided to discuss with their fellow workers, and together they created a plan they thought just might lead to a breakthrough, such as an innovation to improve performance or shorten completion time. They then may have gone to the PM or task lead, who gave them permission to try it. They may recount how they had to work very hard, putting in extra hours to make the new approach work. Many times, these prospects proudly offer the specific benefit measurements of what they had accomplished. They are generally most interested in solving a problem and putting it behind them. These candidates are solution oriented.

This individual had a new idea (innovation), they shared it with others (teamwork), they brought it to the boss (respects organizational authority), they worked very hard to demonstrate this new idea and measure their success with metrics (put in the time it needs). These behaviors sound like the ingredients of an excellent solution-oriented candidate.

Solution-oriented prospects are usually more excited about doing something that has never been done before—accomplishing something that some might not even think possible. They often take delight in observing a process issue and creating a more efficient way of performing the work. They show high excitement when they can demonstrate they have succeeded and will usually offer to substantiate their claims of success with measurements.

Often the quality of work from the solution-oriented prospect will be good enough. But these individuals take most pride in having accomplished a task more efficiently and in less time than anyone had before. Team members in this classification are often a better choice for leadership. But leadership commitments should be reviewed and sometimes tempered with feedback by problem-oriented team members. It requires insight into the personalities of the team members and an understanding of the details of the work to be performed to determine the best team mix (see Figure 8.10).

8.7 Determining Best Team Mix

As discussed, analyzing individual motivation may be used as a guide for establishing the mix of orientation types for a team. As a reminder, an individual is not permanently classified as one of these types. Their current classification is merely the result of a complex combination of the commitments of the program they are working on, their professional maturity, their education, their past experiences, and more.

To be the first-place program, establishing the right mix of these two types is essential from day one. Historically, this often has been achieved with "leadership wisdom" and the trial and error of assigning available professionals to different roles. Unfortunately, some programs have never achieved first-place status, or

Our Maslow-Based Hierarchy Is a Guiding Discriminator

- **Problem-oriented team member**
  - **Motivation encompasses** Physiological, Safety, Love, or Professional Self-Actualization.
  - **Provides product precisely as agreed.**
  - **Plans realistic milestones.**
  - **"Steady Eddie."**
  - **Sometimes insecure when task complete.**

- **Solution-oriented team member**
  - **Motivation encompasses** Esteem **or** Altruistic Self-Actualization.
  - **Vision, optimistic, strategic innovator.**
  - **Most content when task is complete.**
  - **Encourages risks and sometimes fails.**
  - **Impatience may dilute closure.**
  - **Preferred leader if observant, adaptable, and listens.**

Figure 8.10 A team member's self-actualization can be used as a guide to determine if they are more problem oriented or solution oriented (there will of course be exceptions).

have even failed, because they never found the most effective, cost-efficient mix. With the analysis of individual motivations, this best mix can be established from the start.

Figure 8.11 depicts the range of problem-oriented to solution-oriented team combinations that can be derived. One extreme (#3) is more appropriate for work requiring originality, invention, and innovation. The other extreme (#1) is more appropriate for work requiring less improvement and instead routine execution of an existing process. The ideal ratio of these two types depends on where the work of the team lies on this line.

Further guidance for determining the mix required for a task is provided here, with descriptions of the types of task associated with the mix needs numbered 1, 2, and 3 in the figure.

1. Order more of an existing product unchanged from past orders. Exercise a process that has been validated and unchanged. (About 80% problem oriented and 20% solution oriented.)
   » Customer is highly satisfied with what was received from past orders.
   » The program and enterprise are highly satisfied with both product quality and profits from sales.
   » Processes applied are developed, are well documented, and require no change.

Work Content Determines Team Mix

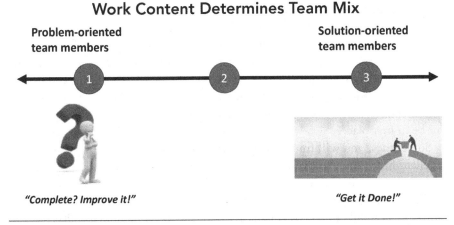

Problem-oriented team members

Solution-oriented team members

"Complete? Improve it!"

"Get it Done!"

Figure 8.11   Finding a good mixture of problem-oriented versus solution-oriented team members for each task is important to be in first place. For example, different mixes are required for work requiring an extension of product capabilities already delivered versus completely new developments.

> » There is low schedule risk.
> » There is fear from both program and customer of changing product or process. High reluctance to "break the mold."
> » Customer and program have high confidence in existing process. Product was thoroughly tested, validated, and proven reliable with use.

2. Improve existing product or process. (About 50% problem oriented and 50% solution oriented.)
> » Increase the performance of an existing product or process.
> » Increase the profitability of an existing process or product.
> » Large change (definition depends on circumstances) in the volume of an order for an existing product or size of execution of an existing process.
> » Request for an add-on or change to an existing and accepted product or process.
> » Update product or process design to correct minor defects.
> » Revise process to make leaner and thus more profitable.

3. New product and/or process. (About 30% problem oriented and 70% solution oriented.)
> » New requirements for performance, reliability.
> » Requires new process or product design.
> » Strict schedule milestone requirements and budget constraints.
> » May require research to support new product or process.
> » May require a business proposal to compete with other potential providers.
> » May be a major revision of an existing process or product design.

Using the above distinctions as guidelines, the modern leader may determine what the high-performance mix should be for their program and task teams.

To be in first place, this determination of mix must be done before starting the work. Leadership must then populate these teams based on the results of motivation analysis. If this is not done at first, the team may lag in completing the work needed. The wrong team mix often leads to the pain of falling behind and having to replace team members. The program in which this occurs will not be in first place.

Sometimes, you will find a prospective team member who appears to be an excellent fit for the work you need. You may feel enthusiastic about asking this person to join your team. But beware—don't assume the answers from the applicant regarding some basic questions that you may believe are trite, almost embarrassing, only to receive an answer that reveals an incompatibility.

Examples of such questions are, "Are you willing to work extra hours if the task is taking longer to complete than you predicted?" "When can you start?" or "Will you subject yourself to a background check?" (see Figure 8.12). Sometimes an answer to one of these questions will be disheartening. After all the hours of interviewing the individual, the response may be, "No, I never work extra hours; I promised my family I would only work 40 hours a week," or "I haven't told my current employer I've been looking, I want to think about this option for a month or two," or "I'm sorry, I will never allow my background to be checked." The author has received these disappointing responses

Recruiting Essentials: Mix Need, Don't Assume

- *Problem* Space + *Solution* Space
- If I could ask only one question . . .
- Don't forget the "obvious":
    - "Willing to support extra efforts?"
    - "When can you start?"
    - "OK with background check?"
    - Etc.

Figure 8.12 The distinction of problem- versus solution-oriented team members can be determined as early as during their interview. The authors found one question that helps make this distinction. Even if the interview goes very well, do not assume the answers to remaining detailed questions will align with program needs.

Recruiting Funnel May Be Used for Large Events

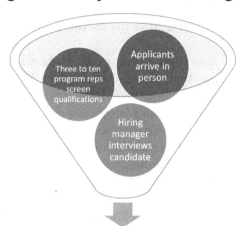

Offer made!

Figure 8.13 There may be times when a new program quickly needs a sizable influx of new team members. This is particularly challenging if the specialty being sought after is scarce. The author recommends enlisting some current team members to develop a "recruiting funnel" that may be used at job fairs, online searches, and more. (The author has found this to be highly successful.)

after spending valuable time and money to arrange and conduct an interview. Make sure that what you may assume to be an obvious understanding with the applicant is vetted.

On rare occasions, you may have to evaluate and recruit a large number of professionals in a short time—perhaps your program was awarded contingent on the effort starting immediately, and you discover the team needs many more participants in a particular talent area. These situations occur frequently for large programs starting up. In this case, a "recruiting funnel" can be assembled and applied very successfully (see Figure 8.13). People already on the program can be enlisted to attend an upcoming recruiting event with the recruiting lead.

This approach is most successful with a large number of applicants, such as a job fair. The members of the recruiting team must be provided a list of questions and criteria to look for in the applicants they review. If based on this preinterview the applicant appears suitable, they are sent to the recruiting lead for a complete interview.

The author had the benefit of four excellent professionals being hired in just one hour based in this process. These professionals turned out to be very valuable to the hiring enterprise, and most of them are still with the company decades later.

During Step 1, a cursory evaluation of the motivation or self-actualization level of each team member should be made by leadership (see Figure 8.14). These initial evaluations should be used as the starting point for determining placement in the team mix.

Certain behavioral traits in new team members should be avoided so as not to impede team progress. Applicants who exhibit behaviors of being highly confrontational or extremely cynical, or who demonstrate a profound reluctance to work with fellow team members, should not be recruited. New team members will observe that leadership insists on selecting only high-quality team members who are compatible with the current team and who will take pride in having been selected.

[During Step 2, the subject of the next chapter, team members will be reminded that they were evaluated to be highly qualified to be on the team. They must also be reminded that they must perform well to maintain this stature. Team members will feel free to do their best and suggest major innovations and continuous improvement ideas when they observe that not only are other team members doing so, but also other team members are forgiven for mistakes—especially mistakes made while vigorously trying. Yet, team members must observe leadership imposing strong discipline for serious infractions of team rules or ethics. Team members will feel unencumbered by knowing their performance will be evaluated fairly, patiently, and with forgiveness. Yet, team members must surmise that constantly striving for above-average performance is necessary to stay on the team.]

Mutually Identifying Motivation Is Essential

- **Discuss goals and aspirations when introduced.**
- **Consider work habits to verify:**
  - **There are NO right or wrong habits!**
  - **Personal conduct:**
    - **Introvert or extrovert**
    - **Team oriented or independent**
    - **Pragmatic, idealistic**
  - **Amounts and types of clarity requested**
  - **Other**
- **Mutually identify current and potential abilities.**
- **Provide tailored assignments to verify and grow.**

> *Mutual awareness, NOT psychoanalysis!*

Figure 8.14 When trying to identify a team member's self-actualization, leadership must know they are not trying to perform psychoanalysis! No self-actualization type is superior to another—it is just a means to match team members with work that they are most passionate about and feel is most achieving their needs. Determining self-actualization should be performed mutually.

Table 8.5 Determining Best Team Mix
SELF-ACTUALIZATIONS FULFILLED

Self-Actualization Level	How Fulfilled by This Success Element
Physiological	Understands leadership recognizes them for their professional preference (often solving a problem thoroughly, even if delivery delayed, etc.)
Safety	Confident working with teams that contain both problem- and solution-oriented members, in proportions depending on the work to be done.
Love/Belonging	Appreciates current work type is considered when team members are assigned. Appreciates adds to team harmony.
Esteem	The act of leadership determining individual motivations to select team mix provides them insight into improving team performance and their rate of promotion.
Professional	Provides relief that members of the teams they work with and rely on for work have predetermined mixture of individual priorities for maximum success.
Altruistic	Invigorated knowing team membership is being designed to shorten time to work completion and assure high success. This provides steady progress toward achieving their altruistic vision.

8.8 Guidelines for the Work Environment

The environment and facilities for a program can be a deciding factor for a team to be in first place.

8.8.1 In-Person Communication

Let's start with communication between the team members. Today's technology affords us a wide range of ways to communicate—text, email, phone calls, video teleconferences, and more make it easy to immediately communicate amongst members of a team. However, communication scientists are constantly investigating why high-valued communication amongst individuals requires more than can be established via any technology. Research shows that the most effective way to communicate remains to be live, in person, face to face, by a large margin and using any measure. Our human species has refined this method for over 200,000 years (see Figure 8.15).

This may sound old-fashioned to some. You may have spent three days traveling, enduring hotels, cancelled flights, bad weather, jet lag, greasy eats, and more,

In-Person Communication for Fast Progress

- 70% to 90% of face to face is nonverbal.
- Provides immediate responses.
- Builds high trust.
- Refined over 200,000 years.
- Easy to use by collocated teams.
- Technology has not substituted.

Figure 8.15 Communication experts insist that the majority of what we communicate face to face is nonverbal. We have fine-tuned this fast, fluent, and highly trusted communication method over the last 200,000 years, and it must be capitalized on to achieve the needed high completion speeds of a first-place program.

just to attend a meeting face to face (the author has). For a team to establish itself in first place and stay there, it is worth it.

Most of us have heard that communication scientists state that 70%–80% of live, face-to-face communication is nonverbal. Controversy remains over what the "nonverbal" substance is, but research shows that this is still the best way for humans to communicate with high clarity and trust.

It is difficult to find a first-place program whose core team it is not physically colocated. This was done partially to allow team members to communicate in person.

With in-person communication, the participants may exchange verbal/written material immediately, quickly answer any questions, and experience the human authenticity that validates the accuracy and completeness of the exchange and any commitments made.

There have been attempts to establish remote video team interfaces that provide the same benefits as in-person meetings. Video cameras in conference rooms now automatically point to who is speaking and even zoom in to their face to capture their expressions. Higher image definition is being provided in the conference room and from desktop cameras.

But communication experts continue to conclude that videoconferencing does not come close to taking the place of actual in-person communication. Yes, there are many good businesses that perform well with distributed sites, communicating via technology. But they would perform better with in-person communication.

It is understandable that some programs require portions of the team to be physically separated. This can be due to the availability of preferred facilities, the location of capable professionals, customer preferences, and more. In these cases, at least the members of the program office should be colocated, with daily face-to-face communication. Members of leadership and other supporting roles should physically visit the other sites to put a person's face and sense of presence behind the phone call, email, text, etc. conducted with them. The author recommends that such visits should occur at least one every quarter for facilities separated by an airplane trip and twice per week for facilities separated by less than a one-hour drive.

Table 8.6 In-Person Communication
SELF-ACTUALIZATIONS FULFILLED

Self-Actualization Level	How Fulfilled by This Success Element
Physiological	Satisfaction that the work they depend on will be completed as promised, based on the trust established during in-person commitments.
Safety	Less fear of misunderstandings regarding agreements and promises made in person.
Love/Belonging	Prefers the social intimacy they observe and participate in from in-person contact.
Esteem	Provides a visible platform to share the authority of their job role. They may find opportunities to develop personal relationships more supportive to their next promotion goal.
Professional	Appreciates that the pace of the program and the speed of their professional development increases with the enhanced trust and faster communication speed resulting from in-person agreements.
Altruistic	These professionals are confident their altruistic vision will be achieved faster with in-person team communication.

8.8.2 Colocated Facilities

A corollary to facilitating in-person communication is the application of team colocation. Obviously, team members must be physically close to each other to easily meet in person. Many authors of good business practices have written how colocation has been an essential element of any first-place program

Colocation Facilitates Speed and Accuracy

- Facilitates in-person communication amongst team members.
- Attempt to have all team members present, including supplier and customer representatives.
- Designate special areas where loud discussions and meetings may be conducted.
- Only highly independent tasks should be allowed to exist in separate facilities (e.g., software unit test separated from product integration).
  - "30-second rule"?

Figure 8.16   A colocated program team is essential for establishing face-to-face, in-person communication; members should be in close proximity so they may meet quickly.

they observed (see Figure 8.16). For example, when the author of this book was assigned to an Advanced Development Division, he was given a desk in a temporary add-on office area. Other engineers sat close to him, with no partitions to separate them, exercising care to not be distracting to fellow workers. The author eventually discovered he was less than a 20-second walk from the division VP office in the same building. Detailed communication was conducted quickly, accurately, and with high trust. This provided immediate exchange with fellow team workers, which allowed this renowned organization to remain first place in the world as a source of exotic, high-performance aircraft.

At another point in his career, the author was assigned the role of managing a program that deployed multiple satellites to provide global telephonic communication. He conducted daily morning team meetings to precisely track their adherence to schedule commitments. On this program he had a "30-second rule," within which he could walk to the desk of any team member.

The one exception was a task team that required a special laboratory that was about 90 seconds away. Members from this team usually attended the morning status meetings, but it seemed they were always the last to know the current status of the program. The author thought their remoteness might cause the rest of the program to fall behind. So he instituted a change that was very unpopular—he asked that this separated team move their desks, phones, computers, and conference room into the colocated facility, meaning they had to walk a longer distance to get to the lab facilities. You can imagine the outcry—"What!? Is this guy subjecting us to some fleeting idealism?" But they reluctantly made the requested move.

The author was relieved to observe that suddenly there was higher program confidence that the remainder of the original schedule would be achieved. The work of this special team became more synchronized with the rest of the program work, and, in fact, they began offering highly valuable improvements that brought in much of their work ahead of schedule.

During Step 1 (see Figure 8.17), leadership must summarize the benefits of colocation for new team members. Examples should be provided of how colocation was necessary for other programs to be first place. When possible, leadership should pinpoint successes of the team they are a part of due to colocation. Leadership should describe how meeting areas will be established in the colocated areas to facilitate discussions without distracting the other team members.

[During program execution in Step 2, leadership must be aggressive about obtaining access to enterprise facilities that provide colocation. When establishing the seating layout for the team, consider setting a maximum time that is allowed for any team member to walk to the workstation of any other member. A limit of 30 seconds or

Colocated, Face-to-Face Fundamental Need

Step 1
• Share documented superiority of face-to-face communication and collocation.
• Discuss existing first-place teams that depend on collocation.
• Request communication conducted in person when possible.
• Insist on collocated work facilities during planning.
• Establish team rules of conduct to avoid distractions.
• Establish easily available meeting areas that do not distract others.
• Leadership exemplify face-to-face exchanges.

Figure 8.17   During Step 1, leadership must emphasize the high value of face-to-face communication to the team and must insist on facilities that promote colocation. Leadership must primarily apply face-to-face, in-person communication as an example to the team.

less has worked well. Leadership should discourage virtual forms of communication when in-person communication is available. This includes discouraging computer and phone discussions amongst team members a short walking distance apart. This practice will eventually demonstrate to the team members that in-person communication is necessary to provide the highest communication speeds, to provide the most complete and accurate communication, and to achieve first-place program progress.]

Table 8.7 Colocated Facilities
SELF-ACTUALIZATIONS FULFILLED

Self-Actualization Level	How Fulfilled by This Success Element
Physiological	Allows team-member agreements to be achieved with high degree of certainty derived from easily accessible in-person communication.
Safety	Are confident that agreements amongst team members will be achieved due to high trust from easily accessible in-person communication.
Love/Belonging	Appreciates the additional personal contact opportunities that colocation of team personnel provides.
Esteem	This is another way of allowing these professionals to provide direct visibility into their work status and accomplishments.
Professional	Allows development of expertise faster with the high speed of resolving issues facilitated by being able to quickly meet counterparts.
Altruistic	Obviously improves work speed and quality allowing program commitments and altruistic goals to be achieved quicker.

8.9 Additional Appeals to Motivation Needs

There are additional rules of operation the PM should establish before starting detailed planning. The most important ones are discussed below.

8.9.1 Milestone Commitments, Not Just Goals

The first is the concept of commitment. This can sometimes be awkward to enforce, even for senior professionals who have worked for the enterprise for decades. However, too many programs have referred to deadlines as "goals." A goal usually has an honorable intent, but it is by no means a *promise* (see Figure 8.18). For a

Commitments Are Currency of Progress

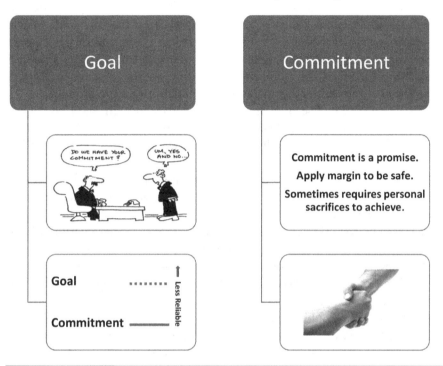

Figure 8.18   Delivery commitments from the team members are essential for a first-place program. Leadership must insist on commitments, not just goals. However, reliable commitments take practice to consistently derive accurately, and leadership must be patient with mistakes made by team members when forming commitments and help them learn from these experiences.

program to be in first place, all its interactions must be synchronized. An organization must know with certainty when the inputs it needs will be completed and available. If these inputs are late, the schedule for the work going forward falls apart and re-planning is necessary. This fault hampers the speedy progress of the program and prevents it from being in first place.

Examine, for example, the extremes of answers a team member may provide when asked when they will complete their next deliverable. They might say, "We will do everything we can to have it by COB tomorrow! We are pretty sure we can make this time; we will do our best." While on the other hand they might say, "We commit to completing the work by 3:00 PM the day after tomorrow."

Does the first answer have value? What is meant by "COB"? Does it mean, 5:00 PM? 7:00 PM? 11:59 PM? There is hope, but little certainty, that the deliverable will be available at any time that day. This assertion is only an optimistic prediction. So, the users of this delivered work cannot plan their work with certainty.

On the other hand, knowing with high confidence that the work will be complete at a specific time, even if a day later than the optimistic goal, allows those who receive these results to plan their work confidently. Having to restart program tasks because of a broken delivery time wastes resources and delays completion of the entire program, as well as jeopardizing team morale.

Final deliveries by the program will be sooner and with lower cost when task completions are promised with clear commitments. Plus, the basic feelings amongst the team members will be more confident and serene—they will feel like they are in control.

So, what does it take to assemble a good commitment? An initial delivery time estimate should be made by the person performing the task, based on their experience and analysis of the details. If this person has little experience with this task, they should consult with others who have performed the same or similar task for verification of their estimate. They can even consult with professionals who are not members of the program but are familiar with the problem type being solved—of course, while exerting appropriate care for program-sensitive data.

A safety margin should then be added to this first estimate—typically (but not always) 20% of the original estimate. The size of this margin will vary depending on how familiar the person performing the task is with the work and whether or not they have consulted a source of actual completion times for the same or similar work. If their estimate is highly uncertain, they should add a larger margin.

Finally, the individual and team should be prepared to work extra hours to make sure the promised completion does not slip.

Leadership must be patient while incorporating the strict use of commitments. Even for some experienced professionals, this emphasis will be new. Making accurate delivery commitments takes practice to do well, and leadership must forgive team members who genuinely try their best to meet their promised delivery time but fail. Leadership should follow up by reviewing with the team member where the mistake was made in their estimate and how to avoid such mistakes in the future. Of course, a team member who is consistently providing inaccurate schedule commitments should be mentored to find the cause and determine a correction.

The practice for team members to provide task completion commitments is essential to all the needs of developing motivations and self-actualization.

Leadership may encounter individuals who predict excessively long completion durations, their strategy being to stake out a comfortable completion duration and so almost always complete it ahead of the committed time. Team members who consistently provide task completion durations that are much longer than needed penalize the rapid progress of the program. This practice can cause the computed final completion date to be later than it should be and require extra team resources to correct this completion date with well-substantiated interim schedule durations. This can pull the effort out of first place and dilute its future competitiveness, so it must be promptly discontinued.

The author has found that this strategy quickly becomes obvious to leadership, and its practice is rarely repeated. Usually, a quick discussion between the offending team member and leadership stops it.

Table 8.8 Milestone Commitments, Not Just Goals
SELF-ACTUALIZATIONS FULFILLED

Self-Actualization Level	How Fulfilled by This Success Element
Physiological	Helps assure team member will deliver required quality on time. Helps maintain essential synchronization between task events to achieve challenging schedule and cost commitments.
Safety	Provides a process to ensure that needed work results will be provided on time. Provides another means to demonstrate that the program execution is high quality by delivering completed work as promised.
Love/Belonging	Enhances cooperation amongst team members when predicting when the work for the various tasks will be completed.
Esteem	Delivering high-quality work on time adds to the distinction of the team member's title. Consistently delivering as promised is another attribute to be considered for promotion.
Professional	Delivering promised product quality on committed time is an essential performance cornerstone of all expert professionals. When a team consistently achieves completion commitments, the program work will be done sooner.
Altruistic	When the team coordinates their work output with commitments the work will be completed sooner. This allows the elements of an altruistic vision to be completed faster.

8.9.2 Clarification of Roles

Clarifying leadership and team member roles appeals to the needs of all the levels of developing motivation and self-actualization. Team-member responsibilities must be precisely defined and allocated in first-place teams. Unfortunately, for many teams, who is responsible for what is resolved over time with trial and error. Conflicts may occur between team members who believe they are responsible for the same thing. Conversely, essential tasks may be left undone because no one was told to be responsible for them. First-place teams cannot afford to waste time and energy because of these mistakes.

From the start, the responsibilities and roles of leadership and team members must be thoroughly defined (see Figure 8.19). These definitions may be refined during execution, but usually the amendments required are small.

Furthermore, any major change in responsibilities must be approved by the program's change control process. This includes promptly announcing approved changes of responsibilities to the entire program team via suitable media (see Figure 8.20).

Leadership must inform the new team during Step 1 that they will be given the opportunity to assist in defining the work plan, assessing needed resources, detecting new risks and issues, and developing plans to avoid and abate them.

Leadership must also inform the team during Step 1 that they will be removing barriers to the fast progress of the team during Step 2—not just as they occur but when they are anticipated. Leadership must acknowledge that when

Clarifying Roles Increases Team Speed

Team Expectations

- Accept uncomfortable targets.
- Acknowledge task ownership.
- Provide "commitments," not "goals."
- Devote needed effort.
- Communicate change of status.
- Complete on time
- Communicate motivations.

Leadership

- Set direction while facilitating motivations.
- Forgives those mistakes made in earnest
- Protect:
    - Against malicious criticism
    - Time needed for personal issues
    - Against force reduction
    - Etc.
- Mentor team member development.
- Sell attributes of reports.
- Maintain buy-in (Step 1)

Figure 8.19 In a first-place program, the expectations of the team members and leadership must be clarified from the very start; relying on mistakes and subtle implications to clarify these roles leads to wasted time, confusion, and often resentment.

Clearly Define Team Roles—Change with Process

Step 1
• Describe detailed roles and expectations of leadership and individual contributors.
• Document in the program plan.
• Solicit refinements from team.
• Describe how this clarity reduces mistakes.
• Use team questions to refine written role descriptions.
• Implement refinements during Step 2 via CCB.

Figure 8.20   The description of leadership and team roles should be documented in the program plan, and feedback from the team should be used to refine these descriptions. Future changes to these descriptions must be adjudicated using the program change process, such as a change control board.

a barrier starts impeding the progress of a program, damage to the schedule has already occurred.

In addition, leadership must consistently and vigorously protect the team and make sure the self-actualization needs of every team member are being fulfilled.

During Step 1, team members must be informed that any time they need for important personal issues will be allocated without question and that they are responsible for helping to select who will cover their work while they are gone. But the enterprise must establish and support the principle that team members will not be allowed by leadership to move to another assignment until program leadership determines that their absence will not jeopardize the success of the program they are currently supporting.

Changes of needed talent in the program must be anticipated by leadership. During Step 1, leadership must inform the team that they will look for new roles for team members if the need for their current contribution is ending.

Ironically, first-place teams are often subject to extra scrutiny and criticism, much of which will have no merit, and leadership must protect against such baseless criticism. If criticism is received in writing, it must be responded to in kind. The first thing the program must do is to ask for written clarification of the criticism, then respond (again in writing) with their understanding of the criticism. This will force the discussion to be conducted with facts and dismiss any criticism that is merely emotion based.

Part of this clarification must be identifying the source of the criticism in order to correctly address any rebuttal, if one is deemed necessary. A person or team that is the source of the criticism must be accountable for their accusation. Then, any facts that support the criticism must be provided. These can include data, reports, comments by leaders, etc. The criticism may be supported primarily by innuendo, which has much less credibility but still warrants a response.

If, based on the available data, the criticism is valid, leadership should post a written admission with gratitude to the source for detecting the problem, including a description of the remedy that will be imposed. If the criticism is found to be unsubstantiated, a written rationale that derives this conclusion must be posted, and future criticisms from the same source should be quickly reviewed for new, supporting substance. But if new evidence does not support the accusation, then additional written rebuttal is not necessary, and the source of criticism should be ignored.

In addition to attending to the needs and safety of every team member (see Figure 8.21), leadership must mentor the development of each member who desires guidance, forgiving mistakes made by team members who are earnestly trying their best. Harsh and degrading responses by leadership to mistakes is self-defeating to the program and the enterprise. At best, this kind of response represents shortsightedness and impatience in leadership; at worst, lack of empathy for the team members. Good leadership should promote the attributes of outstanding team members to the other managers in the enterprise, which benefits both the enterprise and the team member.

Team-Member Responsibilities Start With Fundamentals

Highest Priority

- **Personal safety**
- **Team safety**
- **Data security**
- **Facility safety**
- **Personal emergency**
- **High task quality**
- **Communicate schedule**

Lower Priority

Figure 8.21   Individual team members must be reminded of the priority of their functions, with personal safety and team safety being the highest. This may seem obvious to some, but clearly defining these priorities reduces the time to react to issues.

Team members should be expected to acknowledge the task work and responsibilities they have been given. If a team member later says they did not know they were responsible for some portion of a task, both the team member and leadership must take responsibility for this breakdown in communication.

Team members should be forewarned that at times they will be assigned completion targets that are uncomfortable. (There are some managers who gauge the amount of task work a given team member can be responsible for by how uncomfortable they are! The author has been the recipient of this unique approach.)

Team members must inform leadership of any change in status of their work resulting in changes to delivery content and time, which, among other possible reasons, could be due to new risks or issues they have observed.

During Step 1, new team members must be concisely informed as to what leadership expects from them. They will appreciate this clarity and will be more productive from the start with a firm understanding of the limits of their role and what they should expect from leadership. Team members will feel empowered by knowing leadership places a priority on the clarity of all team roles.

[During Step 2, the expectations of team members and leadership will be documented in the program plan. Suggestions to change the expectations of these roles should be welcomed from any member. It will be the responsibility of leadership to determine if a suggested change should be evaluated by the program change process, which is often adjudicated by a configuration change board for larger programs and will provide a recommendation to either accept or deny the proposed change. The accepted change will be implemented with the approval of leadership, and the entire team will be informed of it via suitable media.]

Clarifying leadership and team-member roles from the start of the program reduces mistakes from erroneous assumptions about who is responsible for what and fortifies the understanding of all team members of what they are individually responsible for working on. Providing this clarification also reduces the possibility of important program work not being assigned to anyone.

Table 8.9 Clarification of Roles
SELF-ACTUALIZATIONS FULFILLED

Self-Actualization Level	How Fulfilled by This Success Element
Physiological	Clear description of expectations at each level allows this professional to be more confident that they are performing their work as expected.
Safety	Prevents misunderstanding of job role so this person is not anxious about possibly not doing enough or exceeding the extent of what they should be doing.

Love/Belonging	Helps establish organizational structure and limits of authority for reference, reducing conflicts about the functions and responsibilities of the team members and increasing teamwork.
Esteem	Provides a clear description of function and authority of team members with this self-actualization. Provides a clear perspective for future promotion.
Professional	Assists in identifying the responsible sources from whom to obtain various information.
Altruistic	Assists in reducing conflict in the team created by mis-understandings about responsibilities. Reduces time to achieve altruistic targets.

8.9.3 Planning and Tracking Progress Successfully: The Program Plan

The program plan documents what must be performed by the team to achieve its customer's desired outcome, and there are necessary steps to creating the program plan that must be taken if the program is to be in first place.

Before starting the program plan, leadership must define both what the program is creating and the status of the team's organization. What program is creating—the final or interim outcome(s) of the program—we are labeling Point B, which will be made clear below. The status of the team, whether "no one yet," "legacy team in place," or somewhere in between, we label Point A. The purpose of the program plan is to describe in detail how to achieve Point B, starting at Point A. This plan may necessarily evolve during Step 2 and thus must be kept current via rigorous configuration control.

Planning a first-place program requires openly and accurately determining its current status and its required outcome and planning the straightest line possible between these two points. These plans are sometimes fraught with low-priority tasks and other distractions.

Frequently, the poorly planned program either has not precisely defined its final outcome or has not realistically determined its current situation, rendering any plan at best partially wasteful and resulting in an unnecessary delay to complete its execution.

Some programs allow the definition of their completion point to evolve throughout the life of the effort, as opposed to clearly describing it up front. Other efforts may precisely define their outcome but are unrealistic about their current status. Both of these errors demote the performance of the program.

Precisely and clearly defining Point A and Point B is critical at the start of the program, providing clarity to all team members on how the program will help fulfill their maturing motivations or self-actualization and help them develop.

With clarity, it removes any uncertainty about what the program will accomplish, which, if unresolved, can be an ongoing distraction that hampers team members from doing their best work. All team participants must be free to do their best work undistracted by disagreement about what constitutes completion of this work. These distractions will prevent a program from being in first place.

Point B should be defined first. If Point A is defined first, this starting definition can prejudice the description of the work to be completed in the definition of Point B. Point B may be the final completion target of the program, or it may be the completion criteria of one segment amongst many that together will result in the completion of the program.

Contract requirements for the program work must be included in the description of point B. Sometimes the contracted work will be divided into sub-portions (referred to in various terms such as "phases," "segments," "parts," etc.), each having defined completion requirements. The description of Point B will often be a superset of the contracted work. Additions to the point B description may include additional requirements and constraints imposed by the program, the enterprise, or the suppliers.

The description of Point B must be stated simply and succinctly. It should not be more than a few sentences long. Vague or overly complex statement examples would be, "Build a world-class fourth-grade math program," or "Create an electric car that goes 250 km on one charge, or 220 miles in medium to light rain, when the rain is less than 2 cm/h for no more than a six-hour period in a 24-hour duration with a reliability of 0.992 over the first five years of life."

Team members must be able to rally around an explicit description that they can clearly comprehend and remember. Well-constructed statements, such as, "Improve the average test score for mathematics for all the fourth-graders in the school district by 10%" or "Build an electric car that goes 220 miles on one battery charge in any weather condition with a reliability of 0.992," are clearer and easier to recall. They allow it each team member to focus on a simple, single team goal.

As mentioned, Point B may be the first of a series of outcomes. In these cases, program teams generate the necessary enthusiasm and dedication to be in first place by concentrating individually on a series of major progress steps, each with a simple and clearly defined closure point, not solely on the final outcome.

For example, the United States successfully put a human being on the moon by first putting a human being in space and safely retrieving them, then safely placing humans in orbit, then successfully locating and docking human spacecraft with another vehicle in orbit, then leaving the Earth's gravitational field and orbiting the moon, and eventually landing on the moon. The team members were highly motivated to complete each incremental step until the final commitment was achieved.

Only after Point B is defined should the team define Point A. This avoids distorting the essential requirements in the Point B definition due to do potential deficiencies in the Point A status. Many times, the team will still be in its preliminary stage of formulation, and the leadership and team members may not even have all been selected. In these cases, completing the selection of team members and organizing the team must be part of the program plan to fulfill the commitment in Point B.

Point A should include a description of any constraints or deficiencies anticipated while pursuing completion, such as limits to the amounts and kinds of team members available, facility limitations, equipment limitations, poor performance history, and more. The description in Point A must be thorough and honest, especially if it highlights big organizational or enterprise challenges to achieving the Point B commitment. If feasible, an accurate description of Point A should be confirmed with an independent review, as an erroneous Point A description may prevent formulating a successful program plan.

Planning and tracking of the resulting plan can be accomplished with a number of methods and tools with different strengths (see Figure 8.22). The PM, with the assistance of their leadership team, must choose the best methods, which will depend largely on the complexity of the program and how likely one or a number of parallel development paths may become a new critical path. (The "critical path" is one of a number of serial, interdependent steps that must be accomplished to complete the program. It is the longest such path and thus determines the completion time of the program.) Task-team members should review their team plan and participate in determining if it can be successfully integrated in the program's master schedule (see Figure 8.23).

Table 8.10 Planning and Tracking Progress Successfully
SELF-ACTUALIZATIONS FULFILLED

Self-Actualization Level	How Fulfilled by This Success Element
Physiological	Provides clear knowledge of what they must do to accomplish their task and its part in completing the program work.
Safety	Establishing a well-substantiated plan that is objectively based on thoroughly understanding current status and what the completion criteria are reduces fears of failing to accomplish the work.
Love/Belonging	A clear plan with a simple and unambiguous description of the intended outcome unifies the team. This increases teamwork and provides a more comfortable work environment.

Esteem	Professionals with this self-actualization desire to achieve their current task with high quality as quickly as possible so they may be eligible for expanded responsibility and promotion sooner. Well-substantiated planning allows the program to complete the work quicker.
Professional	Clearly described task commitments allow these team members to confidently identify what they best contribute to improve program performance and accentuate their expertise.
Altruistic	A well-substantiated team plan with simple, clear achievement criteria allows the team to achieve its commitments much faster. This shortens the time to achieve the altruistic needs of this team member.

8.9.4 Find Faults/Failures Early

For any program, faults and failures will occur as the product is being developed. This is true regardless of whether the output of the effort is a physical product, the results of a study, a new process, etc. The program plan must be designed to find these faults as early in the development flow as possible (see Figure 8.24).The cost of corrections to faults or failures increases exponentially as the product being developed becomes more integrated—for instance, running a small test case for a new process before releasing it to a large organization or finding errors in software during unit test instead of later in a more integrated environment are essential steps. These steps allow the program to complete in less time and at a lower cost so it can achieve or maintain first-place status.

Imagine, for example, prematurely deploying a new curriculum into all the schools of a district, only to find that it fails to achieve its targeted performance. Now all the schools in the district must stop and endure a period of waiting while the problem is being corrected. Large amounts of student time would have been saved if this new curriculum had been validated with a small number of students before distributing it to the entire district.

Finding faults early also improves the team's understanding of the strengths and weaknesses of the product they're creating. These early faults may, for example, indicate a weakness or error in the design of the product, and learning this early can greatly reduce the time and expense needed to correct the design. The early faults found may also indicate the need for additional test coverage in the test sequence. Added tests may reduce total testing cost and provide more low-level performance benchmarks for higher confidence regression testing, if needed (see Figure 8.25).

Balance Strengths of Tracking Tools

PERT Tracking

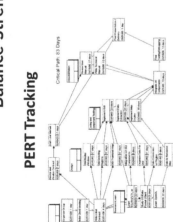

- Clearly shows task interdependencies.
- Tools automatically identify the critical path.
- Caution against managing only critical path.

Gantt Tracking

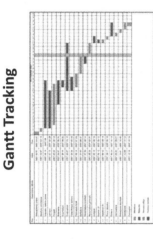

- Better shows tasks planned to execute simultaneously.
- Helps identify tasks falling behind not on the critical path.
- Good for detecting risks on non-critical paths.

Figure 8.22 These are two popular work planning and tracking tools. These and others are implemented with computer software, providing high accuracy, consistency, and a wide range of perspectives for review. Care must be taken to prevent one tool's depiction from concealing risks and issues to the program plan that might be revealed with another tool.

Planning for Success

Step 1
• Define current status and next necessary accomplishment (Point A and Point B).
• Select informative schedule and tracking tools.
• Task teams assist with determining work steps, schedule, and risks.
• Task-team members review program plan to refine and buy in.
• Task teams approve the master schedule.

Figure 8.23 This summarizes some of the important elements of the planning process for the program, and it is important that task teams help develop, review, and approve the master schedule.

Plan Program or Project to Find Faults Early

- Cost of fault correction grows exponentially as product matures.
- Insight from root cause early:
  - Improves product/process knowledge
  - Improves test coverage
  - Lowers total program or project cost
- Thorough early testing simplifies regression testing.

Figure 8.24 Almost all developments of new processes or physical items require a resource efficient and highly effective test plan. A poorly designed test plan can paralyze what would otherwise be a first-place program. One essential tenet is to design a plan to find faults as early as possible in the test sequence. This greatly reduces cost and schedule penalties. A complete regression test plan supported by adequate unit test coverage must be identified to reduce the time to determine root cause of faults and failures.

Table 8.11 Find Faults/Failures Early
SELF-ACTUALIZATIONS FULFILLED

Self-Actualization Level	How Fulfilled by This Success Element
Physiological	Appreciates finding faults and failures early in testing adds to the probability of success of the product or process design. This increases the probability the team plan will remain stable and intact.
Safety	Appreciates that finding faults and failures early improves the likelihood that the program will stay on schedule. This reduces the probability of the program being replanned or canceled.
Love/Belonging	Appreciates that finding faults and failures early reduces the team trauma of having a fault or failure occurring later in a more expensive integrated environment. It reduces criticism amongst team members and maintains team harmony.
Esteem	Finding faults and failures early reduces concern and scrutiny of team dynamics, the program plan, and the individual team members by the enterprise. It reduces the likelihood of the team slipping their committed milestones and forfeiting an image of success.
Professional	Finding faults early allows for an in-depth search of the fault cause and a more detailed understanding of the product mechanism. This allows the team members to develop their special expertise to have a better understanding of the product and to develop solutions faster for future issues.
Altruistic	Finding fault early generally allows for a higher-quality product to be completed faster. This shortens the time to achieve elements of their altruistic vision.

8.9.5 Savings with Reuse

Unfortunately, the value of reuse is often misunderstood (see Figure 8.26). This is true when planning to reuse anything—a documented trade study, a mechanical design, a software program, an electronic circuit, and more. In its extreme, this misunderstanding wrongly assumes that if only a fraction of this product is changed, the cost to make and validate the change will be the same fraction of the cost needed to originally develop the product.

For example, it may be assumed if you have a tested and released software program of 1,000 lines of code and change 100 of these lines, the cost of the change will be 1/10 the original cost of developing this software. This assumption is wrong.

Regardless of what is being developed, there are major costs in originally collecting the product requirements, then designing and executing the testing

Detecting and Correcting Faults Early Needed for First Place

Step 1
• Leadership provides team examples of cost/schedule savings resulting from early detection.
• Leadership reviews and approves unit-level test adequacy for all products being developed.
• Predict expected number of failures from past metrics.
• Provides rationale for why predicted failures may be fewer than past actuals
• Compare new actuals with predicted.
• Credit team-member performances for finding faults/failures early.

Figure 8.25   During Step 1, leadership must educate the team on the importance of early fault detection. Sometimes, tracking the types and numbers of faults and comparing them to those that have occurred in previous, similar programs is helpful. The first-place team must always be given clear credit for finding faults/failures early in the test sequence.

Reuse Saving Is Often a Fleeting Promise

- Most value lost when completion wrapper broken:
    - Even if perturbed very little.
    - Must revisit all requirements analysis, design, test planning, testing and maintenance plans and documentation.
    - Applies to all types of products and support elements.
- Hope of future reusable component "chips":
    - Chip function must be thoroughly documented.
    - Minimum, standardized coupling allowed between chips.
    - Form, fit, and function must be frozen.
    - User confidence must be high.

> *Successfully applied to digital electronics.*

Figure 8.26   A high degree of care must be applied when assuming the savings of reusing past work when developing schedule and cost estimates. Even after making small changes to the existing product, most or all of the original work to flow down requirements and perform unit/system testing must be accomplished again. The actual savings derived from reuse is usually much less than hoped for.

of it. The reader must understand, as soon as you "break the wrapper"—change the product by even a very small amount—almost all requirements analysis, test planning, and testing must be repeated. In addition, all associated documentation must be updated. The small portion of the product being changed usually interacts with the rest of the system being developed. The reader must appreciate that all the effects of the change on the rest of the system are unknown. So, requirements analysis and then testing of the updated product must verify its impact on the entire product. Usually, this work must be repeated to nearly the full extent performed when the product was originally built.

Instead of the cost required to replace 100 lines of a 1,000-line software program being 10% of the original cost, when including the needed review and update of requirements flow down, changes to the test plan, updating all associated documentation, then executing this updated test plan, the update ends up being closer to 80–95% of the original cost, based on actual data. (The actual savings varies, depending on the complexity and criticality of the product being changed, as well as whether its components have been designed for reuse.)

Reuse can be applied to a wide range of products, processes, documentation, facilities, and even personnel. The PM must make a special effort at the start of the program to identify all potential reuse opportunities (see Figure 8.27). However, when estimating cost savings due to reuse, the program team must evaluate the entire development and applications life cycle to derive an accurate figure.

Carefully Consider Reuse

Step 1
• Determine reuse opportunities (product, process, documentation, facilities, personnel). • Determine explicitly what portion of each opportunity can be reused. • Evaluate all original development work and costs for the product to benefit from proposed reuse to predict savings. • Conduct peer and leadership review of predicted savings prior to incorporating in program plan.

Figure 8.27   The estimated savings resulting from the reuse of the process or product must be realistically and thoroughly evaluated. Peer review of the estimated savings, preferably by individuals independent of the program, should be performed to be safe.

Table 8.12 Savings with Reuse
SELF-ACTUALIZATIONS FULFILLED

Self-Actualization Level	How Fulfilled by This Success Element
Physiological	Are comforted by the complete and realistic evaluation of any reuse opportunity to reduce program cost and schedule risk.
Safety	Less concerned about not achieving program completion times and cost estimates due to erroneous estimates of savings from reuse.
Love/Belonging	Glad to see team contentment is higher because team observes realistic evaluation and application of product reuse. This adds to the pride these team members have for their leadership.
Esteem	This realistic process gives these team members permission to evaluate reusing past completed work. Successful application of reuse gives them the opportunity to further demonstrate their suitability for future promotion.
Professional	This gives these team members the opportunity to demonstrate their expertise by evaluating reuse opportunities in detail. It demonstrates their respect for shortening schedule times and lowering costs from any source.
Altruistic	Successful reuse can significantly shorten time to program completion and reduce cost. This allows accomplishing the altruistic needs of these team members sooner.

8.9.6 Understand All Contracts

Before starting the program, all contracts must be reviewed for completeness and for any wording that may be misinterpreted (see Figure 8.28). This review must be of all contracts, including the contract the program has with the customer and any contracts between the program and the suppliers.

It is highly valuable to have the contract reviews attended by participants not assigned to the program. These independent reviewers will not have assumptions that the contract wording has a hidden meaning based on personal relationships between members of the contracting teams. They will not, for example, assume that portions of the contract may not be enforced.

For example, on one actual program, there was a simple line in the customer contract stating, "All subsystems shall be demonstrated in orbit." In this case, the customer actually expected the contractor to turn off the onboard control computer in a satellite while in orbit to verify the operation of the backup system.

Written Agreements Must Be Complete and Unambiguous

- Enlist independent reviewers.
- Contrive most disadvantaged interpretation of each contract statement.
- Review ALL contracts and subcontracts.
- Request customer review *(when acceptable).*

Figure 8.28   All contracts and other written agreements must be scrutinized in high detail. Reviewers independent of the program are of high value. Some statements in the contract may be ambiguous, and an attempt must be made to interpret them in a way that is most disadvantageous to the program. Customer review of the contracts can be advantageous if legal.

For those in aerospace deliberately turning off the flight computer while in flight is unthinkable. Members on the program team failed to suspect that this statement would be taken literally by the customer. Fortunately, this requirement was negotiated to avoid this action.

Table 8.13 Understand All Contracts

SELF-ACTUALIZATIONS FULFILLED

Self-Actualization Level	How Fulfilled by This Success Element
Physiological	Evaluates contract reviews as another valuable step to make sure that all needed information and substance are identified and agreed upon between parties.
Safety	Less threat is perceived that needed work areas have not been identified and assigned or that there is a misunderstanding in an agreement between the parties.
Love/Belonging	These team members take comfort in observing less worry in the team about adequacy of subcontract deliveries or not knowing what information must be delivered to subcontractors/vendors. This adds to team harmony.

Esteem	Understanding all products and services that must be provided by subcontractors/vendors and establishing agreements that successfully recognize them is an essential part of demonstrating higher-level leadership. Team members with this self-actualization recognize that demonstrating this ability is essential for promotion.
Professional	These team members need a precise understanding of the agreement with subcontractors/suppliers to reliably plan and provide their expertise. They appreciate these reviews helps establish this understanding.
Altruistic	These team members understand that erroneous assumptions and misunderstandings between contractors can lead to large cost overruns, schedule delays, and poor future relationships. Avoiding misunderstanding with reviews will shorten the time, reduce the costs, and increase the credibility of achieving their altruistic vision.

8.9.7 Successful Software Development

Some programs will require the development of software as part of their work. If developing new software logic is not a common activity in the sponsoring enterprise, then managing software development can be foreign to the leadership of the program.

In this instance, the task leader for software development must not just be competent in leading the development of the software, they must also be able to communicate software development status, issues, and future work in layman's terms, and they must do so with language the rest of the program team understands (see Figure 8.29).

This requires an additional ability the software task lead must have to exercise their role. This individual becomes an essential interface between the rigors of the software development and the low software development experience of the rest of the team. They are in a sense the software "ambassador" for the program.

Some leaders may understandably believe that software development has been around long enough to be managed like a more traditional technology, yet software technologies are still constantly emerging. Rapid changes to the way software is designed, developed, and applied are occurring, and software-development methodologies are maturing and changing in major ways.

In addition, computer hardware attributes measured, for example, in terms of computational speed, nonvolatile memory capacity, data transmission bandwidth, reliability, fault tolerance, and reduced cost are increasing at a very high rate. New hardware design approaches are being materialized and implemented in all these areas. A first-place software team must understand the availability of these new options.

Software Development Lead Must Be an Ambassador

- **Must fluently communicate status, plans, and issues to non-SW team.**
- **Must have:**
    - **Experience with program product domain**
    - **Experience-based intuition that detects risks early**
- **Assures software development plan is complete, current, *and* *followed.***
- **Senior SW engineers are not always best candidates.**

Figure 8.29   With the quickly emerging new roles and changes in software, the software development task lead must be able to fluently communicate the details of software development milestones, processes, and issues to the rest of the program team in layman's terms. They must also make sure that the software development plan is complete, up to date, and followed.

Due to the vast increase in the speed and density of modern computer hardware, software developers can now accept the resource overheads of using easy-to-express, object-oriented, high-order languages to write their code. High-density neural network hardware has even been developed to support the application of artificial intelligence in embedded, real-time applications.

Furthermore, software engineering has unique characteristics that may be perplexing to competent engineers experienced in more traditional engineering and scientific subjects. For example, applying software usually requires adhering to a strict set of rules that are human made and not established by nature. Adhering to these rules when developing software usually must be 100% complete. No approximate, "back of the envelope" drafts are allowed. When a non-software person encounters these arbitrary disciplines when involved in software development, abiding to these characteristics may be very frustrating for them.

Software has no physical manifestation. A software program listing is only a design document, it is not the series of electronic "ones" and "zeros" that represent the computer instructions. A schematic of an electronic design or a design print for a mechanical part are also design documents, but they lead to an actual electronic circuit or a mechanical part you can hold in your hand and compare with the design document. There is no comparable physical manifestation for a software source program listing.

In addition, the techniques and nomenclature used to develop software are still evolving. The terms and definitions used in software development—terms such as "computer loading," "structured design," "object-oriented software design," "polymorphism," and "artificial intelligence"—can seem mysterious and ambiguous to the layman.

A good software development lead (SDL) in a program team will remove the ambiguity for the work being done and clarify work status and future work needed in terms that are understood by all team members. The SDL should have had experience with the type of product being developed so they can communicate fluently the software function and status with the rest of the team. This lead should have enough related software development experience to anticipate and avoid development issues before they occur.

In addition, the SDL should make sure that a software development plan (SDP) is created and used. This SDP must be rigorously followed by the software development team and must be kept current via the program change process. Because software has a unique texture compared to other technologies, and usually plays a major role in the functionality of the product being developed, it is absolutely necessary that an SDP be created—*and followed*.

The SDP must be the road map for the software developers on the team. It must be the first source of documented direction reviewed whenever a team member has any question about what the next step is or how the development milestones are defined and accomplished.

For this reason, a good SDP must be short and focused on only the development process for the program. If it tries to provide a solution for every potential development problem or turns into a tutorial justifying the processes being used, it will become too big and unusable. This will seriously jeopardize the program's ability to be in first place.

A devastating assumption made by some PMs is that all software and associated development is the same. They may wrongly assume that a good software engineer will be proficient in developing software for any application. Figure 8.30 illustrates the major software domains and summarizes each domain's uniqueness.

When software applications first appeared in industries, the breadth of applications, computer hardware, and computer languages to support it were small, and during this time, the software "programmer" had a limited role. But *programmers* have become *software engineers*—the software programs they develop are now much bigger and perform many more functions than in past decades.

In addition, modern software engineers now have a far greater understanding of both the development and computer hardware/software execution environments for the software they create. They have a better understanding of the

Software Application Domains Require Specialists

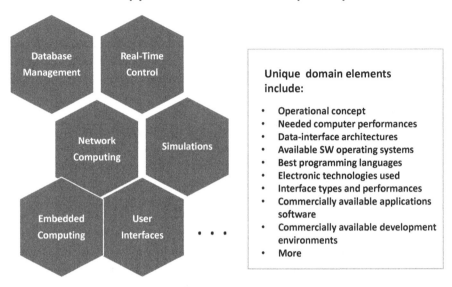

Unique domain elements include:

- Operational concept
- Needed computer performances
- Data-interface architectures
- Available SW operating systems
- Best programming languages
- Electronic technologies used
- Interface types and performances
- Commercially available applications software
- Commercially available development environments
- More

Figure 8.30   Program leadership must understand that the days of general-purpose software programmers are over. Software engineers are now specialists in various applications domains and have current understanding of the functional requirements of the domain, the electronic architectures, and capabilities used, and the best software development tools, operating systems, and programming languages. Care must be taken to select software development team members who are specialists in the application domains the program needs supported.

applications domain they are serving, and many become specialists in these domains. For example, they may understand the connection of certain business variables in a spreadsheet that computes profitability or the advantages of the use of quaternions versus direction cosines in a navigation computer. To assist them in achieving an excellent software design, they must understand both the functions of the algorithms they are implementing and the electronic architecture the software will execute in.

Another feature of modern-day software development is the distribution of costs. Because of today's greater involvement of software in the functionality of many products, the need for it to provide accurate results and execute reliably have become critical. As a result, very little of the cost of developing software currently is used for writing code (see Figure 8.31). Program leadership must understand that most of today's software development cost results from accumulating and managing software requirements, developing a maintainable software

Small Amount of Software Cost Is Coding

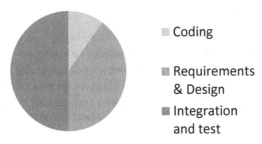

- Coding
- Requirements & Design
- Integration and test

- 10% or less of SW development cost from coding.
- 2–4% of total cost for coding critical real-time SW.
- Future SW maintenance may be significant additional cost.
- Emerging SW technologies are reducing costs.

Figure 8.31   Many professionals who do not develop software are surprised to learn that most of the software development costs result not from coding but from identifying software requirements, designing the software algorithms, and performing unit and integrated testing.

design that achieves these requirements, and then executing a series of tests that verifies that these requirements have been completely achieved. Leadership must include the additional cost for any special facilities/tools needed to track software requirements, design the software, write the code, then test it at the unit and integrated levels.

Software professionals with recent experience in the specific application domain are needed to design a low-cost software development and verification flow. The ability to achieve high time and cost efficiency with a plan to thoroughly test the functionality of the software units and integrate them into the total product can make or break a program. Developing a short, low-cost path to completely develop, test and validate the software is essential to be a first-place program (see Figure 8.32).

The reader must appreciate that, due to the greater involvement of software in modern systems, fault detection and recovery logic has grown dramatically, vastly increasing the cost of testing and verifying software. In some systems, testing this fault detection and recovery software is more expensive than testing the primary function of the software.

During Step 1, new software developers will be motivated by learning that leadership appreciates that software schedules are usually under pressure as a

SW Development Fundamentals to Be in First Place

Step 1
• Hire a seasoned SW ambassador to manage.
• Recruit SW experts with experience in needed domains.
• Scrub proposed SW reuse life cycle for real savings.
• Focus on evaluating requirements changes, design update, integration and test repeated for savings.
• Insist on clearly named, independent SW modules.
• Write a software development plan (SDP) and use it.
• Maintain SDP with configuration control process.
• Involve SW developers in planning, schedules, choosing methodologies and tools.

Figure 8.32   It is a great advantage to hire a software development lead who has experience in the functional domain of the program and will hire developers with adequate experience in this domain. Their experience will help them anticipate potential problems before they occur.

result of slips in the requirements development steps before their work. In addition, they will be freed by knowing that software specialists and leadership have a role understood and respected by the rest of the program team.

Software development team members will be freed by knowing their leader can fluently communicate the content of the SDP, including the software development milestones and other software issues, to the non-software members on the program team—they will be relieved to know they will not have to perform this function and will be able to dedicate all their energy to performing their assigned task. Software developers will feel less encumbered to do their best work knowing that all program leadership will understand the work and benefits of complete software design and testing.

[During Step 2, software developers will know their software development steps and associated benefits are appreciated by the entire program team. They will be highly motivated by the freedom they are given to negotiate the development, test and maintenance methodologies, and tools used to achieve rapid software completion. They will also be motivated by their freedom to assist with generating the software development plan and schedules. The software development team will be motivated by knowing the entire program team understands their challenges and appreciates the benefits of their expertise, approach, and innovations.]

Table 8.14 Successful Software Development
SELF-ACTUALIZATIONS FULFILLED

Self-Actualization Level	How Fulfilled by This Success Element
Physiological	Highly appreciates that software developers have a written plan they all must follow (SDP).
Safety	Relieved that the software development team must agree upon and follow written SDP. They observe that a software development lead that can describe software details to the layman as well as clarifying SDP milestones greatly reduces risk to successful software development.
Love/Belonging	Supports ways of developing a close relationship amongst the software developers and the non-software professionals on the team. This leads to more teamwork and less criticism.
Esteem	Appreciates that fluent communication of software issues, status, and plans with the rest of the program is essential for success. This gives them a firm foundation to perform their job well and demonstrate their special performances to be promoted.
Professional	Understands they need successful software development for them to demonstrate their special expertise. Reduces their concern about future delays.
Altruistic	A supportive relationship between the software development team and the rest of the program is essential to be in first place. This relationship allows the program to achieve the altruistic needs of this team member sooner.

8.9.8 Valuable Planning and Tracking

As mentioned earlier, it is absolutely necessary that all the program team members have a uniform understanding of and focus on what their next accomplishment must be (Point B). In addition, they each must have an accurate, thorough, and honest evaluation of their current status (Point A) (see Figure 8.33).

The next step is to create a plan to achieve Point B not only with high quality, but also quickly and with the fewest resources. Sometimes, to achieve this, an independent audit of the description in Point A should have been performed. Team-member participation in these definitions and planning is necessary. All this planning is needed to be a first-place program (refer to Figure 7.3 on page 104).

The importance of the frontline team members' participating in planning details cannot be overemphasized. A real example is of a PM of a critical program

Accurate Plan Depiction—Tracking Essential

Step 1
• PM, task leads must have common understanding of next completion—Point B—*before determining current team status.* • PM, task leads must thoroughly access current team status—Point A. • Task leads identify all work steps, resources, schedule durations. • Team members review resulting task plans. • Using modern computer schedule tool is necessary. • Innovations, process improvements must be valued.

Figure 8.33 Rigorously following the guidance of first identifying the final accomplishments (or next accomplishments in a multi-stage program)—Point B—and only then assessing the current status of the program—Point A—is essential to achieve the plan for high program speed and efficiencies needed to be in first place. The task team leads must then determine the steps and schedules needed to complete their portions of achieving Point B.

that had a major delivery coming up soon. Unfortunately, the software verification work was behind schedule due to late software requirements. The PM pulled together the software team and tried to deliver a tactful approach of asking them to work around the clock to complete the needed work. This, of course, would require some individuals having to work the dreaded graveyard shift.

The PM started explaining the milestone requirement and reviewing the current schedule status. Then, to his surprise, the software team spontaneously took ownership of the conversation and amongst themselves immediately recognized the need for around-the-clock development, and volunteers selflessly came forward for the different required shifts. They even targeted the completion time and established schedule margins if development problems occurred.

The PM was stunned. The plan they derived was much more efficient and complete than the PM would have developed if solely designing the plan. The software team took full ownership of the schedule challenge, then organized and implemented a solid solution.

This spontaneous and ideal team-member planning result occurred after many months of the PM attempting to establish an inverted pyramid organization. The software resulting from this work performed successfully after this challenging task was completed on schedule. The software team learned much about efficient organization and planning from this exercise, and the pride of the team was further increased—they had shown the boss they could do it themselves, and better!

Program planning can be represented, tracked, and updated in a variety of ways. It is highly recommended that it be performed using a computer-based tool, regardless of the size of the work. A computer-based tool allows for better top-level visibility of the work status and establishes consistency in the tracking method and status shown.

Unfortunately, tracking of program progress by the stakeholders is usually biased, which is a natural, even subconscious, tendency. The use of computer tools for tracking helps to maintain a less biased record of completion status and work to be done. There are numerous ways of displaying a plan for the task work to be done. Two ways will be discussed here, each containing its pros and cons. Both methods have been implemented with computer software with the bonus of automating certain labor-intensive manual analytical steps.

The more traditional way to plan and track a program is with the Gantt format, developed in 1917 by Henry Gantt. As mentioned, it was first used for managing the building of the Hoover Dam. It lists the task steps to be performed, with schedule durations ascribed to each task. In addition, interdependencies amongst tasks can be shown with some scheduling tools (refer to Figure 8.22 on page 160). It is harder, however, to define the critical completion path with this format than with other formats.

There are of course other development paths executed in parallel with the critical path, and if the milestones in one of these other paths are delayed, this parallel path may become the new critical path. The Gantt schedule format provides equal information on the status of all development paths parallel to the critical path, making it easy to observe issues on these parallel paths and prevent delays so they do not become the new critical path.

The PERT (Program Evaluation Review Technique) format more clearly shows task interdependencies with a graphic format. PERT charts were created in the 1950s to help manage the creation of weapons and defense projects for the US Navy, and this format is useful for critical path management. Displaying the task interdependencies graphically is very helpful when these interdependencies are highly complex. In addition, computer tools that use this format automatically determine and illustrate the critical path clearly in its graphical output.

However, the PERT format often makes it harder to track other parallel development paths that may become the new critical path. Some program leaders have made the mistake of daily tracking only the critical path tasks without having identified and mitigated issues on the parallel development paths that were at risk of becoming the new critical path. First-place program leadership must "watch the flank" for emerging development risks in the parallel development paths and abate them before they become issues, as attending only to issues on the current critical schedule path will not allow a program to be first place. Also note that, if the tasks on the critical path are accomplished in less time than scheduled, another task series may become the new critical path.

Table 8.15 Valuable Planning and Tracking
SELF-ACTUALIZATIONS FULFILLED

Self-Actualization Level	How Fulfilled by This Success Element
Physiological	Team members at this level are given the opportunity to incorporate their first-hand knowledge of problems and potential solutions in the planning. This increases the probability of completing successfully and on time.
Safety	These team members will be relieved that an appropriate computerized tracking paradigm (e.g., PERT, Gantt or other) is applied for keeping plans and tracking up to date. This reduces risk of losing control of schedule.
Love/Belonging	These team members appreciate that this planning approach highly integrates team efforts. These approaches make more visible the team-member interdependencies.
Esteem	Thoroughly planning and accurately executing a complex team plan is a major capability needed for higher-level roles. These team members will be encouraged to perform this work well.
Professional	These team members need a well-defined program plan to know where to exert their expertise with maximum benefit. This planning also gives them more insight into where in the development path they may have most opportunity to contribute and grow.
Altruistic	Valuable, detailed planning gives these team members confidence that the commitments of the program will be achieved and provides insight into where their altruistic needs are being met.

8.9.9 Consider a Scheduler

A first-place program must maintain a current and unbiased understanding of its completion status (refer to Figure 8.33 above). Good leaders are inherently optimistic and positive about both the completed work and the work remaining (recall the characteristics of professionals in the solution-space category). However, leadership sometimes overlooks or is even unaware of some of the remaining issues to address when nearing the closure of a milestone.

Therefore, a special team role of *scheduler* is of high value for any program that wants to be first place. Enlisting a scheduler will increase headcount but will usually bring value to the program that is many times the investment.

The responsibility of the typical scheduler is to periodically review and determine the program status, including identifying risks or issues that will prevent certain milestones from being completed on time, querying and obtaining mitigation plans for risks and issues, and more. This person (or small team) must identify and track the critical path and the parallel development paths and report their status evaluation regularly to leadership (see Figure 8.34).

This role may be part-time and may be performed by a team member with low seniority. However, the scheduler must be tenacious, even brazen, when canvassing the program for status. They must be fully empowered by the PM to query the status and completion readiness of any element of the program team, including suppliers and enterprise support.

The scheduler must have the intuition to detect if the status they are receiving from any of the task teams is somehow censored or incomplete, and they must be forward enough to dig deep into status reports from the various task teams to learn all the facts. They must inform leadership if they feel any individual or team is withholding important status information.

In addition, the scheduler is often the most forthright with bad news to leadership. Their job is to be completely factual and frank. It is sometimes hard to tell the boss there is something in trouble in their program, but the PM may not have known about a subtle issue that might cause the completion of a milestone

Consider a Scheduler
Part-Time Team Member to Professional

- Must be empowered to investigate any task issue.
- Uses consistent tracking processes and objective measures.
- Must have excellent perspective on all schedules and potential impacts.
- Objectively summarizes pros and cons of status.
- Usually most forthright with bad schedule news.

Figure 8.34 Paying someone to independently assess and report on the program schedules may seem like an extravagance, but this will usually save a large amount of waste, cost, confusion, and embarrassment. It is important that the scheduler be given the authority by the PM to probe deeply into all plans and schedules. Team members should be informed that the scheduler will report to the PM any instance in which they think a team member may be holding back the details they need.

to be delayed. For the scheduler to announce a potential slip is especially hard when the program is nearing the completion of a major portion of the work, as the PM and leadership team highly anticipated success by this time.

Ideally, the scheduler was involved in developing the initial program schedules. They subsequently should be responsible for updating (often resulting from discovered problems) and publishing the master schedule. In particular, they should highlight any schedule risks, issues, and avoidance/abatement status for work on the critical path.

The scheduler should be engaging, sympathetic, and professional. This is an excellent role for a spirited and energetic new employee in the business management area—and the insight they gain will be highly valuable during their future career.

Table 8.16 Consider a Scheduler
SELF-ACTUALIZATIONS FULFILLED

Self-Actualization Level	How Fulfilled by This Success Element
Physiological	Understands that work assignments will be more stable and bring more value due to highly accurate scheduling and unbiased collection of status.
Safety	Believes the expectations of their work will be less prone to confusion due to the independent scrutiny of its completeness and status.
Love/Belonging	Is comforted by fewer occurrences of team strife resulting from misunderstandings in scheduling and inadequate collection of progress information.
Esteem	Appreciates that lack of stability in the program plan due to inadequate schedule detail and/or inadequate collection of progress status will be low. This gives them more opportunity to highlight the benefits of their role and authority.
Professional	Provides more opportunity to develop innovations and to recommend process improvements without interruptions in the program or process due to frequent rescheduling or reevaluating work status.
Altruistic	Provides assurance that the program will be planned and executed completely and will confidently achieve some or all of their altruistic vision.

8.9.10 Applying Multiple Books

The use of multiple books to track a program may seem to the reader to be deceitful and will dilute the trust of the team. However, team members are usually aware of its use and support it. Most team members are happy there are margins

Multiple Books Can Be Used to Deliver on Time

- Plan 1—*Idealistic* **Cost and Time to Complete**
  - **Assumes ample staff**
  - **Assumes facilities on time and complete**
  - **Assumes needed supplies delivered complete and on time**
  - **Assumes few test failures**

- Plan 2—*Realistic* **Cost and Time to Complete**
  - **Consults actuals from past similar programs**
  - **Incorporates typical delays addressed by experts**
  - **Incorporates margins added by program, enterprise, and suppliers**

- **Manage via** *Idealistic—Plan 1*
- **Promise** *Realistic—Plan 2*

Figure 8.35   Maintaining separate cost and schedule books for team members, team leadership, and the customer may seem deceptive, but usually, all participants are aware of its use and abide by its constraints. This is a highly effective tool for delivering work on time within cost estimates.

imposed on the schedules and cost constraints they have promised to comply with. They fully commit themselves to achieving their given targets, and they understand that late deliveries and overruns are devastating to customer satisfaction and the reputation of the team.

Making the extra effort to develop two levels of planning for program schedules and cost allocation can be very beneficial (see Figure 8.35). The multiple books referred to are actually two plans, as follows:

Plan One: Optimistic (Idealistic) Cost and Time to Complete

This schedule and cost plan assumes that no issues or failures will occur during the execution of the program; all needed supplies, information, and other inputs arrive on time and are satisfactory; all needed enterprise and contractor facilities and equipment are available when needed and function as required; and no failures occur during testing.

When the program wants to put its most optimistic plan forward, this is the one to show. No one can say it is wrong until a problem occurs during execution.

Plan Two: Realistic Cost and Time to Complete

This schedule and cost plan is tempered with actual past cost and schedule performance data from programs similar to the current one; this comparison is used to adjust the schedule durations and cost amounts initially estimated—even if there is a possibility that the application of improved processes will shorten and reduce these estimates.

When this plan is developed, it will be beneficial for independent subject-matter experts who have been involved with similar developments to review the cost and time estimates for accuracy. These reviewers may insert additional costs or schedule durations based on what they have found to be typical from their experience.

Special attention must be paid to any portion of the Plan 2 cost and time estimates that cannot be verified with actual development experience. In this case, schedule and cost margins added to these areas must be higher due to greater uncertainty about the work required. Additional emphasis should be placed on tracking these areas during execution of the work to verify adherence to plan.

When using two books, the PM and the customer must agree on and track the *realistic* schedule. The task leads and team individual contributors must track their work against the *optimistic* schedule, incorporating all their margins and extra working hours to achieve milestone dates. The PM must insist on the team achieving all optimistic schedule milestones and must treat any unsalvageable slip as a highly delinquent late completion or delivery by the program, even though the PM and the customer have applied additional margins to the delivery milestones and cost they are tracking in the realistic schedule. The intent is that the actual delivery dates and costs used to complete the work are within the committed values agreed on between the program and the customer.

Three Books?

There are instances in which *three* books can be used for estimating and managing cost and schedule. As with the use of two books, the team members are usually aware of this strategy and comply with it, because they appreciate that it is used to protect them and not to be deceptive. With this strategy, separate cost and schedule plans are developed for the customer, the task leaders, and the team members, each with successively lower expenditure targets and schedule durations allocated.

The author successfully used this technique on a program that required deliveries of more than 10 complex systems, with early incentive payments promised for each. This program successfully achieved 100% of these incentives. It is interesting that, during this accomplishment and as with other applications of this approach, there were few times in which it was necessary for a team member to work many extra hours. There were rare instances when a team member did slip their delivery beyond their promised date, and the task team lead treated this slip with the same high urgency and focus as a delivery slip under any other system. But the task leads never slipped their committed delivery times beyond their margins or exceeded their cost commitments.

Table 8.17 Apply Multiple Books

SELF-ACTUALIZATIONS FULFILLED

Self-Actualization Level	How Fulfilled by This Success Element
Physiological	Appreciates that this benefits the team performance if they don't feel they are being manipulated to work unduly hard.
Safety	Understands multiple books almost ensures deliveries on time. These team members are willing to support this approach.
Love/Belonging	On-time deliveries brings pride and contentment to the team. The team members usually understand there are multiple levels of scheduling with this approach but supported it knowing it will protect delivery times and reduce last-minute delivery panics. This increases team moral.
Esteem	Realizes that being a member of a team that consistently delivers the promised products on time is a major credential for being considered for promotion.
Professional	Consistent on-time deliveries provide these team members with a stable setting that does not distract from the values their professional expertise is providing.
Altruistic	Consistent on-time delivery by the program adds to the perceived potency of these deliveries which adds two more achievement of part or all of their altruistic vision.

8.9.11 All Motivated to Clearly Plan

During Step 1, new team members observed that leadership strove to use all resources efficiently. They also observed that leadership placed a major emphasis on creating thorough and stable basic plans. From the start, this provides the team members a clear program structure and a map to how the needs of their self-actualization will be achieved.

Team members will appreciate that this planning can only be achieved by clearly describing each needed accomplishment. In addition, team members see that leadership is shrewd, thorough, and complete about assessing the current status of the program. They will observe that leadership removes barriers to progress that may arise, including excessive bureaucracy, lack of facilities, inappropriate team mix, overabundant or insufficient headcount, outdated processes/techniques, poor work environment, and more.

In addition, team members will enthusiastically join leadership in finding the most resource-efficient path to complete the program tasks, and they will strive to contribute to the success of this effort with work that appeals to the needs of their professional motivations.

To be energized to make a special effort and do their very best, most team members do not need to have the work they do appeal to 100% of their motivation needs, just that whatever percentage is provided remains consistent. This in turn provides a stable foundation for the team member to measure personal improvement.

All members of the task team must be involved in supporting the task leader in developing the task plan. They should review the work scope and schedule estimates for accuracy and completeness, and all suggested changes to the plan from task members must be considered. These suggestions must be discussed, implemented, or denied with rationale. This is necessary for the team members to maintain their team buy-in and is also the way of developing the most efficient and effective plan for the task.

As mentioned before, those actually performing the task have the best understanding of the details of what must be accomplished, how to accomplish it, and how to avoid the accompanying risks. They also have the best idea of how to improve processes and apply innovations.

Repeatedly ignoring recommendations from a team member indicates that either the team member is consistently offering ideas with little thought or the team lead is refusing to consider the suggestions. If either situation occurs, it must be corrected.

In addition, recall that sometimes the team will evaluate the immense size of the work ahead of them as being almost insurmountable. Leadership must enthusiastically remind the team those big accomplishments result from a series of many little ones (see Figure 8.36).

8.10 Chapter Highlights

- Selecting a great PM.
- Creating an excellent organization.
- Managing suppliers.
- Selecting best task leads.
- Interviewing team-member prospects.
- Determining team mix.
- Best work environment:
  o In person
  o Colocation

- Commitments, not just goals.
- Role clarification is essential.
- Finding fault/failures early.
- Value of reuse?
- Contract reviews.
- Software development guidance.
- Use multiple books.
- Apply a scheduler?
- Successful planning and tracking.

"One Step at a Time"

- **When the team cannot anticipate all the steps needed to be successful.**
- **When the team knows there will be unanticipated problems.**
- **When this is the first time this work is being attempted.**
- **Recall the words of Don Bennett, who explained how he climbed Mount Whitney with one leg.**

Figure 8.36 Often a program team will be bewildered by the immensity of the task they are undertaking. Usually this is the first time what they are doing is being attempted, and many anticipate there will be unexpected problems. Leadership must freely remind the team members they will prevail—"One step at a time." [For video, see https://www.youtube.com/watch?v=JPq590mz5cU]

Chapter Nine

Step 2 (Execution): How to Do It

9.1 Essential Fulfillment of Motivation Needs During Execution

The work of leadership is intense and evolving during Step 2. For example, leadership must consistently look out for and remove barriers to fast team progress. They must track and facilitate changes in the motivations of the team members. They must listen to and incorporate comments to improve planning and identify risk/issues from many sources. They must adjust the mix of team personnel as the work progresses, and they must consistently identify and communicate the next important accomplishments to be achieved.

In addition, they must be keenly sensitive to the human elements of their team, transparent with status, listen to and understand all inputs from team members, resolve conflicts, give second chances, protect the team from undue criticism, and never imply defeat. They must be a consistent example of good behavior and team ethics, doing so even off-campus and after the program is completed (refer to Figure 7.2 on page 101).

As mentioned earlier, the experiences accumulated during Step 2 should be used to refine the program setup established during Step 1. This setup includes organization, team mixes, team assignments, individual assignments, schedules, needed accomplishments, and more. In addition, the team members must be repeatedly kept sold on what they are doing. This includes again asserting the high value of their good performance and their results (refer to Figure 7.5 on page 111).

9.1.1 The Application of In-Person Communication in Program Execution

Recall that face-to-face, in-person communication has been our primary means of communicating over our 200,000-year history (refer to Figure 8.15 on page 144). The activity of writing our thoughts, using a general set of symbols with grammar, only started about 2500 BC. Before this time, we simply drew pictures. Our species has depended primarily on in-person teamwork in tribes to survive. So, by necessity and natural selection, the fluency of face-to-face communication has become highly refined and is the very method we should not ignore.

The high value of face-to-face communication still outweighs the recent emergence of communicating with technology. Writing an email does provide a way of succinctly recording our thoughts, and it has the impact of a written commitment, almost a contract. It allows a person to say something without having to endure the sometimes distasteful feedback of the visible listener. It allows you to make your request and review the message carefully before sending.

However, communication amongst individuals and small groups using email prolongs a final resolution. Face-to-face, in-person communication, on the other hand, demands real-time understanding, compromise, and results. This high speed and sense of urgency is needed for the team to be in first place.

Emails, text messages, and other social messaging do allow disseminating information to many people with one transmission with ease. This media allows diagrams, photographs, moving pictures, and more to be attached. But program leadership and team members must be judicious about the application of new communication technologies. When used thoughtfully, these technologies can save huge amounts of time when distributing information and can reduce communication ambiguities amongst the receivers. But the fastest and most trusted method of compromise and communication remains to be face to face.

During Step 1, leadership will have reminded the new team members of the practical necessity for in-person, face-to-face communication during transactions. It would eventually become evident to all that conducting these exchanges only via technology is unacceptably error prone and slow for a first-place program.

The high reliance on in-person, face-to-face communication may be uncomfortable for some team members at first. Some may have relied heavily on computer- and telephone-based communications while supporting past programs. For some team members, it may need to be repeatedly used and practiced before it is valued. However, most team members will eventually be impressed by how much less time and work they require to coordinate and complete team tasks. Plus, in-person agreements provide additional trust to all participants that what was agreed upon will be fulfilled.

Leadership must be an example by employing in-person, face-to-face transactions when performing their tasks during program execution. Leadership must discourage the use of computer communications, virtual meetings, and other applications in lieu of opportunities to transact in person. The use of laptops, smart phones, and similar devices must be limited as much as possible to taking notes or presenting materials during program team meetings. Catching up on emails, messaging, and completing work material not associated with the meeting agenda distracts the meeting members and greatly reduces the team member's value to the meeting.

During both Step 1 and Step 2, leadership must provide rules that limit distracting conduct in colocated areas. This conduct includes loud verbal exchanges, loud phone conversations, and persistent casual discussions not related to work. Meeting rooms and other separated areas must be provided in the colocated area to allow team members to conduct conversations without distracting others. Leadership must provide a constant reminder of this to the team by example, demonstrating a special effort to keep their voice low while in a common area. Team members must be reminded to ask other team members to join them in a conference room for extended conversations.

Many times, a task team will need to use laboratories, large integration areas, or other special facilities that are not colocated in the core program team area. In this event, an attempt should be made to provide the team members working in these facilities with desk space in the main colocated program area. The extra time and effort needed by these team members to transit between the team's work area and the special facilities must be recognized and accepted. This sacrifice will be more than repaid by the savings in time and effort from their work being tightly coordinated with the work of the rest of the program.

As mentioned in the last chapter, during Step 1 setup, an effort must be made to keep any ancillary facilities such as laboratories, data centers, integration and test areas, prototype trial areas, and more as close as possible to the program's central colocated work area (see Figure 9.1).

Team members at all levels of self-actualization or those still in the process of developing their self-actualization will learn their motivational needs are being met. They will observe that leadership has attempted to make the execution of their work as unencumbered as possible with direct communication, and they will be relieved that team-member communication and equipment is immediately accessible via colocation and close proximity to special facilities. They understand that this will allow them to achieve their own motivational needs much faster, with fewer burdens.

9.1.2 Strict Adherence to Program Plan

As discussed in the previous chapter, every program must have a written plan describing the organization and operation of the program for all team members. It

Facilitate Maximum In-Person Communication

Step 2
• Collocate the program team as described for Step 1.
• Leadership shares examples of how face-to-face simplified work and improved progress in other teams.
• Discourage computer-based communication and meetings.
• Leadership must exemplify the speed and accuracy of in-person communication.

Figure 9.1   The vast majority of face-to-face communication content is nonverbal. Applying this type of communication whenever possible is essential for the program to be in first place. Over decades it has been demonstrated that the core of most first-place teams was colocated to facilitate in-person interaction. Computer and even telephone-based communication should be discouraged when in-person engagement is possible.

Program Plan Must Describe All Work

Example Outline:

- **Executive Summary**
  - **Program purpose statement**
  - **Description of how to reach commitment**
- **Organization**
  - **Organization chart**
  - **Roles and responsibilities**
  - **Change management**
  - **Facilities**
  - **Subcontractors and vendors**
  - **Rules and expectations**
- **Scope Management**
  - **Scope summary**
  - **Requirements management**
  - **Configuration management**
  - **Deliverables**
- **Schedules**
  - **Master schedule**
  - **Schedule control method**

Figure 9.2   The program plan must include or reference documents that describe all program work. It should be the first reference any team member accesses with a question about the program work plan or process. It must be updated and maintained per the team's configuration control process. The major subjects that should be addressed are shown. *[Figure continues on next page.]*

must be kept current and be the first reference that team members go to when they have a question about the program. It should describe the program organization and the functions and responsibilities of each task team (and functional departments if they exist in the organization), the team and key staff roles, schedules, metrics, common processes, and protocol used in design reviews, peer reviews, change process, failure review process, meetings, general working rules, ethics, and more.

A first draft of the program plan should be completed after a review by the new task team leads and initial team members before the kickoff of the program work. When possible, these team members should include representatives from the customer, subcontractors, vendors, and the sponsoring enterprise.

The processes described in the program plan must be followed rigorously (see Figures 9.2 and 9.3). This format will vary depending on the substance of the program. Often the enterprise will have an outline template they request the program use to start the creation of their plan. Changes and improvements to

Program Plan Must Describe All Work (cont.)

- Cost
  - Estimation process
  - Budget allocation
  - Budget control
- Quality
  - Monitoring
  - Control
- Human Resources
  - Acquisition
  - Development and mentoring
- Program Interfaces
  - Stakeholders
  - Reporting and communication
  - Team interdependencies
  - Metrics collection
- Risk Management
- Procurement
  - Subcontractors
  - Vendors and services
- Program Information Management
- References
  - Integration and test plan
  - Quality plan
  - Safety plan
  - Headcount plan
  - Product support plan
  - Software development plan
  - Risk management plan
  - *More*

Figure 9.2   Continued from previous page.

Program Plan = Operator's Manual

Step 2
• Inform all team members of program plan. • Team members review and suggest improvements. • Review process for revising and communicating updates. • Assign individual responsible for making sure plan is current. • Establish process for quickly notifying team of approved changes to plan. • Leaders set example of strictly referencing and adhering to plan.

Figure 9.3   Leadership must set the example of strictly adhering to the contents of the program plan. Team-member representatives must critique and provide additions to the plan while it is being developed. At least one team member should be responsible for making sure the plan is current throughout the life of the program.

the plan must be made by a well-described, detailed process, described in the program plan. The change process is often adjudicated by a configuration change board or equivalent.

Rigorously following the program plan allows for accurate process performance data to be collected for process improvements. Because each evaluation and change to the plan must follow the same series of process steps, these changes will, on average, be made much faster and use fewer resources than would be by following a different change process for each change.

Having all the functions of a program follow a common program plan synchronizes the interdependencies of the work and allows the program to proceed at the fast pace needed to be in first place. Useless wait times are kept to a minimum, and by having access to a common plan, task team members can even learn and appreciate what the other members of the team must complete.

An additional benefit of a documented program plan is that it provides a stable baseline for process improvements. If there is an attempt to improve a process but the baseline process is not consistently followed, the credibility of a suspected process issue is lessened, and the benefits of the improvement cannot be accurately measured.

During Step 1, leadership will have informed new team members that there is a program plan that must be followed by all team members. Leadership will have emphasized that special efforts would be made to keep this plan simple, concise, and up to date and would be amended via a strict process, usually using the program configuration change board. A summary of the process for updating the program plan would have been provided to the new team members at this time. Leadership will have emphasized how adherence to the program plan would limit wasteful ambiguities on how the work is performed and provide a resource-efficient process that synchronizes all task work and ensures acceptable product quality.

During Step 2, a team member must be assigned to be responsible for keeping the program plan current. This person must be given the authority to identify discrepancies between what is documented and what the program is currently doing and must notify all team members of changes to the plan via a posted announcement immediately accessible by all team members.

This responsible individual should have the authority to make sure the complete, required change process was followed to update the plan. Leadership must constantly be an example by fastidiously referencing and adhering to the contents of the program plan to answer organizational and process questions.

Team members will observe that task work is performed faster, with fewer mistakes, and with high quality by adhering to the directions in the program plan. They will appreciate that this adherence allows them to fulfill the needs of their self-actualization sooner.

Table 9.1 Strict Adherence to Plan

SELF-ACTUALIZATIONS FULFILLED

Self-Actualization Level	How Fulfilled By This Success Element
Physiological	Appreciates that the program plan describes when and how the work is performed. Understands that following the plan lessens rework of the tasks they are performing and is mandatory.
Safety	Is relieved that following the program plan is mandatory and that changes to it are only allowed via the change control process (e.g., by the CCB). This provides stability for the work they are doing.
Love/Belonging	Because the team is strictly following a common plan, there is less opportunity for disagreement amongst team members due to poorly described roles and responsibilities.
Esteem	Appreciates that following well-documented and current processes while measuring success helps identify process steps that need improvement. This is necessary for leadership to justify their role and to consider them for promotion.

| Professional | Appreciates that following a well-documented process strictly and measuring its results with metrics provides guidance for process improvement. This work may provide clear targets for this professional to exercise their expertise to further improve the program. |
| Altruistic | The well-documented process clearly identifies where this team member's altruistic needs are fulfilled. Following these processes with changes only allowed by strict process control increases the likelihood of achieving their altruistic needs quickly. |

9.1.3 Leadership Removes Barriers

Removing barriers to the progress of a program team is a major role of leadership. For a team to slow or stop their progress due to issues that could have been foreseen and solved earlier is devastating to a program trying to maintain their first-place position. What's worse, many times these issues are human made—bureaucratic restrictions of low value, inadequate facilities, frugal approach to purchase of tools and automation, inadequate forward planning, and more (see Figure 9.4).

Leadership Identifies and Removes Delays to Progress

Step 2
• Learns of barriers; "Managing by wandering around."
• Establishes open door for concerns from all team members.
• Insists team members support planning and risk management.
• Challenges institutionalized rules/tools of no value.
• Looks ahead 6+ weeks for needed inventories, personnel, facilities, etc.
• Readily approves proven tools; automation cheaper than manual.
• Immediately remedies interpersonal issues.
• Always responds promptly.

Figure 9.4　Leadership must look well ahead of the development schedule for barriers to progress and then eliminate them. Often, these barriers become apparent during discussions with individual contributors. Leadership's doors must always be open to listen to concerns from all team members, and team members must never feel there may be negative consequences from bringing forward a concern. Delays caused by prolonged conflicts amongst team individuals can seriously hamper progress and must be mitigated immediately.

For barriers to be removed, they must be first known. One excellent way to detect the most impactful barriers is for leadership to communicate with their team members at their working level, often supplemented with "management by wandering around." This will always provide more useful information to leadership than just relying on status reports from intermediate leadership, despite the best intentions of the authors of these reports.

In addition, an active open-door policy must be maintained by all leadership. Any team member must know that if they are concerned about a potential future obstruction to the team, they can discuss it with any member of leadership, including the PM. Leadership must make it clear to all team members that these inputs are highly valued and are not a burden, regardless of how much or how little an impact to progress they may really have. Inputs of concerns and worries from those team members performing the tasks are critically needed in a first-place program.

Still another source for identifying the most urgent barriers to the program comes from observations by the scheduler, a team role discussed in the previous chapter. The scheduler may become aware of consistent inhibitors to progress simply based on repeated complaints they hear from the frontline workers while collecting status. The scheduler may have a broader perspective on a single barrier to the wide range of activities they status, which may allow them to summarize it better than those working the details.

Unfortunately, some leaders are reluctant to report issues in their team to the PM, and gratitude and thanks must be offered to these leads who do come forward to identify future impediments. Task leads should be reminded that doing so will improve the performance of the entire team and are highly valued. In addition, it is important that leadership take prompt action when presented with potential barriers. Often there is little time to prevent the program from being slowed by a barrier, and urgency by leadership demonstrates to the team the high importance of avoiding and/or abating risks and issues as soon as detected.

As mentioned earlier, sometimes barriers are a result of institutionalized rules imposed on the program. These may have originated from the supporting enterprise or customer and were originally designed for all potential situations, but sometimes these rules provide little or no benefit to the program, given its specific needs. Leadership should be prepared to intelligently debate, with supporting data, the option to partially or completely not impose some institutional rules.

The same may apply to enterprise- or customer-mandated tools and processes that have little value and hamper the progress of the program. Again, an alternative plan with supporting data should be provided. For a program to ignore challenging this source of inefficiency usually results in team consternation and delays.

The team and team leadership should constantly look ahead two to eight weeks for barriers that may impede progress. Barriers identified further out in time are more speculative, and spending the resources to abate them usually have a low return. There are of course exceptions that extend this duration for very impactful barriers that have a high likelihood of occurring.

Part of looking ahead is making sure inventories and facilities will be available when needed, such as additional seating, assembly and storage-area floor-space, laboratory and test equipment, computers, and technology support. Often enterprise facility managers provide assets to the program management that is first to make the request and is the most persistent. Don't allow your team to fall out of first place due to delays of this kind. This caution also applies to any audits, reviews, approvals, etc. that are mandated by contract, the enterprise command media, the customer, or the suppliers. Plan ahead to have the necessary personnel and facilities available so these reviews are conducted and completed on time.

Leadership must always pay close attention to suggested tools, automation, software, and other means to shorten completion times. It may be uncomfortable for a seasoned professional to delegate to a computer program a process that in the past had been performed well manually. And to the leader, the price of some of these recommended tools may seem exorbitant. But, in almost all cases, the savings resulting from these tools will be much greater than the price of the tool, considering the cost of labor saved and factoring in additional costs from typical mistakes made during work performed manually. Leadership must be certain that the recommended tool or automation performs the work needed, has a legitimate pedigree, and ideally has some track record of successful application.

To maintain their credibility, it is recommended that leaders admit any past attempts to remove barriers that failed. These admissions should not be looked upon as disgraceful—the fact that a leader recognized and tried to remove a barrier, and was candid about failing, garners much added trust by the team.

Part of the work of knocking down barriers is for leadership to respond immediately to ethics infractions. This quick response removes any ambiguity and confusion in the minds of the team members that these infractions may hold back program progress. Failure to immediately address clear ethics infractions can even cause some team members to question the value of their own ethical behavior and the integrity of the program they are supporting.

Part of leadership's responsibility is to bring prompt solutions to any rare, disruptive interpersonal issues amongst team members. Some of these situations can be embarrassing to the other team members and must be resolved quickly. Resolution must follow the due process established in the program plan and any additional written guidance in the procedures of the supporting enterprise. These issues can include highly aggressive verbal fighting, alcoholism, unacceptable sexual advances, stealing, and, unfortunately, more, and prompt decisive action must be taken by leadership in a first-place team. Left unresolved, these issues will poison the enthusiasm of the team and slow progress.

[As with most of the communication discussed in this book, in-person, face-to-face exchanges bring much value to all the above. From listening to the concerns of team members to negotiating with enterprise facility managers, this direct level of communication adds much value to the exchange and greatly increases the likelihood of a successful resolution.]

Table 9.2 Leadership Removes Barriers
SELF-ACTUALIZATIONS FULFILLED

Self-Actualization Level	How Fulfilled By This Success Element
Physiological	Appreciates leadership dialogues with frontline team members directly to identify risks and obstructions and remove them. Appreciates facilities are available on time to support their work.
Safety	Appreciates leadership has an open-door policy that allows risk and process issues to be brought to leadership candidly and without retribution. Relieved to observe that immediate action is taken by leadership to analyze and mitigate these reported problems. This increases the probability the program will stay on track.
Love/Belonging	Is gratified to see leadership and frontline workers communicating directly. This results in a tight bond that leads to high program performance. Increases respect/admiration for leadership of these teams.
Esteem	Allows assigned tasks to be completed on time. Leadership serves as an example to these team members of the importance of removing barriers to inspiring leaders.
Professional	Obstructions removed to allow these team members to show and develop their in-depth expertise faster. Provides needed facilities on time so that these team members may proceed without interruption. Encourages these team members to consistently evaluate new computer-based tools that may better perform tasks performed manually in the past.
Altruistic	Appreciates that leadership removing barriers facilitates a high rate of progress for the program to achieve altruistic needs sooner.

9.1.4 Plan Changes Only via Procedure

Team members will only confidently follow the contents of the program plan if they know it is current. Team members want to be assured that the plan they are following is "the law" and that all other team members are also following it.

Therefore, all team members must know that anyone who desires to amend the plan must follow a strict process that includes thorough reviews (see Figure 9.5). Everyone on the team must have complete confidence in this update process, and it must apply to all team members on the program as well as those staff members associated with the enterprise, the vendors, subcontractors, and the customer. Approved updates to the program plan must be disseminated quickly, in a way that is clearly known and easily accessible by all team members. A good policy to follow is that an update is not considered to be valid until it can be verified that all team members have access to it.

Changes to the program plan can affect any of its contents—for example, changes to product performance requirements, work schedules, team organization, functions and responsibilities of a team, internal or external organizational interfaces, and more. Often in a large program, the CCB is used to evaluate and issue changes to the program plan (see Figure 9.6). This same process is usually used for changing the other documents in the program, once the first draft of these documents has been approved and placed under configuration control.

Typically, the CCB or equivalent change committee comprises a committee of senior program team members plus team members who represent the different portions of the program that may be affected by the proposed change. For big programs, this committee may include the PM or their representative, system engineering leadership, one or more voting members from the customer, and the leadership associated with the area of the proposed change. Additional members

Program Plan Changes Only with Process

Step 2
• Change procedure described in program plan.
• Often change via change control board (CCB).
• Regular and emergency change process (such as CCB) conducted.
• Team members learn changes to documents, processes, designs are via strict process.
• Leadership fastidiously applies change processes to be an example.
• Team members learn all their work is recorded and revised with procedure.

Figure 9.5 The change process for the program plan and all other documentation should be described in the program plan. Often this process includes adjudication and approval by a board. Team members take comfort in knowing their documented work is protected and may only be changed using this procedure.

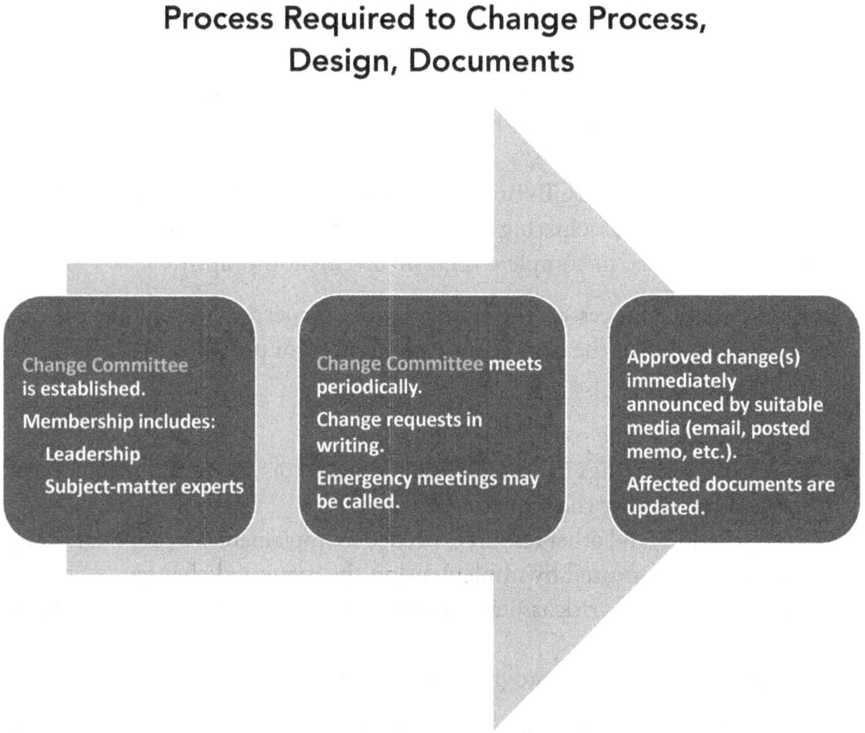

Process Required to Change Process, Design, Documents

Change Committee is established.

Membership includes:

Leadership

Subject-matter experts

Change Committee meets periodically.

Change requests in writing.

Emergency meetings may be called.

Approved change(s) immediately announced by suitable media (email, posted memo, etc.).

Affected documents are updated.

Figure 9.6   This is the flow of a typical CCB, which usually includes members of leadership and senior-level experts. The board usually meets periodically, with the option to call a special meeting if delaying evaluating the change will slow the program down. A method must be established to immediately announce an update to all team members and then subsequently change the associated documentation.

may include, among others, the scheduler, the business lead, the contracts lead, and the chief engineer.

For a small effort, the CCB or change committee may consist simply of the PM or their designee, the business lead, and the management for the product area for which the change is being proposed. What is important is that the change review and approval process used be consistent and known by all members of the program team. This change process must be documented in the program plan.

Some common guidelines for a CCB or similar change committee to follow:

- The CCB or change committee meets regularly, often weekly, for medium and large programs, possibly less often for small programs. The chairperson must prepare an agenda of proposed changes to be evaluated, making sure this agenda is strictly adhered to during the meeting.

- Sometimes, a program team needs to have a change approved as soon as possible so as not to delay progress. In this case, a special CCB or change committee may be convened, often called an emergency CCB or change meeting, which typically convenes within 24 hours of having contacted all board members or their backups.
- Usually, emergency CCBs or change meetings are allowed to be conducted with members participating remotely via technology, allowing the emergency committee to complete their involvement promptly.

For most change processes, the team member requesting the change provides a written description of the change on a standard form provided by the program. This form typically asks for:

- A description of the request to change
- The estimated savings in cost, schedule time, errors, poor performances, etc. accrued by making the requested change
- Cost, schedule, and other resources needed to implement the proposed change
- Predicted risks created by implementing the requested change
- Abatement plan if a risk associated with implementing the requested change becomes an issue
- Consequences of not approving the requested change

Usually, the CCB or change committee members will sign the application when approving the proposed change, but provisional approval can be made that includes a written description of any action that must be completed before the requested change is approved. Also, if any requested change is denied, a written summary of why must be provided.

Each change meeting should follow the same guidelines used for any other program meeting (discussed in depth in Section 9.1.6 on page 203). The CCB or change committee meeting work products should include a meeting agenda, record of attendance, minutes, any action items, and the current decision regarding the proposed change. It is the responsibility of the chairman to make sure all work products are satisfactorily completed per the CCB or change committee requirements stated in the program plan.

Typically, the CCB or change committee chairman will immediately notify all hands of approved changes by some expeditious media (often via email or central posting), within some maximum duration described in the program plan (this has been less than 24 hours for the teams the author has been involved with). Then the affected document(s) are updated to reflect the authorized change, within some duration, usually specified in the change process described in the program plan.

During Step 1, team members will have taken comfort in knowing all their work would be recorded, strictly applied, and only updated with a specific process described in the program plan. They would be impressed that all changes to data, process descriptions, designs, organizational descriptions, etc. were performed with a documented process that leadership insisted is strictly adhered to. New team members will have appreciated that this strict control was necessary for team progress to be maintained at a high rate. All team members will have learned that changes to configurations would be incorporated only after thorough review, with official process, by team members most knowledgeable about the area being addressed and its predicted impacts.

During Step 2, leadership and team members must fastidiously follow the change procedure described in the program plan, and leadership must set a visible example by always doing so. Provisions will usually be established in the program plan for periodic reviews as well as emergency reviews of change requests by the CCB or change committee.

Team members will be encouraged to put forth their best creative efforts, knowing their results will be recorded and protected by strict controls, free from the fear of their valuable work being lost or indiscriminately changed. This reassurance is necessary for a team to remain in first place.

Table 9.3 Plan Changes Only via Procedure

SELF-ACTUALIZATIONS FULFILLED

Self-Actualization Level	How Fulfilled By This Success Element
Physiological	Appreciates the program plan is protected and can be only changed with process. Provides incentive to rigorously adhere to the plan.
Safety	Removes the fear of part or all of the program plan being lost or indiscriminately changed. Assures all processes established in documentation remain stable and are only changed after thorough evaluation.
Love/Belonging	Observes that team anxieties remain low by rigorously preserving the program plan. This reduced tension allows for more personal exchanges and supports more teamwork.
Esteem	Provides an essential rule base to which they can demonstrate conscientious adherence. In addition, provides a stable framework for them to demonstrate exceptional capability and hopefully be promoted.
Professional	Provides exact processes in the program plan for creating, distributing, and storing their work. These team members are gratified their work can only be changed by a rigorous, well-documented change control process.
Altruistic	This policy allows faster completion of the program and faster progress toward their altruistic vision.

9.1.5 Using Metrics Effectively

Metrics provide measurements about the performance of the program, but sometimes the data selected is not the most valuable to the team.

Often, the metrics selected track data that is already being tracked elsewhere in the program—for instance, a program metric of the output status of a series of items being manufactured may also be tracked by the task team responsible for the product and even additionally by the suppliers. So simply replicating the data from these other sources and labeling it a metric robs valuable team resources and provides no added value.

As important, often just the *output* of a process is measured to verify conformity to plan. But what is usually more valuable to the program is to measure the *inputs* to a process to verify their conformance to required performances (see Figure 9.7). Measuring input metrics can provide the highly valued ability to predict failures in the outputs and make corrections to prevent them before they occur (see Figure 9.8). This action can totally eliminate the expense, team trauma, and resulting delays caused by a major failure during the progress of the program.

Figure 9.9 illustrates the typical tracking of a metric of an input to a process. Usually, this input has a high and a low performance acceptance limit; as long as

Process *Input* Metrics Often More Valuable than *Output*

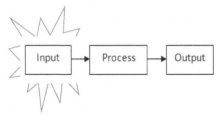

- **Some programs only use metrics to confirm that output quantities/qualities achieve planned levels.**
- **Many times output metrics are already being recorded by another team or supplier.**
- **Monitoring process input metrics can predict unacceptable outputs.**
- **Predicting instead of reacting to unacceptable outputs can save vast amounts of schedule duration, cost, disappointment, and team reputation.**

Figure 9.7 Tracking input metrics is usually more valuable because trends may be used to predict future failures. Tracking output metrics usually detects faults after they have occurred, delaying work progress. Also, output metrics are sometimes redundant to records collected by other organizations.

Input Metrics Often Have Higher Value

Step 2
• Team identifies critical input metrics to predict failures. • Monitor for failing trends within acceptable range. • Predict and mitigate output failures *before* they occur. • Avoids cost, schedule impacts, embarrassment.

Figure 9.8   Input metrics can predict product failures before they occur. Often root cause can be rectified before work schedules are interrupted, resulting in zero impact to program schedules.

the measured input performance is within these limits, the input is assumed to be acceptable and will support an acceptable output value. But usually, when an input value falls out of tolerance, it does not do so instantly. Instead, it eventually reaches an acceptance limit over multiple creation cycles. Good input metrics with vigilant analysis will detect this bad trend. Given the curvature of the trend,

Smart Metrics Can Mitigate Major Cost and Schedule Losses

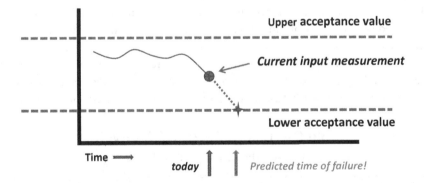

- **Measure** *inputs*.
- **Look for** *failing trends*.
- **Correct root cause of failing trend before product performance unacceptable.**
- **Extrapolate failing input trend to predict time of product failure!**

Figure 9.9   Input metrics must be monitored for failing trends. Often these trends can be extrapolated to predict time of product failure if not rectified.

the team can even predict when this input value reaches the acceptability limit and the entire product fails testing! The author has observed this to be repeatedly accomplished in many excellent programs with good metrics management.

With correct application, metrics have very high value. Many excellent programs have used input metrics to predict product failures before they happened. If root cause can be determined for the failing input, it can be remedied before the input value falls out of acceptable limits and the process output fails. The program then continues without interruption, with little impact to cost and no impact to schedule. Using metrics to prevent work stoppage is a major part of all first-place programs.

Of course, trends in data values can only be tracked when multiple copies of something are being measured. But even if the program is creating only one final item or system, there are usually many subitems needed to make it. For example, there are multiple integrated circuit chips used to build one circuit card, or there are multiple student performance measurements required to compute an improved capability in the school district. Trends can be detected during testing of the multiple inputs for these items.

During Step 1, team members were tutored on the correct use of metrics to predict future failures and were motivated by learning that metrics would be used to reduce work effort, expense, and time to completion, and not just flag out-of-limits measurements. Team members will have appreciated that the good application of metrics would avoid the embarrassment of late deliveries.

During Step 2, team members are asked to identify the critical input metrics and monitor their trends for early problem detection. Team members will experience the exhilarating benefit of using metrics to mitigate a developing issue before it impacts their schedule commitments and has a major impact on cost. They will be encouraged to focus on the metrics of inputs to important manufacturing or process flows because of their ability to predict failures well in the future. They will value metrics, when correctly used, as another essential tool to achieving milestone completions on time. This comprehensive use of metrics is necessary to be a first-place program.

Table 9.4 Using Metrics Effectively

SELF-ACTUALIZATIONS FULFILLED

Self-Actualization Level	How Fulfilled By This Success Element
Physiological	These team members appreciate that the metrics they use or develop are not a waste of effort due to redundancy. They appreciate proper metrics avoid major impacts to program schedule and cost
Safety	These team members are encouraged by using metrics to predict failures before they occur, thus eliminating expensive delays and risk to program success.

Love/Belonging	These team members take delight in working in an organization that has the ability to detect failing trends in process inputs and avoid delays in work completions. This adds pride and confidence to the team and increases teamwork.
Esteem	These team members highly appreciate the immense power in detecting failing trends in input metrics and correcting them, preventing costly delays to the program. Demonstrating the ability to assemble and manage this system is a major advantage when considered for future promotion.
Professional	The effective use of metrics helps professionals developing an expertise to perform at a higher level by detecting impending failures early and avoiding system failures.
Altruistic	This process shortens the time to achieve the altruistic vision of these team members and adds credibility to these goals, given the high demonstrated management quality of the program.

9.1.6 Conducting Valuable Meetings

During the execution of a program, it is necessary to bring together groups of individuals with varying expertise to analyze and resolve complex problems in person. As discussed, the most expeditious way to completely communicate, compromise, and achieve trusted agreements is when team members meet face to face.

Due to the high enthusiasm by some to use new technology and the apparent savings of team-member effort that may result, computer-based meetings are becoming popular, sometimes even amongst team members on the same floor in the work facility. Information is exchanged, but, unfortunately, final agreements made this way are often tentative or put off to a later meeting. A virtual meeting environment is often a lot less impactful than an in-person environment to bring quick closure.

There is a risk of team progress being delayed when meetings are conducted virtually. In-person meetings are necessary to achieve solid, trusted progress and closure at high speed. The added advantages of face-to-face, in-person communication discussed earlier apply during meetings, and they are necessary for a program to maintain a first-place position.

Some programs must coordinate and integrate the work of participants who can only regularly communicate virtually, usually because their home facilities are a large distance from each other. Given this situation, funds and efforts should be provided for the participants to periodically travel to meet in person. This will at least establish a foundation of trust that will increase the rate of progress achieved in the virtual meetings. These in-person meetings should be

Valuable Meetings Require Preparation!

One Meeting Lead.
- Responsible for arranging and conducting
- Responsible for meeting products and closure

- **State meeting purpose during opening.**

- **Only attendees of specific value invited.**

- **Present and follow prepared agenda.**

- **Record names of attendees.**

- **Record meeting minutes.**

- **Record action items, including responsible person and estimated completion time.**

- **Post-meeting records to be accessible by program team members (as allowable).**

- **Meeting lead manages action items to closure.**

Figure 9.10   Any meeting must result in more value created than is lost from time invested by the meeting members. Each meeting must have one lead, who must apply a meeting process documented in the program plan. The meeting lead is responsible for planning the meeting, conducting it, and bring it to closure.

conducted at least once a quarter if separated by thousands of miles to as frequent as one every week if separated by less than a one-hour drive.

A productive meeting is an expensive event. It takes a significant amount of time to adequately prepare for it and then to collect and disseminate its results. Team members must devote the time to attend the meeting, and they must prepare and present status on their response to an action item (see Figure 9.10).

Sometimes an attendee's participation is critical to the purpose of the meeting for only a short time but is of little value during the rest of the agenda. If the meeting lead makes sure the various agenda items stay within their planned time limits, the value of this attendee's participation is usually still greater than the value of the time they are not involved.

The meeting must clearly provide value to the program that is greater than the total value of the invested time and attention, otherwise it should not be called.

An essential part of achieving value from a meeting is following the process described in the program plan. Important elements should include:

- **Meeting Lead.** A person must be assigned to be responsible for arranging and successfully conducting the meeting, and, in addition, managing the closure of all action items. They announce the purpose of the meeting, create the agenda (preferably with specific durations allocated to each item), and make sure the agenda is followed. They check that all work product the team members have committed to providing are received, acceptable, and—when appropriate—disseminated. They determine who will be of value to invite.

- **Attendance List.** The names of the requested attendees will be in the invitation, and the names of those who actually attend should be included in the minutes. This can be important if team members or leadership later ask who was involved when decisions were made.

- **Meeting Agenda.** The agenda must be prepared before the meeting by the meeting lead and included in the meeting invitation. The agenda must include a concise statement of the purpose of the meeting, and the meeting lead is responsible for making sure this purpose is achieved. The meeting lead might refer to the purpose statement during the meeting to make sure the subjects being discussed are in support of it. Each agenda element may have a time duration assigned to it. The meeting lead must make sure that time constraints are adhered to or that there is ample justification to amend them.

- **Meeting Minutes.** The minutes are a written record of what was discussed, by whom, and what was decided. They should include the highlights of the discussions, including who participated in them and what their position was, agreements reached, conclusions and solutions that were derived, new items discussed that were not on the agenda, and agenda items that were not discussed. The minutes should also include the agreed-upon time, place, and purpose of a following meeting, if one is planned. The meeting lead or their designee must record these minutes during the meeting and must publish them via common media, such as a program website; this will allow all program team members to learn the results of this meeting quickly.

- **Action Items.** These are specific work assignments to program team members that must be completed to obtain information to allow the program to progress. The meeting lead will be responsible for adding actions to this list, keeping it current, and managing all the actions to closure. The first version of this action item list becomes part of the meeting minutes.

Each action item should contain a description of the action item, the name of the person responsible for completing it, and a completion due time. It is the responsibility of the meeting lead or their designee to track each action item to its closure. Care must be taken by the meeting lead when choosing the granularity of action items. If they are too detailed, the meeting can be overwhelmed, and it will become too cumbersome to completely close all of these items. This can lead to the action items' losing credibility. During a good one-hour meeting, no more than five to ten action items should be recorded. They should address top-level issues that are key toward maintaining the progress of the program and be achievable by the agreed-upon times.

At the start of the meeting, the meeting lead should scan the attendees to make sure they were invited or otherwise bring value. Leadership should resist the urge to invite team members only to represent their associated task with no specific contribution. If a member of leadership is interested in the outcome of a meeting but does not want to attend, they should consult the meeting minutes.

During Step 1, new team members were informed that all meetings would strictly follow a basic process designed to provide a value greater than the investment of time by the participants. Team members must have bought into the concept that all meetings would be conducted in a time-efficient manner, guided by the process described in the program plan. They will have appreciated that meetings would only be called to achieve progress content or rates that could not be achieved by other means.

Table 9.5 Conducting Efficient Meetings

SELF-ACTUALIZATIONS FULFILLED

Self-Actualization Level	How Fulfilled By This Success Element
Physiological	These team members are glad meetings only take the time necessary to add unique value to the program so they can then return to finishing their work on time.
Safety	These team members are pleased that the meeting preparation process assures coverage of all necessary subjects and that remaining issues are assigned to action items, which reduce future issues in the program.
Love/Belonging	Personal meetings enhance the teamwork and camaraderie of the team. These team members appreciate that in-person communication is more effective for resolving risks and issues than the use of technologies.
Esteem	These team members place high emphasis on showing results for their title. They support incorporating a process that creates high-value results while minimizing cost.
Professional	These team members want their contribution to be precise and quickly achieved. Conducting well-run in-person meetings aids in achieving this.
Altruistic	Conducting effective meetings is another characteristic of a program that is conducted well and concludes on time. Both of these performance characteristics are important attributes when making progress in achieving an altruistic vision.

Strive for Simple, Multipurpose Solutions

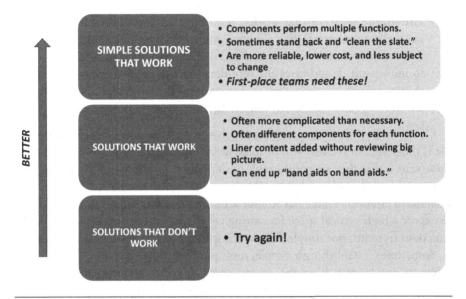

Figure 9.11 Simple solutions are the best, especially when one solution fulfills multiple needs.

9.1.7 Three Traditional Solution Levels

A common characteristic of first-place programs is that their solutions are simple and solve multiple problems. When innovating, the program team must be encouraged by leadership to find simple solutions. To provide perspective, three common levels of problem solutions are described (see Figure 9.11):

- **The solution that does not work.** This solution requires little introduction. In the highly exacting environment of conducting a first-place program, a solution that only partially solves a problem is usually considered to have failed. Problems must be solved completely for the program to proceed confidently.
- **The solution that works.** These are usually acceptable to the program, but sometimes very complicated. For example, beware of a solution that is a compilation of solutions for each of the intermediate symptoms associated with the problem. Some solutions can appear to be a series of Band Aids® on the observed symptoms, hoping the root cause of the problem will finally be defeated. The program may become overwhelmed trying to manage a large number of solutions to intermediate symptoms while still not having

eliminated the starting cause of the problem. A solution to the root cause will be simpler and require fewer resources.

- **The simple solution that works.** Ironically, this kind of solution can take more effort to develop than a more complicated solution, yet the simple solution is much easier to understand and maintain and is usually less expensive to implement. It addresses the root deficiency or cause of a problem rather than attempting to abate a series of secondary symptoms. Because it addresses the starting cause, it is often simpler and its operation is more reliable.

Often, an ingenious simple solution solves more than one problem. An example is the design of the rear seat of some newer model cars. The basic function of these seats is that they are comfortable to sit on for a wide range of passenger body types and for all road conditions. But in addition, the seat backs can be folded forward to establish a large flat storage area, or the seat bottom can be folded up to expose a high vertical space for storing tall items—three distinct and valuable functions from just one simple design, using only a couple of simple moving parts.

Sometimes, establishing a simple, multipurpose design requires deleting past attempts and approaching the design anew. Overly complicated designs are often a result of a team trying to salvage the original design.

Simple solutions benefit the needs of all levels of self-actualization, as well as those new professionals still determining their self-actualization. The team understands that simple solutions are the most enduring and that these solutions usually use fewer resources. Team members with a Professional self-actualization that includes inventing simple solutions are of high value in an effort to be the best.

Simple Is Best but Usually Hardest

Step 2
• Leadership must encourage simple solutions solving multiple problems.
• Degree of simplicity should be distinguished when reviewing proposed solutions.
• Compute additional program savings resulting from simple, multipurpose solutions.
• Development of simple, multipurpose solutions should be credited to team individuals in meetings and in their performance review.

Figure 9.12 Sometimes the simple solution requires more effort to develop but reduces the total expenditure of time and money expended by the program.

During Step 1, team members would have been counseled to not just accept any solution to solve a problem but to strive for simple solutions. Simple solutions should have been defined in detail and good examples provided. New team members would have perceived that simplicity of solutions is a very favorable attribute and would have been made aware that leadership appreciates that simple solutions often require more effort to originate.

During Step 2, leadership should emphasize simplicity when reviewing proposed solutions to problems. Special recognition should be provided to team members who propose a solution that is simple and solves multiple problems. Team members will observe that simple solutions are easier to understand, reduce mistakes made during use, provide greater operational reliability, reduce the need for added maintenance resources, and more (see Figure 9.12).

Table 9.6 Three Traditional Solution Levels
SELF-ACTUALIZATIONS FULFILLED

Self-Actualization Level	How Fulfilled By This Success Element
Physiological	Simple and effective solutions are easier to implement and help ensure that their work will be provided as promised. This helps ensure high productivity.
Safety	A simple solution that works has fewer ambiguities and less confusing. This reduces risk to implement.
Love/Belonging	Team pride is increased when simple, multipurpose solutions are found. This increases teamwork.
Esteem	These team members appreciate that simple, multipurpose solutions are considered to be of more value by the program and upper management than are complex solutions. They support simple solutions because they are a sign of quality leadership.
Professional	These team members take extra pride in offering a simple answer to a problem, especially if it solves multiple issues. Simple answers to complex problems are often the hallmark of a consulting expert.
Altruistic	Simple solutions usually reduce the time and cost to the altruistic vision of these team members.

9.1.8 Innovation—Gold at the Door

Thus far, we have identified the organizational and process elements needed for a program to be first place, highlighting the value of commitments as opposed to goals and showing how to establish a committed task delivery time, which includes margins and the willingness to put in extra effort to achieve it. But sometimes, even with a conservative and well-thought-out estimate, a completion milestone becomes in jeopardy. When this happens, an innovation in the design of the product or the way the task is being performed may preserve the commitment.

Innovations must be a necessary part of the diet of a first-place program (see Figure 9.13). Not only are they important for adhering to delivery commitments, but they also may improve the quality of the product being developed and/or lower its cost.

Leadership cannot direct the inspirations that cause innovation; they must, however, encourage new ideas, consistently emphasize their high value, and have their door open to them from anyone at any time. They must **never** express even a subtle negative response to a new idea, as this reaction can destroy a team member's enthusiasm to bring forward brilliant proposed innovations to the remainder of the program.

For example, the author has conducted highly focused meetings with top-notch technical talent to solve challenging program planning or technical issues. In the heat of suggesting potential solutions, actions were taken by team members during these meetings with a plan for the team to reconvene the following day. I would return to my office content in knowing the best minds were working a solution.

Innovations Fuel Faster Completion and Higher Quality

- **Enthusiastically receive and walk through all suggestions with provider.**

- **Valuable innovations are derived from any individual, any time.**

- **Recognize even innovations not used.**

- **Innovations offered should be considered when team member performance evaluated.**

Figure 9.13 Innovations, including process improvements, are a necessary infusion for a program to be in first place. They usually reduce cost and time to market and even increase product performances. They are often derived from an inspiration that may occur at any time in any team member.

However, often later that evening, a team member would appear at my door and say, "I know this sounds crazy, but . . . ," and I would know the suggestion that followed was potentially of very high value and always merited careful evaluation.

When someone brings forward a new idea, I admit my mind too often rushes to determining why the idea will not work. Probably I'm afraid of wasting my time evaluating a suggestion that may end up not adding value. But this is very wrong! Every new idea must be given consideration. What is proposed may in itself have merit or may provide an entry point to another valuable innovation after further discussion.

Your first response to suggestions should be to clarify questions you may have and confirm your understanding of the idea by repeating it back to the originator. If the idea clearly has no way of becoming valuable, then both parties should walk through its application in more detail and mutually recognize and acknowledge the deficiency, if there is one. However, you may want to consider the idea further, discuss it with colleagues, the business group, and more—by being patient with all proposed innovations, you and your team member may find a jewel!

Innovations can come from team members of any self-actualization level, or a new professional who may have not yet discovered their self-actualization. The team member need not be a specialist in the area for which they are offering a solution.

The author recalls one very solid software engineer who would come to his office every few days with what he thought might be a better way to design a controls algorithm he was implementing. He would usually knock at the author's office door early in the evening and start off by saying, "I am very sorry to bother you, but I have an idea that is about ready to make my head explode!" (This drama would of course get the author's attention.) This team member would then promise he would not take much time. The author always took the extra effort to talk through this person's idea together and identify the pros and cons. In this way, they would come to the same conclusion if the idea brought the value hoped for. Usually, we eventually agreed the proposed idea was not practical or brought little value but were satisfied in having tried to find value.

One evening, this team member brought forward an idea that seemed feasible and made sense. There was no reason to dismiss this proposal. The following morning, the author shared this proposed innovation with the other task leaders, and weeks later it resulted in saving the program millions of dollars plus considerable schedule time. The team member who offered this idea was simply gratified at being recognized by his fellow team members for making a highly valuable contribution. Previous positive responses to his suggestions, whether adopted or not, enabled this team member to keep developing and presenting ideas until one was accepted.

The arrival of innovation ideas is truly unpredictable. They can occur at any time, in an individual with any self-actualization. An estimate should be made of the resulting savings to schedule, cost, risk, or improvements to product performance garnered from those innovations if implemented.

So how can a leader motivate innovations? How can they get team members to generate brilliant ideas on demand? The answer is simply, highly respect, highly regard, and award new ideas. And as mentioned, hold the door open to them all the time.

Enthusiastically receiving innovation ideas must be a part of the program culture. Showing impatience or discontent in response to a new suggestion can permanently damage an individual's enthusiasm to imagine and propose a new idea. If the timing of the program is such that there is not a need or feasibility to implement a new idea, this will become apparent during the talk through of the idea, but keeping the idea for further discussion might bear fruit at a later time.

With the permission of the originators, all innovation and continuous improvement ideas should be shared with the program team. Even well-thought-out ideas that are not implemented should be shared. This gives recognition to all team members trying to provide improvements, and it emphasizes the high value the program attributes to these improvement ideas. In addition, the number and success of the innovations brought forward by each team member should be considered when reviewing their work performance (see Figure 9.14).

Encourage Innovations, Process Improvements to Be First Place

Step 2
• Innovations cannot be commanded but "open door" wide.
• Avoid skeptical body language. Mutually walk through the idea.
• Respect every proposal, regardless of source.
• Publicly recognize good ideas, even if not used.
• Compute and share savings/benefits from ideas implemented.
• There are no "#&@%!" ideas—*appreciate and encourage all.*

Figure 9.14 Demanding that an individual or team be creative is usually futile. It is better for leadership to place a high value on creativity, then keep the door wide open to any form of it. Leadership must treat each suggestion with respect and give it due process, rewarding the good ones. All improvement suggestions must be valued as special and cherished.

During Step 1, leadership will have informed the new team members of the high value the program places on innovations and continuous improvement proposals, motivating them by leadership's appreciating the value of their creativity. Leadership will have reminded the team that innovations and continuous improvements are always helpful and are sometimes required to achieve cost, schedule, performance, and risk commitments.

During Step 2, team members must be recognized for their innovation and continuous improvement contributions, even if not applied. When a team member is recognized, the resulting savings in cost, schedule needs, and future risks, plus improvements to product performances, should be computed and shared with the team. Special awards should be presented to team members who have created innovations or improvements to team processes that have had highly valuable impacts.

All leadership must be enthusiastic about considering proposed ideas that are brought forward. A standard minimal process must be applied when evaluating recommended improvements. All suggested improvements must be treated as valuable, even if not applied. It is important for leadership to consistently encourage innovation and continuous improvement in the teams. A high level of innovation and continuous improvement is necessary for a program team to be in first place.

Table 9.7 Innovation

SELF-ACTUALIZATIONS FULFILLED

Self-Actualization Level	How Fulfilled By This Success Element
Physiological	These team members appreciate that innovations can help deliver their finished output sooner and with higher quality. They are encouraged by their improvement ideas always being listened to and valued.
Safety	These team members appreciate that innovations can provide the schedule and performance margins that may be needed when issues are encountered later in the program. They understand that receptiveness to all proposed improvements increases the probability of team success.
Love/Belonging	These team members understand that the beneficial use of innovations often enhance team allegiance to the team member providing the innovation. This increases teamwork.
Esteem	These team members appreciate that innovations often provide schedule margins that allow the finished product to be delivered on time. These innovations may also reduce cost. These qualities are important when maintaining stature and providing justification for future promotion.

| Professional | These team members are often the source of effective innovations. Many team members believe that innovation is the most valuable contribution from participants with this self-actualization. These professionals take pride and self-fulfillment in providing well-supported improvement ideas. |
| Altruistic | Innovations reduce the time and expense to complete the program. This allows all or parts of the altruistic vision to be accomplished sooner and with more confidence. |

9.1.9 Incorporating Team Rhythm

Some may feel that meeting events should be conducted only when their need is high. The following analogy will illustrate why regular team meetings are necessary for a program to be in first place.

Imagine you and others are told to get into a rowboat and propel yourselves across a river as fast as possible. You are each intelligent and value what you believe is the positive impact of the way you row. You all jump into the boat and start rowing as fast as you can, using what you believe is a compatible cadence, and the others are trying to do the same. Yet the path of the boat weaves all over the water. Oars are bumping into each other, anger and fear rising. "We can't even travel in a straight line!"

But now an additional person gets into the boat, sits on the stern, and yells "stroke" at an even, moderate cadence. All the oars go into the water and are pulled at the same time, and the boat now moves in one direction, at high speed, quickly crossing the river. This team is successful because they have adopted "team rhythm."

A first-place program needs team rhythm, which is achieved by having regularly scheduled meetings with fixed agendas. Participants provide their input with common formats in discussions of such topics as funds expended, schedule completion status, achievement of required product performances, risk and issue status, and many more. These periodic meetings may be convened daily, weekly, monthly, or some other regular duration. Sometimes, a meeting may be invoked as part of some non-periodic event—for example, a peer review before the delivery of a work product or when assembling a failure review board for a serious test failure.

Periodic meetings are used to maintain a uniform team understanding of the program's current status and to coordinate the detailed plans to achieve the next milestones. They also provide each team and the individual team members an accurate reference to evaluate and improve their own rate of progress. Each meeting should have an agenda and maintain a list of action items (see

Figure 9.15). They should follow the process discussed for good meetings earlier in this chapter (see Section 9.1.6 on page 203).

It is important to repeat that only team members who provide or gain value from the meeting should be invited. Individuals must not attend a meeting just to represent a task team. If other members of this task team want to know the outcome of the meeting, they should consult the minutes and action items documented by the meeting lead.

The size of these periodic meetings will vary—for example, if the PM conducts monthly all-hands meetings, the entire core team might attend.

The following have been observed by the author and his colleagues in different industries as typical periodic meetings that are conducted in a program.

- **Progress to plan meeting.** Many programs have a daily meeting, often at the start of the workday, to review whether work scheduled for the preceding day had been accomplished. The scheduled completion milestones for

Programs Need Common Beat

- Regular meetings **with constant agenda**
  - Daily examples
    - Progress to plan
    - Issues and workaround plans
    - Risk and avoidance/abatement
    - Help needed
  - Weekly examples
    - Failure review closure review
    - Change control board
    - Program report to enterprise
- Event-driven **meetings**
  - Peer reviews
  - Product deliveries
- Standard formats **for planning and tracking**
  - Cost
  - Schedule completion
  - Achievement of required performances
  - Risk management
  - Request additional assistance

Figure 9.15 Regular in-person meetings are needed for a program, big or small, to be in first place. Meetings should follow the general meeting guidelines, using predetermined formats for participant inputs. Any program team must follow a common rhythm to be highly successful.

the current day are also reviewed and amended if necessary, as are ongoing issues with avoidance and abatement plans. Requests may be made by team members for more resources, special assistance, facilities, and other items. These requests may be made for assistance from inside or outside the program. These daily meetings are often useful as another means for the customer to stay current on development progress.

- **Business meetings.** These meetings are usually conducted weekly or biweekly. All task-team leads and functional department leads attend with their business specialists to review performance to cost and schedule commitments. Usually, work progress highlights to date and work planned to be performed over the next reporting period are shown. New risks, issues, and workaround plans that have been identified since the last meeting are usually introduced, with a focus on their potential impact on program schedules and cost. This meeting provides another opportunity for task-team leadership to request help.

  Common program tracking methods and formats for tracking, schedules, cost accounting, product performances, risks identified or issues mitigated, and more are used. This meeting provides the program team, the enterprise, the customer, and the suppliers a uniform understanding of the business status of the task teams, lessening ambiguities in communication amongst these team elements while they are conducting daily work.

- **Change control board meetings and failure review board meetings.** These meetings are normally conducted about once a week, depending on the size of the program. They may be conducted more frequently for emergencies, such as a critically needed new development process or the imminent change of design due to a serious failure. There must be a provision in the program plan to call a special meeting when an urgent issue needing a document change or a failure evaluation requires it.

- **Program task team or department team meetings.** These teams will have periodic, usually weekly, status reviews during which the performance of their team is reviewed. Also, the flow down of information from leadership, the enterprise, and other sources is provided. Problems regarding their team organization are presented, discussed, and resolved. Special problems and needs requiring assistance from higher-level leadership to resolve are usually recorded and provided to the PM.

- **Peer reviews.** These meetings are usually driven by the completion of certain product development milestones. Their agendas should be outlined in the program plan with performance dates shown in the master schedules. Peer reviews can be arduous for those whose work is being reviewed, but when evaluation is targeted judiciously and conducted thoroughly, their value is always worth much more than the time and cost expended.

Table 9.8 Incorporating Team Rhythm
SELF-ACTUALIZATIONS FULFILLED

Self-Actualization Level	How Fulfilled By This Success Element
Physiological	These team members are comforted by having a regular review of team status and platform to announce questions and concerns. This clarity provides confidence their work provides what is needed.
Safety	These team members are comforted by being given regular and current status of the program, including its probability of success.
Love/Belonging	These team members believe regular meetings are also a time for interpersonal exchange, where team members' feelings, not just thoughts, can be exchanged. This adds to team fellowship and teamwork.
Esteem	Team members with this self-actualization appreciate that regular meetings are a necessary part of dividing a big task into its smaller steps to accomplish. This is necessary for the work they are responsible for to complete successfully. With periodic meetings, progress can be accurately measured and shared.
Professional	These team members use these meetings to review the work progress and learn current events. This provides further perspective that allows them to fine tune their contribution for maximum benefit. It also provides a platform for them to share the impact of their ongoing contributions.
Altruistic	For these team members, team rhythm is necessary to fine tune high product quality. This high quality is necessary to achieve their altruistic goals. The way they present their work status and the content of their questions often further encourages the altruistic outcomes they are striving for.

9.1.10 Watch the Flank!

Often a program places its resources on the series of tasks that constitute the critical path—the series of interdependent tasks that take the longest time to complete and therefore determine the completion date. The focus centers on making sure each task along this path is completed on or before its promised time. As mentioned, sometimes the sum duration of this series of tasks shortens, and another task series becomes the critical path, but the program teams may have paid little attention to the steps in this new series. As a result, task issues on this new path may be resolved late, resulting in the completion date of the program being delayed. Or, conversely, the tasks on a parallel path are found to take longer than originally estimated, making them the critical path.

This failure is avoided by program management's not only mitigating issues on the current critical path, but also for those tasks that would be on the new critical path. This focuses on the tasks on the "flank" of the critical path tasks (see Figure 9.16).

The traditional Gantt schedule format illustrates those tasks that must be serviced in parallel with the tasks on the critical path. Sometimes, just a quick review of the forecasted task completion dates in this format will reveal what tasks may find themselves on a new critical path. Other times, a computer scheduling tool will show the new critical path if tasks on the current critical path are assumed to complete earlier than scheduled. Both these techniques can be used to identify what tasks may become the new critical path and should be given special attention.

Another imputes for paying attention to the flank are the concerns voiced by the frontline working team members. The viewpoints from these team members are invaluable! Some of these team members may believe, for example, that a task that is not on the critical path may take longer than estimated or has tremendous risk of not being completed at all. This task, along with the others in

Watch the Flank for Undetected Risks ⇨ Issues

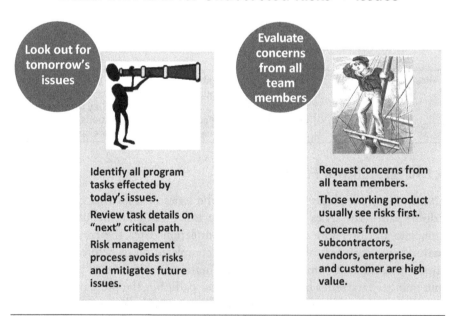

Look out for tomorrow's issues

Evaluate concerns from all team members

Identify all program tasks effected by today's issues.

Review task details on "next" critical path.

Risk management process avoids risks and mitigates future issues.

Request concerns from all team members.

Those working product usually see risks first.

Concerns from subcontractors, vendors, enterprise, and customer are high value.

Figure 9.16 In a first-place program, risk management is as critical as product, cost, and schedule performances. Many have a risk-management team following a detailed process described in the program plan.

a different task series, may actually be the real critical path. Even if leadership is not convinced this concern establishes a new critical path, they should place additional emphasis on making sure the tasks on this potential new path are completed on or before their scheduled completion time.

Keep in mind that the team members on the "front line" may include individuals working for a supplier, the customer, or another part of the sponsoring enterprise. Sometimes, subcontractor or vendor representatives have valuable experience solving similar problems with other customers, and they may have a highly successful and proven assessment of some risks and mitigation approaches. Their guidance can be conveyed in general terms without infringing on the privacy or ownership rights of their other customers.

Another way of staying aware of program tasks that may become the critical path is with the use of a risk-management plan, which is described or referenced in the program plan. It usually requires a risk management team to execute it. This team identifies the high risks and current issues in the program, computing both the likelihood of a risk's becoming an issue and the impact level if it does so. This team typically develops and tracks both risk avoidance and issue abatement plans for each risk and issue identified.

This is a way of making sure the program pays attention to all risks and issues, not just those on the critical path. In most cases, if a lingering problem becomes a risk or a risk becomes an issue, there will already be avoidance and abatement plans established, thus reducing the valuable schedule time needed to react. With these cautionary actions, it is possible the program may assume a new critical path with little or no delay to the original delivery commitments.

Please recall that managing risk in a program is as important as managing cost, schedule, and product performance. The best programs are not caught flat-footed when a risk becomes an issue. They are not surprised and paralyzed by this event, causing the effort to fall out of first place. Instead, they have maintained broad situational awareness and have prepared for risks in tasks on their flank. The program might be disappointed by the occurrence of a new issue but should not be surprised by it (see Figure 9.17).

During Step 1, leadership will have communicated that all team members were encouraged to bring forward worries, concerns, and potential issues. It would have been emphasized that this reporting could be provided casually and sources held in strictest confidence.

Team members must be reminded that many risks and issues they bring forward may be beyond the view of leadership and the risk management team, and so otherwise would not be known. Team members must be assured that all worries, concerns, and questions are welcomed and will be answered. Also, team members should be assured that their value to the team will in no way be discounted by the types and volume of concerns and questions they bring

Encourage Risk Vigilance and Preparation

Step 2
• Encourage all team (including enterprise, suppliers, customer) to forward all concerns/issues.   • Reward sources that identify new risks.   • Verify work duration estimates and know risks/issues on development path(s) becoming critical if current one is eliminated.   • Identify risk identification as positive in a team member's performance evaluation.

Figure 9.17 Leadership must have their doors wide open to risks and issues brought forward by any team member. Team members must be recognized and rewarded for identifying them.

forward. On the contrary, finding undetected risks and issues will be evaluated as a positive attribute in a team member, and should be commended in the presence of the other team members. Leadership should consider using the success of identifying unknown risks and issues as part of the evaluation of each team member's performance.

Team members will be delighted at the high degree of structured planning for potential and actual issues. This will set them free to achieve their self-actualization needs at a high rate and with a high probability of success.

Table 9.9 Watch the Flank
SELF-ACTUALIZATIONS FULFILLED

Self-Actualization Level	How Fulfilled By This Success Element
Physiological	These team members appreciate that they are queried about their concerns regarding the program. They are motivated do their best work by the freedom to offer their worries, concerns and observations of risks and issues at any time.
Safety	These team members take advantage of program processes that solicit their worries and concerns, often not known by leadership or the risk-management process. There relieved by knowing their concerns will be taken seriously regardless of their level in or affiliation with the program.
Love/Belonging	These team members appreciate a greater sense of team unity and confidence that occurs when the program prepares schedule contingencies.

Esteem	These team members place a high premium on completing their assigned program responsibilities with high quality as soon as possible. They are enthusiastic about analyzing and mitigating risks in their tasks that may put them on the programs critical path.
Professional	These team members believe part of their professional duty is to highlight potential issues related to their expertise that may cause the program work to fall behind schedule. They take delight in identifying program tasks that may become on the critical path and with developing effective plans to mitigate them.
Altruistic	Having a work tracking process that identifies potential changes in the critical path adds to the credibility of the program results and ensures shorter time to completion. These features are of importance for achieving elements of their altruistic vision.

9.1.11 Creating Valuable Documents

The effort expended to document program guidelines, processes, designs, test data, etc. is a two-edged sword. Yes, it requires extra time and mental focus that is often uncomfortable, yet, if applied correctly, it is invaluable for achieving program commitments with high-quality results on or before promised times.

Team members are usually motivated to precisely immortalize the excellent work they have completed. They take pride in what they've accomplished and want others to benefit from it, and they are usually enthusiastic about recording and sharing what they've done. In addition, they will appreciate that the documented work will only be altered by a strict process described in the program plan.

Team members motivated by providing high-quality solutions and completing program tasks competently and as quickly as possible appreciate that certain guidelines and restrictions for processes, roles, approvals, workforce makes and more are essential. They appreciate that the list of these guidelines is vastly more complicated than can be committed to memory and that these processes and restrictions must be documented. The challenge of program leadership is to achieve the above-stated documentation gains and legitimize the effort of developing useful documentation (see Figure 9.18).

Outstanding examples of innovation and creativity resulted from the Cold War; many of these developments are in the technologies we use today. One of the big contributors during this time was Lockheed's Advanced Development Programs, called the "Skunk Works." This lean, multifunctional team was noted for creating successful, high-performance aircraft decades ahead of the then state of the art. This organization was especially noted for creating these amazing breakthrough aircraft with teams a fraction of the size that many experts in the industry estimated would be needed. These teams were truly in first place.

Document What's Important and Revise Per Process

- **Document what's important!**
- **Short documents are hard!**
- **Includes:**
  - **Program plan**
  - **Process *(+ key personnel)***
  - **Product design**
  - **Configuration management plan**
  - **Risk management plan**
  - **Verification/test plan**
  - **Software development plan**
  - **More**
- **Follow documented process:**
  - **Saves time and money**
  - **Documented foundation for improving process and design**

Figure 9.18   Succinct, easy-to-absorb documentation is essential in any first-place program. Often, a concise document requires more effort to write but more than repays itself with straightforward clarity and ease of use.

The author spent months in this facility supporting new developments; he assisted this team for a week before he realized that his desk was a mere 15-second walk from the office of the head of this organization, Clarence "Kelly" Johnson. He met Mr. Johnson as part of his indoctrination—another lesson for the author of the high value of colocation: in-person dialogue.

Kelly Johnson summarized the need for documentation in his book, *More Than My Share of It All*,[1] stating, "There must be a minimum number of written reports required, but *important* work must be recorded *thoroughly*."

The following lists important documents that are essential for a first-place program.

Program Plan

As discussed thoroughly already, this document is a detailed description of how the program will be executed. A copy must be given to every team member, and updates must be promptly distributed via amendment pages, updates to the program website copy, or any method that is secure, complete, and immediate.

---

[1] Johnson, C. (1989). *Kelly: More Than My Share of It All*. Smithsonian Books. ISBN: 978-0874744910.

Whenever there is a question or disagreement amongst the team members about the workings of the program, they should first consult the program plan, which will usually reference supporting plans, including the software development plan, the risk-management plan, and others plans for details. A program plan that is well written and well maintained should be immediately grabbed by team members when there is a question about the program structure, or process.

This plan must be as short and to the point as possible; otherwise, it will not be used. The first draft is usually written by the PM and their charter leadership team and later refined by inputs from the new task teams. (Figure 9.2 on page 188 provided an example outline for a typical program plan.)

Requirements

This document varies in size and complexity depending on the size of the program, and it must include all the requirements imposed on the program. These requirements will come primarily from the customer and may include additional requirements from the enterprise, suppliers, and other qualified sources. In most requirements documents, there will be a distribution of primary, top-level requirements and sub-requirements (often the results of requirements flow-down work) to the task teams, suppliers, and sometimes the customer.

Requirements specified in this document include product performances, content and formats of deliveries, delivery dates, cost constraints, reporting contacts and protocol, customer terms and conditions, and more. For large programs, the customer may convey their needs with a combination of a statement of work, requirements specifications, a work-breakdown document, a funding constrained profile, a master schedule of deliveries, and more.

To the extent possible, all program team members must have access to current contracts and requirements documents, although this availability might be constrained by agreements regarding sensitive data or other special requests provided by the suppliers, enterprise, or customer.

Integrated Schedule

This schedule must provide the schedule details that support the program's master schedule, integrating the interdependencies and completion dates of all task teams and the input content and delivery times from the suppliers and often the customer. This schedule is the central focus for the program scheduler.

Schedule margins must be included in all predicted durations when computing committed delivery dates, and a margin policy must be provided by program leadership to task-team leadership and suppliers. This policy may be different for each of these. Sometimes, multiple books are established by the business team (this is discussed in detail in Section 8.9.10 on page 178).

Every program organization must attempt to complete their scheduled work before using any margin; in case the margin is exhausted and the work is still not completed, the team must resort to extra hours and/or incorporate a new innovation to deliver on time. Late deliveries must be treated as a very serious infraction by leadership. Some potentially first-place programs have lost first-place status because of their lenient response to late deliveries.

For special, schedule-critical deliveries from a supplier, a delivery incentive is sometimes appropriate. This can consist of a monetary bonus if the delivery is compliant and delivered on or before the committed time. If delivery ahead of schedule is even more advantageous to the program, then this bonus can be constructed to be greater in value by increments for progressively earlier deliveries.

In rare instances, a monetary discount (penalty) may be considered if the supplier delivers late. However, this imposition should be used infrequently, because it will be interpreted by many suppliers as punitive. Setting this tone can dilute the willingness of the supplier to take risks, innovate, and incorporate lessons learned from past work.

Risk-Management Plan

With the optimism of a newly starting program, it is difficult for the team to stop and conjecture all the things that can go wrong. But as mentioned, identifying, tracking, and abating risks and issues is as important as managing costs, schedules, and product performances. A risk-management plan must be part of the program plan.

For bigger programs, a risk-management team should be established. This team meets periodically to record, categorize, and score the severity of the risks brought forward by the program task teams, evaluating as well any new risks and issues brought forward by suppliers, customer, enterprise management, and even other programs.

Traditionally, the risk-management team will develop a risk-evaluation matrix that records both the probability of a given risk becoming an issue, and the impact of the issue if it occurs. This establishes a hierarchy of importance for avoidance and abating. The most important risks, of course, are those with a high likelihood of becoming an issue and, should the issue occur, has a high undesirable impact on the program. The risk-management team develops a mitigation plan for each risk, with priority given to those risks of highest importance as determined by the risk matrix. In addition, this team will develop a draft abatement plan for each issue that may result.

The risk-management plan is necessary for a program to be in first place. There should be no delay to program progress due to the team being unprepared to respond to an issue. The risk-management analysis and documentation add confidence in the customer and the sponsoring enterprise that the program will successfully be completed on time, as committed.

Expenditure Profile Plan

This plan must show the allocation of program funds to all the elements of the team, including the task teams, the suppliers, enterprise support, and others. These allocations are based on the predictions of the monies required to achieve each milestone, usually including funding margins that the various leadership entities have put aside. The PM and the task-team leaders maintain a record of funding margins with a method and format agreed upon with the business team. The size of these margins will vary depending on the risk and complexity of what each expenditure supports. If some activity exceeds the estimated cost required and exhausts the allocated margin, then it will have a cost overrun, which usually must be covered by monies allocated to other tasks.

Except for extenuating cases, a cost overrun must be considered by the program team to be a serious infraction. Disappointing performances in the supporting technologies or late deliveries by suppliers are examples of weak justifications for a cost overrun, as these should have been anticipated during planning and included in the estimates of margins.

A cost overrun for a program jeopardizes the credibility of its estimates for their remaining work. Cost overruns will often be associated with a program slipping important milestones, preventing it from holding a first-place position.

Software Development Plan

If the program is developing software, a software development plan (SDP) is essential. As discussed in detail in Section 8.9.7 (on page 167), software is providing an increasingly larger portion of the functionality of many new systems and processes. Software is less tangible than other engineered products, has more dynamic parts than other technologies, and is derived from rapidly changing development processes.

The SDP must describe the software development methodology, development tools used, and the plan to develop the software, including the software development milestones. It must describe the development steps, which will typically include software requirements flow down, software design, software coding, peer reviews, software unit testing, integrated testing, and support for its integration into the rest of the program work. The SDP also describes the process for estimating and tracking computer hardware resources needed, including computational throughput, memory requirements and types, interface bandwidth, fault tolerance overheads, and more.

The SDP primarily serves two audiences: First, it is the plan that guides the work of the software developers. Second, it provides an overview description of the software development process, including milestones, for the non-software team members. As mentioned earlier, part of the role of the software development task lead is to clearly answer any questions from the non-software program personnel about software development status and what is described in the SDP.

Some programs or program management may consider the SDP as an unnecessary elaboration, feeling that the software developers will end up "doing it their own way" anyway. Ironically, this concern is one of the major justifications for an SDP. Because of the novelty and complexity of modern-day software development, there is a wide range of approaches to develop it. But the program will only be its best if all the software engineers use the same development methodology, tools, work product formats, etc. This is akin to team rhythm—all members pulling their oar the same way, even if some members do not agree it is the best way.

The good software task-team leader will make sure all developers strictly adhere to the process and methodologies required in the SDP, and that the SDP is maintained under strict configuration control and is changed via the program's configuration update process, typically a change control board.

Only What's Necessary

Program leadership must insist on creating only those documents that are needed (see Figure 9.19). This sometimes will strike seasoned participants as less than what they have created in the past.

Leadership must ensure that each document is kept short and succinct; otherwise, the document will not be used, rendering it a tragic waste of time and effort for the program. In addition, important documents that end up not being used

Necessary, Succinct Documents Are Needed to Be First Place

Step 2
• Inform team, short documents of only what is important.
• Acknowledge succinct documents often take longer to create.
• Establish documents as source of all official status and direction.
• Documents are updated only by process described in the program plan.

Figure 9.19　It is critical that what is documented is followed by the team. If content is found to be inaccurate or needs to be updated, changes must only be allowed via the program's change process.

leads to unnecessary confusion and errors in the teams. Ironically, short documents are often harder to write than long ones.

Leadership must be wary of insisting that documents adhere to a general-purpose format, which may contain sections that have little value for the specific needs of the program. In addition, trying to reuse similar documents from past programs runs the risk of propagating process material that is irrelevant and even erroneous.

None of the preceding documents discussed should be longer than 100 pages, including diagrams, for any program. Documentation must be fastidiously direct and simple. If an author believes that certain detailed process justifications must be provided, then it is recommended that the author reference this description as an external document and not insert it into the main text.

Table 9.10 Creating Valuable Documents
SELF-ACTUALIZATIONS FULFILLED

Self-Actualization Level	How Fulfilled By This Success Element
Physiological	These team members appreciate that devoting extra time to developing succinct and valuable documents pays back multiple times by eliminating confusion and errors.
Safety	These team members take comfort from the stability added to the progress of the program derived from well-documented plans. They pay allegiance to fastidiously following the definitions and directions in the program plan.
Love/Belonging	These team members observe that rigorously following documented plans and information is another means of minimizing arguments and confusion in the team. This improves team harmony and teamwork.
Esteem	These team members attempt to get the work done with highly efficient use of work effort. They believe in the value of good documentation to achieve this. They often act as an example of adhering to the rules, processes, and data in this documentation, to galvanize the team's perception of its value.
Professional	These team members take pride in developing documentation that is direct, simple, and not complicated with low value protocol. They take pride in using their extensive expertise in creating the simplest solution possible. They understand and are willing to accept the added work needed to develop a simple document.
Altruistic	These team members see simple documents as another aid to completing the program commitment as soon as possible and with little or no ambiguity. This allows elements of their altruistic goals to be realized sooner.

9.1.12 Insist on Root Cause

A description of how to determine root cause and its high value are summarized in the following. (More details are provided in the author's previous book, *Project and Program Turnaround.*[2])

When executing any program, there will be times when some product or process does not operate as intended. For example, perhaps the change in the way funds are collected does not reduce the overheads at a nonprofit organization, or the use of a new material for manufacturing construction rivets does not increase the strength of a new bridge.

The process of finding the originating cause of a failure may seem like a low priority to some readers, but failure to determine and eliminate the ultimate cause of a failure on the first try will quickly demote a program from being in first place. The penalty of not finding root cause as soon as possible can be catastrophic—much larger than many PMs anticipate.

When a team uses the wrong process of only guessing at the cause of failure, usually multiple causes are hypothesized, and the team ends up creating a solution for each of the suspected causes. Developing solutions for multiple candidate causes can, of course, cost large amounts of money and time. But what is worse is that unfortunately it is unusual, even given the wide breadth of potential causes that are remedied, that the actual cause will be eliminated.

The program is then allowed to continue, but the failure that resulted in the original anomaly occurs again, often at the worst possible time! The additional time and cost needed to address the issue again will have a major and sometimes devastating impact on the success of the team.

It is amazing how accurately the root cause of a failure can be determined if the right process is rigorously followed (see Figure 9.20), but it is disappointing how few programs follow it. The root cause determination process used must be described in detail in the program plan, and it must be *completely* executed whenever used. If the root cause determination process is not completed, the cause of a fault or failure will probably not be found. The program will end up not eliminating the failure cause, and it will occur again, usually in a more integrated development setting where it is more expensive to remedy.

To emphasize this point, accurately determining the root cause of a fault or failure with a rigorous and complete execution of the determination process will cost only slightly more than just providing a cursory guess. However, the impact of executing the cause determination and repair process a second time will cost over twice what it would have if the cause had been accurately found the first time. Also, further delay further impacts cost.

---

[2] Pavelko, T. (2017). *Project and Program Turnaround.* Boca Raton, FL: CRC Press/ Taylor & Francis Group.

Root Cause Process Must Be Performed Completely

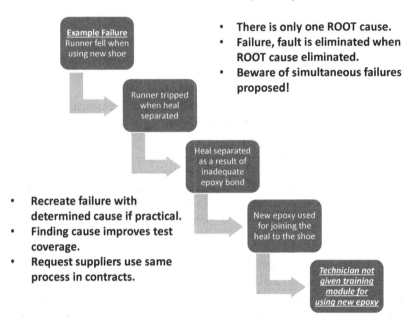

- There is only one ROOT cause.
- Failure, fault is eliminated when ROOT cause eliminated.
- Beware of simultaneous failures proposed!

Example Failure
Runner fell when using new shoe

Runner tripped when heal separated

Heal separated as a result of inadequate epoxy bond

New epoxy used for joining the heal to the shoe

Technician not given training module for using new epoxy

- **Recreate failure with determined cause if practical.**
- **Finding cause improves test coverage.**
- **Request suppliers use same process in contracts.**

Figure 9.20   Finding the root cause of faults and failures on the first try is a cornerstone of a first-place program. Responding to intermediate failure symptoms is always more expensive than solving root cause, because the problem will occur again. Patience must be exerted to complete the entire root-cause determination process described in the program plan.

A good program will continue to use the experiences it has accumulated, correcting faults to improve its understanding of the strengths and weaknesses of its product. This can determine the substance of future product design revisions and guide how the current revision should be applied (see Figure 9.21).

Some industrial-based observations about root cause by the author and his colleagues:

- Root cause is the starting fault or failure that results in the final observed or measured fault or failure. There may be multiple failure symptoms observed resulting from intermediate faults that occur between the root cause and the final failure, but inevitably there is only *one* root cause.
- The test of finding only one starting cause is essential when verifying root cause. When a team offers a combination of simultaneous causes for a failure, they have not yet found the root cause.

Insist on Single *Root* Cause

Step 2
• Execute *full* process for anomalies, faults, failures.
• Avoid mistake of only identifying intermediate cause—fault will occur again after mitigation.
• Use root-cause knowledge to fortify test coverage.
• Maintain metric of faults, failures reoccurring after correction.
• Unverified failures must be avoided!

Figure 9.21   A root cause based on multiple simultaneous faults/failures is never real. Unverified root cause usually results in developing corrections for all remaining candidate causes, which is very expensive. Even with the wide breadth of corrections for an unverified failure, the failure/fault may occur again.

- A technology frequently used for hypothesizing multiple causes for a failure is electronics. It is exceptionally easy to create a wide range of failure symptoms by assuming multiple simultaneous failures in complex electronic circuits.

    One of many such examples where electronics were originally blamed was a failure observed during acceptance testing of a complex device provided by a subcontractor for a satellite application. This subcontractor's failure-review team asserted that the cause was from four electronic circuit components whose performance values were at the edge of their allowable ratings. In actuality, the probability of this happening was virtually impossible, and the PM for the satellite did not accept this explanation as the failure cause.

    As a result, the PM received numerous calls from the subcontractor's high-level executive management. He feared receiving a call from his own superiors conveying the concerns of this important subcontractor, which serviced many programs in his company. However, his phone stayed silent. Three days later, the root cause was accurately determined to be something totally different—contaminated optics. This example highlights the essential need to fix the origin of a failure and not one or more of the intermediate observables.

    Another example is when a capacitor in an electronic circuit had been destroyed due to overheating. It was noted that the potting material used as a heat sink for this component was of insufficient quantity, and therefore too much heat was accumulating in the component. It could have been assumed that the root cause was that an insufficient amount of potting material was used to mount the component, but this was only an intermediate symptom. The *root* cause was that a backup technician mounted this component and had not received adequate training on how to apply the potting material. The corrective action was to administer complete training to the backup technician and to add an independent inspection to check the adequacy of the thermal potting as part of acceptance testing.

- If there is no danger to program cost, schedule, or safety, the derived root cause should be applied to the system that had failed to verify that the failure is re-created.
- The testing sequencing should be examined after the root cause is found to see if test coverage can be improved to find this fault sooner in the development sequence.

A consistent and proven way to find root cause is to list all the potential causes of the failure, then proceed to exclude candidates based on the collected data and other observables during the failure. Root cause is determined reliably by this simple process of exclusion. It is amazing how consistently successful it is. For example, for one program, over 100 failure review boards were convened in which this process was used. These failures occurred at the different levels of component test, unit test, integrated test, acceptance test, and application support. None of these failures occurred again after being corrected. At no time was a determination of cause found to be erroneous.

What is important is that this process must be followed *completely*, as summarized below:

- **Freeze and document the failed setup and create a timeline.** This may be impossible if what is being tested is active when it fails. In this case, stop the test as soon as practical in a configuration that is safe for the test personnel, the test apparatus, and the item being tested. Do not rely on the memories of the team members to determine the configuration of the test when the failure occurred; instead, document the configuration immediately. Also, develop a timeline of the events that were performed and observed by the team before, during, and after the fault/failure occurred.
- **Assign a principal investigator.** This person must organize a failure review team, often referred to as a failure review board (FRB), and lead the process of finding the root cause and correcting the problem. The principal investigator does not have to be a senior member of the program but must understand the root cause determination process. Plus, they should have good planning and leadership skills and have credibility with the program team for being able to organize and lead analytical work. This person is given the authority to be the one person responsible for leading the work

to determine the cause and corrective action for the fault/failure to which they have been assigned. The responsibilities of the principal investigator include giving assignments to team members, establishing a schedule of regular team meetings, conducting the team meetings, and making sure the FRB follows the process description in the program plan. They provide status on the cause investigation and problem solution to the program and provide a final report and presentation on cause and corrective action to leadership for approval of closure.

- **Assemble the fault/failure investigation team.** As stated, it is the responsibility of the principal investigator to assemble a failure review board. The members of this board usually include the associated product development personnel, the subcontractor (if applicable), members from the test organization, and other specialists as needed.

- **Complete a timeline of events**. The team conducting the test when the failure occurred must construct a preliminary timeline of the events that occurred before and after the fault/failure. It is important that the team perform this is soon as possible after the failure, while their memory is still fresh. This timeline should include everything that may be relevant to the fault/failure being analyzed, even if its relevance appears to be minor.

- **Record all random observables.** These include any and all observations by team members that could have some relevance to the fault/failure that are not included on the timeline. Examples could include, "It rained for an hour two days before the failure of the suspension bolt," or "Printer software was updated 24 hours before erroneous reports were printed." These observables will be used as part of the evidence base to evaluate candidate causes.

- **Create a hierarchical breakdown of potential fault causes.** All potential causes of the fault/failure should be recorded by the failure review board. These potential causes are usually the result of brainstorming by the members. A recording format should be chosen that allows the potential fault causes to be categorized under the different fault areas—fault trees and Fishbone diagrams are formats commonly used. Every potential fault/failure cause should be identified, and listing a large number of candidates should not be a concern. Many will be disqualified quickly.

- **Attempt to disprove all potential causes with the data.** The FRB must incorporate all data, including test records, timeline, and observables, and attempt to disprove each potential fault cause, documenting the argument and supporting data that disproves each candidate cause. Occasionally, while attempting to disprove the cause, more data is needed, requiring more tests.

- **What's Left?**
  - **One potential cause remains that cannot be disproved.** This is usually what happens—this remaining candidate is the root cause! (I appreciate

that this process of elimination appears to be simplistic, but after thousands of applications by many managers in a wide range of applications, it has been observed to be completely successful. The faults and failures the author and his colleagues have solved this way have never occurred again.)

o **More than one potential cause remains that cannot be disproved.** The FRB must review all test data, timeline, and observables to verify that all data was considered when eliminating fault candidates. Further testing may be indicated, if practical, to further eliminate remaining candidates down to one cause. If this reduction cannot be accomplished, complete corrective action must be applied to all the remaining fault candidates. This is often referred to as a "worst-case" corrective action. This will correct the problem, but the FRB will not know which of the remaining faults corrected was the root cause; plus, the correction work will be more expensive due to its greater extent.

o **All potential root causes are disproved by the data.** This outcome is very rare, and it indicates one of three problems. The appropriate remedy should be taken to resolve this.

» The failure data collected is in error, causing the actual cause to be wrongly disproved.

» The FRB did not identify all the potential causes of the fault/failure, and the real root cause was never identified as a candidate.

» The measurements indicating there had been a fault/failure are in error—a fault/failure never actually happened.

In rare instances, after performing all the above, a single failure cannot be found. These very rare instances become what are commonly referred to as an "unverified failure," and these are to be avoided tenaciously in all programs! They have been given no formal corrective action because the failure cause was not known, and no action has been taken to prevent it from occurring again. And, of course, at this point there remains an unquantified probability that the failure will occur again.

Root-cause determination reminders:

• Root cause must be found and corrected for a fault/failure, otherwise it will occur again.

• Care must be taken not to confuse the root cause with the intermediate faults that are observed between the root cause and the observed failure symptoms.

• There is always only ONE root cause; a cause requiring multiple failures occurring simultaneously is statistically impossible.

• Determining root cause for a failure that recurs will inevitably be much more costly and will result in a greater loss to the progress of the program than applying the complete determination process the first time.

- It is highly recommended that suppliers (subcontractors, vendors, etc.) use the same root cause and corrective action process as the program—this reduces errors in communicating fault determination status and ambiguities when comparing data. This stipulation can be written into subcontracts and purchase agreements.
- It is recommended that, if possible, the root cause be applied to the system that failed to verify that the failure symptoms are re-created. This can help guarantee root cause was found.

During Step 1, leadership should have provided examples of how repairs to defects in process and product can be highly wasteful and team progress can be unnecessarily delayed if the root cause determined is wrong. The root cause determination process used by the program would have been reviewed in detail.

During Step 2, the program must rigorously follow the root cause determination process documented in the program plan. This is been already stated multiple times. In addition, the program must maintain a metric of corrective actions that did *not* remedy the problems they were designed to eliminate. These failed corrections, if any, must be reviewed to improve the root cause corrective action process, so that future corrections will always remedy faults and failures the first time.

Also, a metric of numbers and types of unverified failures must be maintained. In a well-run program, the occurrence of these failures should be very rare—hopefully never. If they occur, enhancements to test process details, data recorded, etc. must be implemented so that root cause may be found. Allowing further development to proceed with unverified failures is highly risky.

Table 9.11 Insist on Root Cause

SELF-ACTUALIZATIONS FULFILLED

Self-Actualization Level	How Fulfilled By This Success Element
Physiological	Some low-experience team members with this self-actualization may be perplexed by the emphasis on always determining the root cause. With experience, they will observe the large penalties to cost, schedule, and team morale that occur if faults/failures are not eliminated the first time. They will then highly support accurate root cause determination.
Safety	These team members feel threatened by a fault or failure that occurs again after the team believes they eliminated it. They are enthusiastic about incorporating a rigorous process to eliminate the root cause, even if more laborious than desired.

Love/Belonging	These team members see that a successful root-cause process helps reduce emotions in the team. They observe that there may be resentment resulting from a lengthy root-cause process but realize that the anxiety and embarrassment that occur when a failure recurs is worse.
Esteem	These team members evaluate that a thorough root-cause determination process is necessary toward minimizing the time to complete the program. It also provides more assurances that the resulting product is accurate and successful. This helps to maintain the stature of the role of these team members and their favorable credentials for future promotion.
Professional	These team members see a well-documented and thorough root-cause determination process as necessary toward achieving their schedule and quality commitments. They enthusiastically apply it.
Altruistic	For these team members, enforcing assurances that deliver the product on time with promised performances not only achieves their altruistic vision sooner but adds credibility to their vision.

9.1.13 Mistakes to Avoid When Controlling Configuration

Poor product or process configuration control causes huge and detrimental penalties to a program, particularly when the configuration of a process or a product is different from the configuration tested. An old saying goes, "Test as you use and use as you test"; this is very true (see Figure 9.22).

Mistakes that cause discrepancies include the following (see Figure 9.23):

- **Parts substitution.** The program must be aware of any process steps or product components that have been changed, even with a so-called "equivalent process" or "equivalent part." All such changes must be approved by the CCB or equivalent approval procedure. These same rigors of approval must also be applied internally by the subcontractors and vendors, and this must be included in their purchase agreements or subcontracts.

  The CCB should require some level of regression testing on a product or process after it has been changed, including any change of process or parts with so-called equivalent ones. Even when a new source for a part promises that form, fit, and function are exactly equivalent to the original part, there may still be subtle differences—even if the new part source assigns the part the original part number.

  In all instances, the CCB must thoroughly review any equivalent part to determine the actual differences, which can include dimensions, operation,

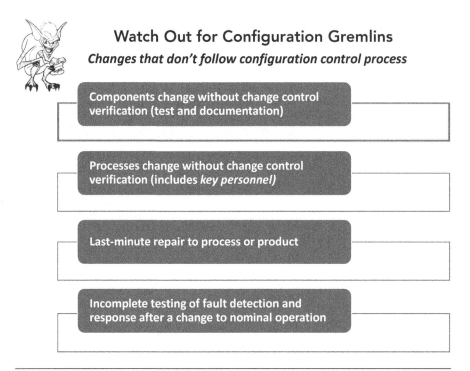

Watch Out for Configuration Gremlins

Changes that don't follow configuration control process

Components change without change control verification (test and documentation)

Processes change without change control verification (includes *key personnel)*

Last-minute repair to process or product

Incomplete testing of fault detection and response after a change to nominal operation

Figure 9.22 There are subtle circumstances during development work when configuration control processes may be neglected. Leadership must be aware of these and prevent them, as not doing so will prevent a team from staying in first place. Suppliers should use a similar configuration control process, with the same high level of rigor as the program. This process should be described in supplier subcontracts.

Avoid Common Mistakes in Configuration Control

Step 2
• Leadership shares examples of common configuration control mistakes and consequences.
• Describes how accurate configuration control provides development speed to be first place.
• Applies simple, strictly enforced configuration change process.
• Leadership must be visible example of following change process.

Figure 9.23 Leadership must support the configuration control rules by describing, with examples, the consequences of not following them.

build material, weight, reliability, installation process, and much more. The CCB must evaluate each of these differences to certify that the substitute part is suitable for use.

- **Changes of process.** Any change in process steps, including deletions or additions used to create the process or product, must go through CCB review. Even something as seemingly innocuous as changing the work shift in which a work step is performed can change the configuration.
- **Changes in personnel.** This is especially true for changes in leadership personnel or specific team members performing critical tasks. For example, a task team may have had a lead who is scrupulous about maintaining consistency in their processes, but who is then replaced by a new lead who is less meticulous. Or a highly experienced technician who performs some special work on a critical part may be leaving the team. This person may have had some experience-based additions to procedures that are not recorded in the work procedures.

  Key personnel changes in the program team or at one of the suppliers must be reviewed and approved by the CCB. It is a good idea to request a list of key personnel, by name, in all subcontracts and other purchase agreements.

  There have been many actual system-level failures whose root cause was an inadequate procedure performed by replacement personnel. Often this person had not received the complete requisite training to perform the job. The CCB must be convinced that all replacement personnel will receive all required training before being assigned a critical role.
- **Poorly tested logic for degraded operation.** For highly autonomous products, more time and money are often spent to develop logic to detect and recover from faults than is spent making the system perform its basic function. During schedule pressures while approaching a final delivery, it is easy for fault recovery functions to not be completely tested during regression testing. Often team members consider this to be testing of a backup function, and therefore it is not given the same emphasis.

  Program leadership must insist that fault recovery functions always receive the same complete level of test and verification that the primary function of the product receives. This must be true both during initial product testing and after changes are made to it at any time.
- **Last-minute changes.** It is human nature to wait until the last minute to apply final changes to a product—we often want to make sure that all final changes are identified so they may be incorporated at one time. Unfortunately, as a result, there is usually a rush to implement these changes, opening the opportunity for some changes to be accepted without complete review and testing. This of course is dangerous.

  Last-minute changes, such as electronic circuit fixes with jumper wires, the late decision to add a new social group to a public survey, or the decision to eliminate inspection steps considered to be of minor importance, are simple examples of how product defects can be created and/or allowed to pass.

Program leadership must insist on conducting the full review and approval processes for all changes, as described in the program plan, even under the high pressures of imminent deliveries. This requires that leadership exert tremendous calm, patience, and objectivity while making sure that acceptance testing and approvals are complete.

The importance of making sure that last-minute changes to a product or process are thoroughly reviewed like any other change cannot be overemphasized! Very often, the root cause for faults and failures in delivered products is due to last-minute changes that are not thoroughly reviewed or tested.

During Step 1, new team members will have been informed of the high emphasis leadership gives to complete adherence to the processes of configuration control. Examples of how easy it is to break the configuration control rules during the panic of last-minute deliveries would have been shown and discussed. Team members would have been reminded that adherence to configuration control process is necessary to achieve all commitments of scheduled delivery, cost control, product performances, and risk avoidance. Typical mistakes made while controlling configuration through the entire life cycle of the program will have been reviewed, including computations of the resulting losses.

All team members must be given a thorough indoctrination into the change process for the program, and typical change examples must be walked through in detail.

During Step 2, the importance of rigorously using a change process such as the CCB must be consistently emphasized, and leadership must be a consistent example of thoroughly applying these processes.

Leadership must highlight any product development issues, schedule delays, or cost overruns resulting from configuration control errors during execution of the program. During this time, it should be determined how to avoid these errors in the future.

Table 9.12 Mistakes When Controlling Configuration
SELF-ACTUALIZATIONS FULFILLED

Self-Actualization Level	How Fulfilled By This Success Element
Physiological	These team members most often place their emphasis on completing the work they are assigned. They are less hampered by concerns that their work results are being changed with lack of process.
Safety	These team members appreciate that experience-based, typical configuration control mistakes are identified and that explicit provisions are established to prevent them.

Love/Belonging	These team members look forward to the team's celebrating their major accomplishments. They appreciate that often configuration control mistakes delay or dilute these accomplishments, and they are very supportive of avoiding these mistakes.
Esteem	These team members highly appreciate that on-time delivery is a major part of the evaluation of their performance. They are very supportive of configuration control–related precautions to prevent delays.
Professional	Many of these team members have experienced the consequences of configuration control mistakes. They do not want their work to be damaged by them, and they are very supportive of measures to avoid mistakes.
Altruistic	These team members appreciate that configuration control mistakes can not only delay the release of the final product but also place its quality in question. They believe that high-quality results, delivered on time, add to the credibility and importance of their altruistic vision and therefore support strict configuration control.

9.1.14 Code of Conduct Increases Business Success

What industry refers to as "ethical behavior" is usually a part or all of a special team code of conduct, which establishes the guidelines and limits of the team's behavior. It may directly describe or imply the moral elements of the team. Modern ethical behavior usually assumes that all team contributors have equal rights to fair treatment. It does not tolerate discrimination, unsubstantiated criticism, intimidation, abuse of power, or any kind of violence or behavior that is considered abusive to the members of the team (see Figure 9.24). Therefore, ethics training and ethical behavior in a team is a way to codify and activate a set of team rules of conduct focused on providing equal fairness and respect for all team members.

It may surprise some that the time and expense used for ethics training in a program is paid back multiple times. For example, with strong team ethics, team members perform their work with less fear of retribution, being taken advantage of, evaluated, or considered for new job roles with less respect than the others. With less fear of being unfairly treated, team members actually complete their work more freely and efficiently, thus reducing cost. The decision to provide ethics training is not only an important moral one, it is also a necessary business decision.

What are some of the elements of good modern ethics in a program? It includes insisting on complete truth and honesty amongst all team members. It demands high respect for the contributions from every team member, regardless of background. This emphasis and respect for honesty means that fellow workers are trusted to provide the most accurate status and estimates they can.

Build the Team Code

- Good team code = Ethics.
  - Honesty
  - Nonthreatening
  - Equal opportunity
  - Nondiscriminatory
- Develops team trust and pride.
- Periodically review—*it's necessary.*
- Leadership must *always* be an example.
- Net business performance improvement—worth the investment!

Figure 9.24 High-quality team ethics is the major part of the team code. Adherence to a team code fulfills our "tribal" needs, which are an inherent part of our human nature.

Good ethics assumes that there is no gaming or posturing amongst the groups or individuals working in the teams. It requires that the program receive all suggestions, criticisms, and work products from the team members in the same open manner, regardless of sex, age, ethnicity, sexual orientation, seniority, etc. Prejudicial, insulting, or threatening expressions in any form are not allowed from any team member; therefore, team members develop a high level of trust and respect for each other.

This high level of ethical conduct must be established quickly and maintained for a first-place program. There are at least three functions needed to achieve this.

- **Regular ethics meetings with distribution of written reminders.** Each team member should attend a one-hour ethics meeting two to four times a year. It is valuable for participants to split up into subgroups and role play ethics infractions, followed by all team members and leadership discussing the appropriate responses. This exercise reactivates an awareness of ethical behavioral limits for all participants. It sends a strong message that being aware of and precisely practicing ethics is a necessary part of being a member of a successful program team.
- **Equal and swift due process.** An ethics violation during the conduct of the program must be adjudicated swiftly and with the same fact-supported due process that is applied to any other infraction. If the program or enterprise is big enough to have a human resources group, the adjudication should be conducted by them.
- **Leadership by example.** All program leadership must exhibit awareness and adherence to the ethics rules, being clear and decisive about not exceeding any ethics limit. This behavior must be exercised during off-campus events, even well after the program has ended. No member of leadership should ever imply that they are somehow maintaining two sets of ethical guidelines. This example is needed to irrefutably emphasize that good ethics is the only behavior accepted by the enterprise.

During Step 1, the team members and leadership would have been requested to generate, in writing, a draft team code of conduct, including ethics rules. This draft would then be refined during Step 2. Leadership will have shared examples of how good team ethics improves team-member trust and have been an essential part of the success of first-place programs.

One recent example of this is the story of an electronics product team that delivered high-performance, embedded computer control systems for critical applications. This team consisted of over 400 electrical engineers colocated in a large building. They had developed a thorough and well-documented code of conduct, which included their description of ethical behavior.

One day it was discovered that expensive computer memory chips were disappearing from some of the high-powered workstations. At the time, these chips could be sold on the black market for high prices. Enterprise security was informed and promised to launch a widespread investigation.

But this team had a strong sense of camaraderie, based on their robust ethical code. So they "hot-wired" the entrance panels to the workstations so that security and team management would be informed by smart phone if workstation entry was attempted. Days later, at 2 AM, phones came alive, and the thief was apprehended. All members of the product team took delight in knowing that adherence to their solid ethical code foiled a serious infraction—a valuable example of how the galvanizing effect of a well-founded ethical team code made them united and more effective.

Leadership must discuss how active team ethics actually increase the speed by which the program fulfills its commitments and how it ensures that high-quality work is delivered. Discussions should include how team members communicate with a higher level of trust with a high standard of team ethics. Additional discussions should be conducted on how trusted communication results in faster, more accurate, and highly trusted exchange of information amongst team members and how this facilitates a faster development pace (see Figure 9.25).

Leadership must emphasis how high ethics ensure that all team members, regardless of background, have an equal opportunity to be heard—that every good idea is evaluated fairly, on its merits and that no good idea is ignored.

Team Ethics Is Part of Team Code

Step 2
• Introduce team code concept during interviews.
• Ask new team members to comment on draft code.
• Show examples how ethics needed for first-place teams.
• Conduct regular ethics meetings.
• Discuss solutions to typical ethics issues with team.
• Leadership takes swift and fair responses to infractions.
• Leadership is example of good ethics, even off campus.
• Team ethical behavior reduces costs, increases moral.

Figure 9.25   Regular in-person team ethics exercises galvanize the awareness of infractions and provides response guidance. Leadership must impeccably demonstrate adherence to the ethics rules, even off the work campus. In addition, leadership must swiftly and fairly respond to ethics infractions.

This openness to all good ideas increases the program development pace and improves product quality.

During Step 2, the team must review the draft code of conduct and ethics guidelines and provide feedback, which must be reviewed, evaluated, and implemented if deemed appropriate by the team. As a result, team will take more ownership and be more aware of ethics guidelines they feel are uniquely theirs.

As mentioned, leadership must exert fair and swift reaction to ethics infractions. This will impress team members that ethics behavior is strongly upheld, and it will relieve the fear in some of nefarious actions preventing them from achieving their self-actualization needs.

Team members will enjoy increased task completion speeds if they can trust commitments from their team members; they will also feel secure knowing that their personal reputations and belongings are adequately protected. They will feel freer to complete their work and achieve their motivational needs if they trust that others are looking out for them, and they will take comfort in having clear team rules ensuring that they will always be treated fairly and without discrimination.

Table 9.13 Code of Conduct Increases Business Success
SELF-ACTUALIZATIONS FULFILLED

Self-Actualization Level	How Fulfilled By This Success Element
Physiological	These team members are galvanized and comforted by the agreements they have with other team members as to what is wrong/unethical.
Safety	These team members are freed from extra precautions they feel may be needed because of mistrust of the deeds and words of fellow team members.
Love/Belonging	These team members experience enriched fellowship when sharing objections to unethical or illegal behaviors.
Esteem	These team members understand that a strong ethical bond in a team actually reduces program cost and schedule length. They appreciate that it is a business imperative for a first-place team they wish to be associated with.
Professional	These team members highly appreciate the emphasis on honesty in communications. They know that to be an extraordinary performer in their field, they must always apply truth. Unethical exaggerations or guesses will destroy their credibility.
Altruistic	These team members believe the high ethical integrity of the program reflects favorably on the ethical value of their altruistic vision.

9.2 Motivating High Tempo

An essential role of leadership of a first-place team is to keep its members aware of the importance of the work they are providing and of their accomplishments. This is essential to maintain each team member's buy-in (Step 1) and to give them the freedom and confidence to take risks to perform exceptionally well (Step 2).

Sometimes, a team member hesitates to make a "big deal" about what they have accomplished. Leadership must tactfully but consistently remind the team of outstanding work they have done. This helps ignite their best abilities, regardless of their seniority or professional level.

9.2.1 They Are Special

A first-place team must be constantly reminded that their capabilities and the work they are doing is special. This must be established during Step 1 and repeated during Step 2. Most often, leadership will remind the team that what they are accomplishing is being done for the first time. This is clearly true not only when developing a brand-new item or system, but also when accomplishing something repetitive and simple, such as increasing the production volume of an existing product. Regardless of what is being performed, the team should be reminded what they are doing is unique and special (see Figure 9.26).

Team members should be tactfully reminded that not everyone who applied for a role on the team was accepted—that they possessed special talents that convinced leadership they would make an important contribution to the product being developed. In addition, team members must be appreciated by leadership for their inputs to plan for performing the work, and that their planning inputs are essential to successfully achieving the program milestones.

Leadership must remind team members that not only will they be expected to perform their assigned work thoroughly, but that also they must be able to respond quickly and effectively to development anomalies, failures, and changes in work priorities.

During Step 1, leadership will have highlighted what is original and special in the program, pointing out the unique capabilities of each team member. This must be done with tact and restraint, depending on the personalities and seniorities of the team members.

Team members must be reminded that they possess important abilities that convinced leadership they should be on the program team. This will not only invigorate their enthusiasm but will also start galvanizing mutual respect with the other team members.

As discussed in Chapter 8 (Section 8.9.2, beginning on page 151), being a first-place program attracts a lot of attention from other programs in the home enterprise and other businesses. Unfortunately, sometimes this curiosity turns into

Point Out Start of Team Value

Recognize first evidence of success.

Figure 9.26   The way a program is started often sets the tempo for the rest of the effort. It is very important that even small successes are shared with the team as soon as they occur.

critique. During Step 2, leadership must visibly defend the team any time they are being criticized unfairly. Criticism that is accurate and constructive should be accepted and appreciated as a supportive gesture. But baseless and malicious criticisms must be responded to with a professional but direct response. Repeated baseless criticisms must be ignored. Keep in mind, leadership will be an example of how the rest of the team should feel about and react to baseless criticisms.

Team members must be encouraged to reply to requests for assistance from outside programs. They must kindly acknowledge all requests for help, and, if they cannot provide it, they must politely inform the requester and, if possible, offer alternate sources of help.

During Step 2, team members must feel the joy and enthusiasm from freely achieving self-actualization needs and being recognized for extraordinary accomplishments. Maintaining the critical balance of individual and team humility with intense team pride is a major role leadership must orchestrate.

Table 9.14 They Are Special
SELF-ACTUALIZATIONS FULFILLED

Self-Actualization Level	How Fulfilled By This Success Element
Physiological	These team members are reassured that they were selected for their special abilities. They are reminded that their performance to date has been of value.
Safety	These team members take comfort in being informed of the outstanding work the program team has accomplished. They feel this favorable feedback bodes well for continuation of the work.
Love/Belonging	These team members take pride in being recognized as being on a special team.
Esteem	These team members take pride in the favorable review of their accomplishments that support the importance of their title.
Professional	These team members take pride in the expertise they have offered to the program that resulted in the compliments—particularly if their contribution resulted in a major part of the success.
Altruistic	These team members usually equate the recognized high performance of the team to the importance of their altruistic vision in the likelihood of its fulfillment.

9.2.2 Share Early Successes

Sometimes when a new project or program is started, weeks may pass before leadership acknowledges team progress. This is a mistake. Leadership must post the evidence of even small progress steps as soon as available. These can be simple intermediate accomplishments, such as "Preliminary task planning is complete," or "We have recruited 80% of our team target."

It is recommended that, as a new program is starting, the PM conduct short daily status meetings with their leadership team. This is an excellent time to share specific progress elements, even if small. To help the team maintain a sense of progress, schedules should have enough detail to identify at least one milestone to be accomplished each week.

The new program team must see evidence that they are quickly demonstrating their high capability and are achieving their commitments on time. Leadership should point out how the power of high-quality communication and teamwork are a part of their success. Leadership should especially highlight accomplishments achieved ahead of schedule, emphasizing the importance of delivering work on or before promised times.

One example of the benefit of sharing early success is of a PM who led a highly talented team of over 40 professionals developing operational logic and software to deploy multiple satellites in different orbits. Completing this work was pacing the critical milestone of deploying the entire gigantic system.

This complex challenge was divided into independent pieces, each with small teams developing and testing their part. These tests were conducted with a high-fidelity and thoroughly proven software simulation. After successfully completing their test plan, they submitted their portion of the final software to a central lead, who integrated it into the whole.

One evening this lead brought the results of his integrated simulation to the PM. He showed data tabulations and plots illustrating how the many completed software pieces actually operated successfully together. He was able to display with engineering data that the intended satellite deployment sequence functioned correctly from beginning to end.

The PM immediately saw a major opportunity to invigorate the team with this early evidence of their success. At their morning meeting the next day, he asked the integrating engineer to present the plots showing this success. The resulting silence in the room was deafening! Some engineers became emotional. They saw for the first time that their work, when integrated, was successful. Despite the many days of extended work hours and exhaustion, they were highly rejuvenated, and they left the room buoyant—they had done it, and their future work would extend this success.

This is an example of a good leader sharing the success of the team as soon as it is achieved, greatly enhancing morale and teamwork. This is much more than a "pep talk"; it is actual evidence of success, presented as soon as available. First-place teams thrive on this feedback to maintain their momentum.

During Step 1, leadership will have assured team members that they would be informed of all progress as it occurred. Team members would have been reminded, with examples, that large accomplishments are achieved by a collection of many small ones. They would have also been assured that small accomplishments would be noted and given credit. Posting these small accomplishments was designed to give the team a constant sense of movement necessary to maintain enthusiasm.

During Step 2, an attempt should be made to identify team progress at least every two days. Even if a milestone is not scheduled for completion during this time, the team should be reminded with informal examples and descriptions of partial completions of their fast progress.

Of course, all communication of status to the program team, which may include members who are not employees of the home enterprise, must adhere to sensitive data restrictions. But even only communicating the accomplishment of top-level milestones without details enhances team morale.

Table 9.15 Share Early Successes

SELF-ACTUALIZATIONS FULFILLED

Self-Actualization Level	How Fulfilled By This Success Element
Physiological	Reduces concerns regarding the value of their initial contributions.
Safety	Provides early encouragement that the program is making acceptable progress and that the program plan is good.
Love/Belonging	Provides early evidence of the value of teamwork. Shows that the organization and team assignments are successful.
Esteem	These team members have increased enthusiasm when hearing their role is contributing to immediate good progress.
Professional	These individuals are encouraged that their early contributions are showing team success. They appreciate that some contributions will take longer to indicate success.
Altruistic	These team members are encouraged that the organization, team assignments, and program plan are showing early signs of supporting their altruistic vision.

9.2.3 Growing Dedication and Providing Guidance

Establishing high team-member dedication requires that leadership study the motivation of each team member and plan an involvement that appeals to their developing motivation or self-actualization needs. A major part of this is reinforcing team-member buy-in and enthusiasm found in Step 1 throughout the duration of the program.

Elements useful to achieving this are as follows:

- **Mentoring.** There are a variety of ways a professional may be mentored. It varies depending on the need, the seniority of the person being mentored, what motivates them, their willingness to be mentored, and more. Even company presidents with tens of thousands of professionals reporting to them have confided to the author that they have a mentor.

  Anyone can be a mentor—assistance need not be administered only by a person with high seniority or by a leader. The choice of a mentor depends on the mentee's needs. For example, sometimes someone with indisputably exceptional social skills or with highly respected basic common sense can be a good mentor, regardless of their level in the organization.

  For a new team member in a large enterprise, trying to determine how something should be done next can be overwhelming, and a second opinion can provide insight, guidance, and confidence. A good mentor can make suggestions that help determine a professional's self-actualization and how to achieve it.

The details of a mentor relationship vary, depending partially on the goals of the mentee and the availability of the mentor. An agreement may range from regularly conducting in-person meetings to the mentor's simply being on call.

A wide range of subjects may be discussed, from detailed planning of career development to addressing an interpersonal issue. The mentor plan may be highly detailed, with written meeting times, development steps, and planned outcomes, or it may be less formal, simply relying on random topics based on the current circumstances of the mentee.

The mentor must promise to hold all information in the highest confidence. This becomes very important and sometimes awkward if the mentor has any relationship with the mentee's leadership. For this reason, it is usually preferable for a person to choose a mentor who is not affiliated with the program they are supporting.

It is important when creating a mentor relationship to establish its purpose. This should allow the mentor and the mentee to summarize what has been achieved when complete. Without a specific completion goal, the relationship might simply atrophy, and the mentee may not receive the help they want.

Table 9.16 Mentoring

SELF-ACTUALIZATIONS FULFILLED

Self-Actualization Level	How Fulfilled By This Success Element
Physiological	These team members must be reassured that their contribution is of value. An independent evaluation of their work is appreciated and encourages them strive for their best.
Safety	These team members often need reassurance that they are doing the right thing. They may not want to wait for a performance review to find their weaknesses. A discussion about their performance can provide early warning of weak areas and plans to improve them. This reduces the fear of being noncompliant.
Love/Belonging	Genuine personal support from a mentor adds tremendously to the feeling of belonging for all team members. Personal dialogue provides understanding and resolution paths that cannot be achieved with only written reviews.
Esteem	While struggling to increase their stature in the organization, these team members often desire to be reviewed for performance by an independent and qualified source. For most, the guidance they receive is highly appreciated and encouraging.

Professional	For these team members, mentoring is usually provided for their analytical technique and for ways of improving their knowledge of the enterprise and exposure in it. Mentoring for these professionals can help sort out where the focus of their expertise should be. This increases their sense of fulfillment.
Altruistic	For these team members, their altruistic vision might be clarified and made more realistic with mentoring. Also, realistic expectations for when elements of this vision can be accomplished may be established. This can improve their enthusiasm to achieve their altruistic goals.

- **A real open door.** Some leaders have had their office door removed and laid by the entrance to their office. This message is clear: "Anyone can walk in and ask questions or discuss an issue at any time. If I am busy, I promise I will get back to you. I will intently listen to you. There will never be a negative outcome from talking to me. If the subject matter is personal, I will cordially request that we move our conversation to a conference room. In this way, we can continue our discussion in a more neutral environment and without being disturbed. Only a few will know where we are and will contact us only if there is an emergency."

  Many have found this approach to work well. This direct accessibility maintains the high degree of team morale and trust necessary to continue to be in first place, and it is another way for team members to bring forth concerns, improvement ideas, and sometimes ingenious innovations.

Table 9.17 Real Open Door
SELF-ACTUALIZATIONS FULFILLED

Self-Actualization Level	How Fulfilled By This Success Element
Physiological	These team members are highly encouraged that they can discuss their fears, concerns, and questions with anyone in leadership without ridicule or retribution.
Safety	These professionals are comforted by the policy that allows them to discuss their curiosities, fears, and apprehensions candidly with any leader. This allows them to have confidence in the future.
Love/Belonging	These team members take comfort in a policy that allows in-person communication by any team member with any leader regarding the future of the program in the future of the role. This adds to team contentment and teamwork.

Esteem	These team members understand that misconceptions and fears in their coworkers and reports can squelch innovations and the sharing of perceived risks/issues. They encourage a program's open-door policy, despite the potential for criticism about their own work.
Professional	These team members value the opportunity for in-person discussions with leadership to clarify the needs and value of their expertise. This helps ensure that they are most effective.
Altruistic	These team members appreciate that they can question leadership about the possible outcomes of the program. This gives these professionals some reassurance of the attention leadership is paying to the possible effect of the program work on society.

- **Triggering strong dedication.** Some modern-day professionals are highly transient, regularly moving from company to company through their career. Someone who does well with this kind of employment path carefully chooses their next role so that it is both complemented by and expands what they've done before.

  Professionals who choose this path strive to build a wealth of experience in the specialty they have chosen. They are usually very concise about the extent of work they commit to perform, deliver what they promise on time, integrate well with the team, and then move on, often after a few years. They concentrate on maintaining a network of professional contacts and often rely on it to locate their next job.

  These professionals take pride in having a wide range of experience and good endorsements from both past employers and colleagues in their specialty. They are, however, without deep roots in one enterprise.

  This type of professional most often has a Professional self-actualization of doing exceptionally well in some particular specialty and being sought after to serve. Some may be partially motivated by Esteem, but this is rarely the driving source. They strive to grow a specialty that they believe will be valuable in the future, thus fulfilling their Professional self-actualization needs.

  But experience has shown that high-value innovations are most often created by long-term employees—those employed by the company for decades, seldom by employees who have been with the company for just a few years.

  Experience has also shown that a good program can be initiated with short-term employees and consultants, but it will not be the first-place contender. To be in first place, the effort must have team members who have dedicated their careers to the home enterprise (see Figure 9.27).

  To fully achieve their self-actualization needs and goals, professionals must have leaders who invest in and look out for their growth—leaders who

Team Dedication Fosters Special Traits

- Close support and trust is forged amongst team members.
- Members spontaneously devote extraordinary efforts.
- Team members work together to find the shortest path to success.
- Individual needs often become secondary.
- Responding to near-term needs of Esteem often secondary.
- Required additional knowledge and expertise learned/ incorporated quickly.
- Innovation sought after and cherished.
- Team depends on and respects best sources of expertise.

Figure 9.27   Team members who feel a high sense of team and enterprise dedication bring forth special traits that are essential for a first-place program. The author has observed that long-term dedication by a team member to a program or enterprise usually increases the extent and depth of the special traits they offer. He has observed all breakthrough innovations come from these team members.

offer themselves as a mentor to the team members during times of uncertainty. This triggers a special high level of dedication from the professional, which is necessary for the program and the home enterprise to be in first place. This can only be achieved when the professional is employed by and integrated with the home enterprise for most or all of their career.

Table 9.18 Strong Dedication
SELF-ACTUALIZATIONS FULFILLED

Self-Actualization Level	How Fulfilled By This Success Element
Physiological	These team members appreciate the enterprise vision that the work they are doing is essential and will be of continued value in other efforts. They are content in knowing there is an enterprise plan to help them approve their capabilities, fairly promote them, and increase their compensation.
Safety	These individuals will be comforted by knowing that the enterprise encourages their long-term employment and will assist them with developing good performance in the future.
Love/Belonging	These team members appreciate that the enterprise is establishing a long-term relationship with them by attempting to maximize their value. This effort often results with in-person review and guidance.

Esteem	Many of these team members appreciate that long-term dedication to the enterprise can lead to steady promotion, with a wider span of influence and more respect for their job title. They appreciate the benefits of this route, as opposed to starting over in different enterprises.
Professional	These professionals are pleased that the enterprise provides avenues to increase their knowledge and capability in their specialty, and they enjoy their developing good reputation in the enterprise.
Altruistic	Many of these team members appreciate that achieving important altruistic outcomes requires long-term dedication by the enterprise and its employees. They appreciate the understanding and respect of their altruistic vision they have received from leadership. Some may believe they have gained additional leadership subscription to this vision as a result.

- **When it's scary.** When a program encounters a major issue, leadership must remain calm, composed, and positive that a solution will be found. Team members look at the PM and leadership to see their reaction, and their body language will be revealing.

  Leaders must not jump to a conclusion regarding the cause of an issue. They must both establish the principle of and be an example of learning more about a situation before determining action. This response will maintain calm in the team and remind them that good decisions are based on a thorough understanding of facts.

  Leadership must exude confidence that the team will successfully solve the given problem. By expressing this conviction, the team will.

- **Have their backs.** There will be times when a problem occurs during work being performed by a team member with less experience than the others. The temptation, understandably, will be to reassign this problem to a team member with more experience, but this must be avoided.

  The earlier-discussed concept of one responsible person per task should only be violated in the most extreme situations. A corollary to this guideline is that the single person is the same person. Leadership must show high confidence that the team member with the assignment will solve the problem, showing patience and giving this team member ample time to work through the issue.

  Sometimes, leadership may see the need to help this team member with assistance from someone more senior—someone to "tag along" during problem solving, acting as a sounding board to assure the team member that they are doing the right thing or provide a second opinion on the plan forward. But leadership must make it clear that the team member originally assigned remains responsible for deriving the solution.

This approach is important for the morale of the entire program team. It allows lower-seniority professionals to develop while being responsible for real, critical problem solutions. It gives more senior professionals the opportunity to tactfully mentor and make suggestions without preempting the responsibility for completing the work. This is a capability essential for future leadership roles.

The entire team will observe and appreciate that leadership is not giving up on the responsible team member. They will realize they needn't fear being abruptly removed from an important role without a chance to redeem themselves—that once they are given a responsibility, they will be allowed keep it to completion. They will learn that problems along the way will be used to improve problem solving and leadership capabilities, without penalty to the program.

Sometimes an entire team needs to know how much leadership respects and cares for them. For example, a large, highly technical development program involving hundreds of professionals risked delaying a critical delivery milestone because of a complex pointing stability problem. This team, consisting of over 20 controls analysts, worked feverishly to solve this problem.

The team had been working this issue for months, often seven days a week; they were exhausted, and mistakes were beginning to happen. To the chagrin of the customer, the PM told the team to take the upcoming three-day weekend off. In this intense development environment, a three-day getaway was a major luxury! But the team was exhausted and way overdue for a rest. Leadership had their back, despite the criticism they might incur for delaying the delivery.

Of course, all stakeholders assumed the final delivery date would slip by three days. But program leadership team was pleasantly shocked when they saw that, two days after the team's return, this complex problem was solved. What was predicted to be a three-day slip to the program schedule was now a day ahead of schedule!

This team of analysts were given time to clear their minds, rest, and create a successful solution to their problem. They were given the time to take ownership and show the bosses how really good they were. But as important, they appreciated that the boss was empathetic and would insist on protecting them.

Table 9.19 Calm and Have Their Backs
SELF-ACTUALIZATIONS FULFILLED

Self-Actualization Level	How Fulfilled By This Success Element
Physiological	These team members will be delighted that assigned tasks will be the responsibility of one individual, who will be supported to complete it.
Safety	These individuals will be relieved that work responsibility will not be transferred to others because of initial concerns about work performance. They will be relieved when leadership demonstrates that their health and safety is their first priority.
Love/Belonging	These individuals will favorably experience that leadership personally cares for them and their team members. This promotes a more personal relationship between team members and leadership.
Esteem	These individuals will be delighted that if they make a mistake, they are still expected to be responsible for the work and will be provided assistance if needed to complete it.
Professional	These team members are comforted in knowing their high quality/expert contribution will continue to be their responsibility, even if they encounter problems.
Altruistic	These team members respect that responsibility for tasks will not be moved to another team member if problems are encountered. They understand that progress toward their altruistic vision occurs sooner when the originally assigned responsible individuals are allowed to complete their task.

- **Everyone gets a second chance.** There is a tendency of some contemporary leaders that is very disturbing in light of modern leadership. This leader may proudly claim that they "make the tough decisions." If this leader's superiors are not paying careful attention to the circumstances, they may be impressed and even relieved by the strength of this proclamation. Unfortunately, often this phrase refers to firing someone for not achieving a certain performance level. But the fact is that immediately dismissing a professional because they have not achieved certain performance metrics is too simplistic. A leader who does this usually has not exerted the care to evaluate the individual and the entire circumstances.

  In general, a team member does not achieve an acceptable performance level for one of two reasons: they do not want to, or they want to but do not know how. If someone does not want to do the work, leadership must discuss this apparent lack of motivation with them. Occasionally, this lack of motivation is due to misunderstood communication between leadership and the team member. Otherwise, the enterprise and this professional may be better off if they are offered another assignment where they can fulfill the needs of their motivation.

However, if the employee's mistake falls into the second category, they should be given a second chance to perform the work acceptably. Note, this is a "second chance," not just "another chance." Neither this individual nor the team can be left with the impression that repeated mistakes will be tolerated indefinitely.

If a professional really wants to perform their best, they will thoroughly scrutinize their past mistake and make sure it never happens again. They may ask leadership and peers for some insight and guidance, but they will take responsibility to complete the job correctly.

Many of us have life examples in which someone had the sensitivity and wisdom to let us try again. Some people really don't care and respond by doing just as poorly the second try; but if they really care, this second chance can lead to high value to them, their manager, and the team.

A real example is of a young man who crewed on a racing sloop alongside a more seasoned crew member and the boat captain. The captain happened to be very competitive, thus very vocal about deficient performance. In fact, his sailboat was painted black, and yes, his last name was Cook!

The young crewman was eager to do his best, but he was also inexperienced. During a race of over a dozen boats, their boat was in first place, and they were the first around the windward mark, where they were to deploy their spinnaker. This is a very critical deployment event where a race can be lost.

The young man attached the halyard and sheets to raise and control this big balloon sail. He was positive he rigged the sail correctly, but when he deployed it, it was upside down! Not only did the boat lose, but there was endless heckling from following boats—"spinnaker upside down?!"

The rant from Captain Cook was endless! The young man felt like the lowest of amateurs, and he doubted he would ever be invited to crew on any boat again. But to his surprise, at the end of the day, Captain Cook invited him to crew on his boat the following weekend. During that week, every night the young man would review in his head the details of raising the spinnaker. He would run through the procedure many times, trying to make it as quick and as foolproof as possible. He thought that maybe sometime in his distant future, he might be asked to deploy a spinnaker again.

To everyone's surprise, the next race was almost identical to the previous one. Captain Cook and his black boat were in first place, and they were approaching the windward mark. The young man thought for sure that the more seasoned crewmate would be asked to deploy the spinnaker—but Captain Cook asked him to try again. Surprise! As the boat rounded the windward mark, he set up and deployed the spinnaker perfectly and in record time. The captain even yelled out, "What happened to you? Did you take some kind of smart pill?!" Captain Cook's black sailboat and crew won the race.

Because of the patience, wisdom, and yes, willingness to take a little risk by this captain, the young man did not despair. He learned the power of always trying to do your best and was vindicated. And his dedication to Cook and crew was now irrevocable.

This is an example of one of the best qualities of leadership—carefully thought out, patient intuition, even some risk, but with a result that has multiple, permanent wins.

Providing a second chance not only applies to inexperienced employees but also to senior employees attempting a new task. For example, an excellent senior technical staff consultant may want to try a leadership responsibility, and they may make some basic leadership mistakes while trying to develop this ability. Successful leadership habits are mostly learned, not inherent in an individual. This senior professional may learn from their mistake and not re-create it if given a second chance.

Table 9.20 Everyone Gets a Second Chance
SELF-ACTUALIZATIONS FULFILLED

Self-Actualization Level	How Fulfilled By This Success Element
Physiological	These team members feel free to improve their work process or consider innovations, knowing that a mistake will not disqualify them from continuing to be responsible for the work they were assigned.
Safety	These professionals will be relieved to know that one mistake will not result in their being removed from completing their assigned task.
Love/Belonging	These team members will feel personal support to complete their assigned responsibility. They will not feel abandoned because of a mistake.
Esteem	These team members will feel free to incorporate innovations and process improvements with less fear of either being evaluated as being too risky or being reassigned.
Professional	These professionals will feel much freer to incorporate risky innovations or other improvements that may have a high payoff to the program.
Altruistic	These team members realize that their altruistic vision may not be completely realistic. A second chance will help them clarify it and give it higher value.

- Stand up for them. The PM will be continually asking for team-member innovation, hard work, and dedication to closure. Yet they must vigorously protect their team when they are being challenged. This protection must be fair, be based on facts, but be prompt and evident.
  - **Outside criticism.** Programs that are in first place are targets for probing and criticism from other organizations. This sometimes stems from jealousy or disbelief that the team being scrutinized is doing so well. Erroneous conclusions include that exaggerated metrics of success were published, that the program is receiving special help from the sponsoring enterprise, that the program captured high-performance professionals from other programs, and more.

    As discussed above, such accusations must be responded to promptly. First, leadership must determine if there's any truth to the accusation, and if so, must apologize for any negative effects and announce a plan to remedy the problem. But if the criticism has no basis, leadership must issue an immediate response, in writing, with all the facts that counter the accusations. If the criticism continues and there is no new information to support it, it should be ignored.

    What is important is that leadership immediately express, with conviction, strong, justifiable support for the team. This will assure the team they are being cared for and protected.
  - **Individual's poor work performance.** This subject has been addressed earlier. As stated, a team member's performance may be poor because either they do not know how to do the assigned task, or they simply are not motivated to do the task. What is important is that leadership approach this issue with respect and patience, not anger. This team member may simply not have the training or background to understand how to do the work.

    If the team member's deficiency is simply lack of knowledge, leadership should devise a plan to improve their skills. This plan may require that they spend extra personal hours for special training. A team member motivated to be successful will make the needed sacrifices. The investment leadership extends to the team member will usually increase the dedication and hard work they provide to the program and the enterprise.

    If, on the other hand, the team member cannot be motivated by any task on the program, then the mismatch should be obvious. In this case, leadership should make a reasonable effort to find a fulfilling role for this team member in another program or even in an outside enterprise. The team member should leave the program and sponsoring enterprise without feeling like they were treated unfairly.

○ **Reduction in workforce.** Most programs are executed in a corporate business structure. In the US, the success of corporations is measured quarterly with such top-level metrics as orders, sales, cash flow, EBIT, and more. Many corporate leaders make these parameters the measure of their performance and, for some, even their self-value.

When there is a downturn in business that requires budget cuts, they often jump to the most obvious solution—reduce headcount. Frequently, those employees assigned to the troubled business sector are the ones let go, instead of those employees in other business sectors who are poor performers. This practice may not fairly compare the ability and contributions of all the employees in the enterprise, but it is expedient. Some corporate executives may even respect the PM for making a hard decision.

Unfortunately, the leadership of this troubled business missed a highly valuable opportunity—their hard decision may have really been a short-sighted one.

Leadership must take this opportunity to keep their best performers when there is a reduction in the size of the business. This response requires more work, including objectively evaluating the motivation needs and performance level of each team member.

One approach is for executive management to insist on moving the professionals affected by the reduction into other programs in the enterprise, allowing the normal attrition and employee evaluation process to dismiss poor performers. Of course, this may not keep the quarterly business metrics as high as they would be if leadership just let go of those employees associated with the failing program, but in the long run, it ends up keeping the better performers. This approach also might be seen to be fairer. More important, the dedication to the enterprise will be enhanced for those who stay as a result of this fairer action. This is an example of making a short-term sacrifice for a long-term, much bigger return.

One real example of this approach involved a large program, with thousands of employees, that was very successful. However, the customer suddenly no longer needed the product, and with short notice, canceled the program. After what had been a very successful program, the people on this team no longer had jobs.

Some executive managers might have given these team members time to find new jobs in the enterprise, but if they could not, they would be laid off. This resolution is acceptable in most enterprises.

But the executive vice president for this business insisted that all other programs in the enterprise absorb these surplus professionals. Resumes were polished and distributed throughout the enterprise.

The rewards from this action were immense. Yes, some programs were forced to grow beyond their budget, but they had an infusion of sometimes superior talent. Existing members in these teams even took notice, and many upped their game. Now, if one of these receiving programs had to reduce their headcount, it would let the lowest performers go. The effect was to increase the performance of all the programs forced to inherit professionals.

But of even greater impact, the loyalty of those hard workers who were saved increased enormously. They felt respected and appreciated, and their gratitude enhanced their enthusiasm to support the enterprise with the best job they could do and best innovations they could create, for many decades afterward—an excellent return on investment! This dedication, coupled with the ongoing fulfillment of self-actualization needs for the team members, is the biggest source of making a program in first place. It brings forth the best work from the team members, the most brilliant innovations and improvement ideas, and the best future leaders.

o **Personal crisis.** For a team member to do their best, they must feel that if some unexpected personal crisis occurs, they will have the freedom to resolve it. In the past, some programs evaluated a team member's personal crisis as a hindrance to be resolved quickly, even at the expense of incomplete closure for the team member's issue. This is a shortsighted response and must be avoided. The personal needs of each team member must be given a high priority and be highly respected.

A team member must be allowed to dismiss themselves for any urgent personal reason. Examples can be a family health crisis, a child behavior issue, the need for child-rearing support, the loss of a family member, a major house maintenance issue, work burnout, and many more. Team members must be requested to take the time needed to solve their problem and come back when they are ready, but keeping the program informed of their status and when they plan to return. They should also assist in handing their tasks to other team members to continue work progress while they are gone.

Many leaders might think this gives their employees license to abuse the policy and take more time than they need. But experience shows exactly the opposite! Many team members do not take the personal time off they should have.

It is the obligation of good leaders to maintain a sense of the well-being of all their team members. It is not the role of leadership to solve a team member's personal problem. Leadership should, however, reassure the team member that the program and enterprise will do whatever they can to preserve their safety and happiness during a crisis, without the threat of demerit or other retribution.

Table 9.21 Stand Up for Them

SELF-ACTUALIZATIONS FULFILLED

Self-Actualization Level	How Fulfilled By This Success Element
Physiological	This team member's enthusiasm will be increased by knowing that, despite being given high demands, they will continue to be supported, even if their performance is subpar, there is a reduction in workforce, or they have a personal crisis.
Safety	These professionals will be relieved to know that there will be continued support from the program and enterprise to maintain their employment, regardless of their personal issues, temporary poor performance, or business circumstances.
Love/Belonging	These team members will be excited by the personal support given them by the leadership team and the enterprise. They appreciate that this improves team morale and teamwork.
Esteem	These team members will be relieved by the continued support they receive for maintaining their role and development of their status, even while making errors in their work or enduring personal issues.
Professional	These team members have gratitude for the understanding and protection they receive from the enterprise and leadership. This includes leadership's highlighting the relevance and performance level of their work.
Altruistic	These team members are delighted by the stability of team assignments derived from leadership's protecting their roles. They appreciate that their altruistic vision cannot be achieved with frequently changing team structure, team assignments, and personnel.

- **See in them what they may not.** There is often a good amount of query, trial, and error for a person to determine their professional self-actualization needs. Many times, an independent evaluation by leadership of what they do well helps determine this (see Figure 4.8 on page 62).

  Their leader has two major advantages in this regard. First, they have an independent view of what this team member does well. They have had a chance to examine the attributes of this person over time and in many different circumstances while operating with different team members. This perspective can often provide an accurate insight into the real self-actualization goal of the team member. Secondly, the leader has a wider perspective of roles and opportunities in the program to allow the team member to expand their capability. They usually have the authority to provide special assignments to the team member, allowing them to grow and determine if this is work they want to pursue.

Leaders often will see potential in a team member that the team member is not aware of. Leaders should discuss these observed potentials with the team member to determine if they are willing to work in these new areas. The team member often will be surprised by this suggestion, but if the option being offered is even a little attractive to them, they should try. If this potential new professional direction successfully matures, and if it brings new value to the team and the team member enjoys the work, the gratitude from the team member may be insurmountable. This result can be a gigantic step forward for an individual to understanding their real self-actualization.

Sometimes, the team member will not do well in a new work opportunity given them or may not want to pursue a new career path, even though they may have some inherent talent to do so. Leadership must understand that the growth opportunities they provide may not always be successful. However, if the attempt fails, the team member will still gain insight into both their capabilities and the limits of their interests, which is progress.

This attention by leadership is beneficial in multiple ways. Certainly, it is of immense help to the growth of the professional—it greatly improves their dedication to the program and the sponsoring enterprise and, therefore, the value of their contributions. Their expanded capability certainly adds to the total capability of the enterprise.

But also, the other team members will observe leadership's attention to the growth of the team individuals and that it is being applied equally to all. They will see that leadership wants to help them discover what they do best while bringing the most value to the enterprise. Team members will appreciate that leadership makes a special effort to ensure that each team member fulfills their motivation.

During Step 1, leadership will have informed the team members that they would be required to keep leadership informed of current program status and issues. Leadership would also have confirmed that they would answer any questions candidly and to the best of their ability, earmarking any information they don't have and striving to attain it.

In addition, leadership will have informed team members that they would make efforts to develop any emerging capabilities observed, assuring team members that these development opportunities would not be forced, but provided only after discussion and mutual agreement.

During Step 2 maintaining a wide-open door regarding any subject will be a high leadership priority. Team members will be motivated by the respect, fairness, and attention they receive from leadership.

Team members are comforted by knowing that leadership is not only trying to fulfill their current developing motivation and self-actualization needs but is also identifying and helping to develop new abilities.

Table 9.22 See in Them What They May Not

SELF-ACTUALIZATIONS FULFILLED

Self-Actualization Level	How Fulfilled By This Success Element
Physiological	These team members may become aware of hidden talents they have that might enhance their transactional status.
Safety	These team members are comforted by observing examples of leadership's trying to cultivate the talents in fellow team members. They will understand that leadership is trying to develop them in the same way.
Love/Belonging	These team members are impressed and comforted by the extra effort leadership makes to identify subtle talents in the individual team members. They feel more belonging because of this special attention.
Esteem	These team members are motivated by the gain to the value of their professional image and the success of their assigned task if they cultivate subliminal talents in their coworkers and supports.
Professional	Often these team members are surprised that there is a perception that they may have talents they were not aware of. They may want to attempt to work in these areas to determine if there is an added specialty they should pursue or if they can augment their current specialty with this attempt.
Altruistic	These team members realize that when leadership attempts to develop emerging abilities in other professionals, the total talent of the program is increased. This will reduce the time to achieve parts of these team members' altruistic vision.

9.3 Chapter Highlights

- Key habits are needed during execution.
- Face-to-face communication is essential.
- Program plan must be adhered to.
- Removing progress barriers.
- Change design/process via procedure.
- Metrics can be very powerful.
- Recall three solution levels.
- Innovation is essential.
- Team rhythm is needed to synchronize the work.
- Watch the flank for sneak attacks.
- Develop documents that are necessary and used.

- It is imperative root cause is found.
- Avoid typical mistakes when controlling configuration.
- Motivate high team tempo.
- Grow team and enterprise dedication.
- Develop emerging team-member talents.

Chapter Ten

Program Closure

10.1 Criteria

Creating and executing a detailed plan for closing a program is necessary to maintain the target cost and schedule commitments (see Figure 10.1).

A list of what is necessary to declare the program work completed must be established during the start of the program. This list should be reviewed and approved by the customer. It may include:

- Verification that all specified requirements are achieved.
- Status and rationale for any requirements not achieved.

All remaining questions answered regarding the work performed from customer, enterprise, and other sources regarding sensitive data restrictions. Questions should be provided in writing and answers received in writing within a specified time limit.

- All contract-required meetings, reviews, and deliverables completed.
- Any deliverables that were not delivered are listed; describe why and what the resolution is.
- Completion time established, in writing, to return any facilities, services, equipment, etc. provided by the program to the customer, enterprise, suppliers, and vice versa. Describe penalties that will result from delinquent returns.
- Review to what extent and how long product support is provided after closure. This description should be in the contract with the customer.
- If the customer's need for additional product support is unknown at this time, a retainer can be negotiated. There may be a fee included.

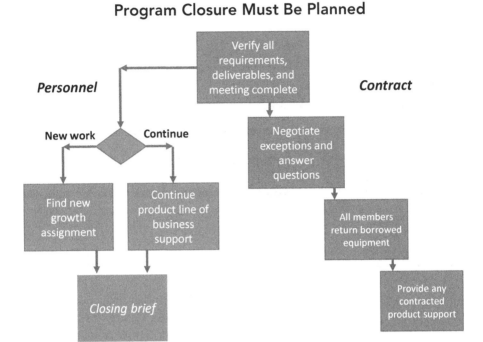

Figure 10.1 Criteria for completion of the program work must be predetermined. Otherwise, some team members may want to refine results beyond what they have already acceptably provided. Closure includes addressing any final contract requirements as well as assisting team members with finding their next assignment.

10.2 Is It Enough?

Sometimes there is reluctance to complete work on some deliverables by the more problem-oriented team members. This hesitancy can unnecessarily bleed away profits if unchecked. Program leadership must shrewdly evaluate if all contract/agreement-required content and performances have been delivered. If so, further work must be stopped.

10.3 Forward Plan for Team Members

The work is complete and the program must be dismantled. Dismantling should be planned for and executed with care to preserve the morale and career growth of the individual team members. There may be future tasks associated with the completed work. For example:

- Continued product support/maintenance of the work completed under agreement and contract.
- Continued customer support in other capacities—of course, funded by the customer.

In addition, there may be temporary overhead-funded tasks to support the enterprise that need service while the team members are being placed into new positions. These may include writing command media, participating in developing new business proposals, attending special classes, and more.

Finally, the team members leaving the program should be given a final closing review by leadership. This should include:

- Asking what work or part of the work was most satisfying to them.
- Asking if they feel that their developing motivations or self-actualization was partially or completely fulfilled.
- Asking them to comment on the amount of satisfaction they have received from knowing their motivations have been acknowledged and given guidance to develop.
- Asking them to summarize how the program has developed their professional ability and their concept of self-actualization.
- Asking if they feel that the work assignments allowed them to develop. What was accomplished.
- Asking them to summarize their unique contribution to the integrity and well-being of the program and the enterprise.
- Asking them what was good and bad about the way the program in total was run?
- Asking if they would support an extension of the program that just ended or a similar one in the future.
- Asking them to select which individuals would be good candidates for future leadership, with specific justification.

Leadership should also discuss with the team member:

- What emerging new interest/talents were detected by leadership in the team member? Does the team member want to continue to pursue these?
- What future options does leadership see for the team member? Are there any special work experiences or curriculums they would like to pursue? What are the potential growth paths that could result?

Table 10.1 Strict Adherence to Plan and Closure
SELF-ACTUALIZATIONS FULFILLED

Self-Actualization Level	How Fulfilled By This Success Element
Physiological	Establishing clear closure criteria before the end of the program brings clarity to the completion time and allows participants to plan ahead for their next involvement.
Safety	These team members will be aware of what identifies the end of the program and therefore can adequately plan ahead for the next assignment.
Love/Belonging	This allows these team members to be resigned to ending the program. Team members realize that part of the camaraderie of a program must end when the work is done.
Ego	These team members will learn the clear criteria that identifies the end of the program. This information can help them summarize their specific contributions and give them a head start to investigate new assignments and promotional opportunities.
Professional	These team members will have a clear description of the criteria for completing the program. This will help them make sure the contributions they have completed are adequately implemented and documented.
Altruistic	These team members can use the completion criteria to help measure the success of the program's achieving their altruistic vision.

10.4 Chapter Highlights

- Criteria for closure.
- Verification that enough has been done.
- Forward team-member plans.

Chapter Eleven

Building the Sponsor's Reputation

11.1 Establishes a First-Place Portfolio

With enterprise leadership's understanding human motivation in its programs, including its needs and how to manage it, the stature of the enterprise will be greatly increased, and this enterprise will become the leader in its business area.

Recognizing the motivations of the individual team members and appealing to their needs greatly enhances the unique innovations and productivity of the programs in the enterprise. It results in making the programs the best amongst competitors, in first place. Increasing the number of first-place programs in an enterprise greatly propels its reputation to a high level.

11.2 Gives Enterprise Teams Feeling of Being First Place

When the motivation needs of the individual team members are detected and appealed to, the program will perform at its best.

By experiencing being on a first-place program, team members will become familiar with its composition and will be determined to re-create it in the future. They are delighted when they observe that each team member is given authority to plan, lead, and complete their assignment. They are gratified that management supports their motivation needs, their search for their self-actualization and their resulting high work effectivity. They are further grateful that leadership is making the effort to evaluate their special talents and is helping them grow into their complete self-actualization.

11.3 Identifies Future Leadership

In the fast pace of a first-place program, the ability to motivate and lead the team to derive a high-quality closure will be evident.

Senior leadership must take note of new leaders, such as task leaders who led the delivery of contract-compliant goods with high quality, on or before the committed delivery date. These individuals will likely be excellent choices to lead future enterprise programs.

11.4 Provides Improvements and Innovations for Future

Innovations in the development processes or in new products developed and proven by a first-place program are of great value to future programs in the enterprise. By encouraging and implementing such innovations, an enterprise can become outstanding, building on the legacy of past successes.

11.5 Increases Morale and Allegiance

If a program is one of many in an enterprise, its success in being first place is contagious! The team members of all the enterprise programs take pride in being a member of an enterprise with one or more first-place contenders.

Most leaders are sensitive to the fact that first-place programs seem to contain some kind of special essence that makes them so successful, and they strive to identify what that is. By observing a program managing human motivation to achieve this essence, they will follow suit. This will result in the performance of the entire enterprise improving.

11.6 Demonstrates High Capability of the Brand

The excellent reputation of the enterprise brand is greatly increased if it contains one or more first-place programs (see Figure 11.1). The fact that the programs in this enterprise are using advanced leadership processes, including evaluating and managing human motivation, demonstrates that it is always stretching to improve

First-Place Makes an Outstanding Enterprise

- **Increases profits.**
- **Develops culture of achieving commitments.**
- **Gives employees feel of being On-Step.**
- **Identifies effective new leaders.**
- **Provides powerful process improvements/ innovations for future.**
- **Prevents mistakes in future programs.**
- **Increases enterprise morale and allegiance.**
- **Demonstrates high capability of enterprise brand.**

Figure 11.1   An enterprise should strive to have as many first-place programs in its portfolio as possible. This benefits the enterprise in many ways.

itself. It shows that it is open to continuing to find ways of improving its completed work and enhancing the satisfaction of its customers and the growth of its employees. This is the kind of business a customer wants for the work they need.

11.7 Chapter Highlights

- Establishing a first-place enterprise.
- Improvements and innovations for future.
- Increasing enterprise morale and allegiance.
- Establishing high-quality brand.

Glossary

Buy-in	The state of mind in a team member in which they believe the work they are doing is necessary and worth their effort.
CCB	Change Control Board. A team of senior leadership and specialists who review and approve all proposed changes to the program.
Critical path	The series of interdependent tasks estimated to require the most schedule time in a program schedule.
Failure	An occurrence when a process or product failed to perform as designed.
Fault	An anomalous occurrence in a process or product. This item may not have failed but the occurrence was unexpected.
FRB	Failure Review Board. A team of relevant product developers and subject specialists convened to determine the root cause of a product fault or failure.
Gantt schedule depiction	A schedule creation and tracking technique created by Henry Gantt in 1917 that reveals the schedules for all the work to be done to complete a task.
In person	Any interpersonal activity in which the participants are physically close enough to each other such that they may comfortably conduct a conversation.
Issue	An occurrence that is a disadvantage to the program.
Margin (schedule, cost, performance, risk)	Added amounts of one of these items inserted in planning to absorb the impact of unexpected issues without changing the commitments in the master schedule. These margins typically exist in the task-level plans.
Master schedule	The top-level schedule for a program. Integrates all the lower-level schedules for the individual program tasks.
MBWA	"Management by wandering around." The simple activity of leadership enhancing their understanding of work status by being physically present where the work is being accomplished.

Mentor	Usually an individual with large amounts of successful experiences in a particular subject who conveys what they have learned to a professional with little experience. Goal is to increase the rate of productivity growth in new and/or inexperienced team members.
Metrics	Repeated measurements of specific performances of a program during its work. Useful in confirming conformance to planned amounts and identifying trends.
On-Step	An extraordinary high level of program performance that puts it in first place. Usually, these programs are ahead of competitors or those performing similar work by a very large amount.
PERT schedule depiction	Program Evaluation Review Technique. A schedule creation and tracking technique that emphasizes the interdependencies among tasks.
Program plan	The master plan for the program. Contents includes schedules, organization, functions and responsibilities, product requirements, milestones, special guidelines, constraints, and more. Often this document will reference other detailed supporting documents.
R&D	Research and Development. Work devoted to develop new theories, algorithms, processes, techniques and more used to develop new concepts and products.
Reuse	The use of a process or product that had been originally developed for an earlier application. Usually applied in an attempt to reduce program costs, schedule time, and risk.
Risk	Something that would be a disadvantage to the program that may occur but has not. If it does occur, it becomes an issue.
SDL	Software development lead—the task lead for development of software for a program.
SDP	A document that describes in detail the development process for any software being developed for the program.
Task lead	The person responsible for one of a number of tasks needed to complete a program. They are singularly accountable for the success of the task they are responsible for. They usually report directly to the program manager.
Task team	Group of program team members performing a specific task. They are led by a single task lead.
Team mix	The relative portions of various expertise, experience levels, motivational types, and more in a task team. This book describes the best mixtures of problem-oriented and solution-oriented professionals.
Turnaround (program)	A special activity of stopping a program from falling behind its plan. Often requires reorganization and new planning.
WBS	Work breakdown structure. A graphical depiction of the pieces of work needed to be accomplished to perform the program task. Usually presented with a hierarchical format.

Index

A

action items, 198, 205, 214, 215

B

barriers, 53, 59, 66–71, 83–85, 89, 101, 107, 113, 152, 181, 185, 192–195, 263

buy-in, 66, 67, 85, 99, 100–103, 106–110, 113, 115, 122, 182, 244, 248

C

change control board, 153, 216, 226

change process, 153, 155, 169, 189–191, 196–198, 226, 238

closing criteria, 265

closing review, 267

code of conduct, 58, 70, 71, 83, 85, 89, 93, 106, 109, 118, 239–243

cognitive evolution, 38

colocation, 145–147, 182, 187, 222

commitment(s), 1, 9, 10, 19, 21, 27, 32, 41, 44, 58, 65, 66, 70, 80, 83, 87, 89, 99, 101–105, 109, 112, 125, 133, 136, 137, 144–151, 157, 158, 181, 183, 186, 202, 209, 210, 213, 216, 219, 221, 238, 242, 243, 246, 265, 271

configuration control, 64, 156, 188, 196, 226, 235–238

critical path, 17, 158, 175–178, 217–219

cultural, 55, 115

D

dedication, 2, 26, 30, 64, 69, 87, 119, 157, 248, 251, 252, 257–264

degraded operation, 237

E

early successes, 246, 248

ethics, 64, 83, 84, 88, 89, 108, 118, 133, 142, 185, 189, 194, 239–243

ethics infractions, 194, 241–243

ethics meetings, 241

evaluation, 17, 38, 80, 83, 102, 103, 120, 131, 142, 173–177, 190, 211, 216, 220, 259, 261

expectancy, 41, 49

F

face-to-face, 143–147, 186, 188, 195, 203, 263

failure review board, 214, 216, 231, 232
fault trees, 232
feedback, 4, 13, 29, 109, 111, 137, 153,
      186, 243, 247
first-place portfolio, 269
Fishbone, 232

G
Gantt, 17, 175, 218
gradualists, 37

H
Hawthorne Effect, 40, 41, 49
Herzberg Factor, 39, 49
human factors, 61, 62

I
infraction(s), 125, 142, 194, 224, 225,
      241–243
in-person (communication), 6, 64, 69,
      95, 143–148, 182, 186, 187, 188,
      195, 203, 215, 222, 242, 249
integrated schedule, 223
inverted pyramid, 66–69, 174

K
key personnel, 237

L
leadership selection, 70, 71, 106

M
Maslow, 44–49, 61, 73, 78, 85, 86, 89,
      93, 94, 97, 138
Maslow-based, 73, 85, 138
meeting agenda, 187, 198, 205
meeting lead, 204–206, 215
meeting minutes, 205, 206
meetings, 64, 106, 144, 146, 187, 189,
      198, 203–206, 210, 214–216, 232,
      241, 246, 249, 265
mentoring, 62, 64, 122, 248, 249
metrics, 9, 64, 94, 137, 189, 200–202,
      255, 258, 259, 263
military organization, 14, 15, 52
modern leader, 53, 60, 61, 140
motivation hierarchy, 61, 82, 83, 88

O
On-Step, 1–6, 9, 11, 19–25, 28, 29, 36,
      39, 43, 48, 51–54, 61–64, 71, 80,
      83, 86, 113, 119, 271
open door, 102, 193, 250

P
parts substitution, 235
peer review(s), 164, 189, 214, 216, 225
performance history, 9, 158
personal crisis, 260
PERT, 17, 175
potential, 11, 29, 55, 60, 77, 85, 92, 95,
      107, 109, 119, 124, 139, 142, 158,
      164, 169, 172, 178, 193, 210, 216,
      219, 220, 228, 231–233, 262, 267
predict, 17, 37, 70, 150, 200–202
principal investigator, 231, 232
problem oriented, 65, 66, 78–82, 95,
      97, 103, 135–139, 266
process improvement, 69, 107, 108
program closure, 265, 266
program plan, 4, 8, 9, 64, 67, 104, 121,
      132, 153–160, 187–191, 194–199,
      204, 206, 216–224, 228, 229, 232,
      234, 238, 263
protection, 258

R
risk management, 64, 218, 219

root cause, 64, 161, 201, 202, 207, 208, 228–234, 237, 238, 264

S

second chance, 108, 255–257
six-level, 58, 70, 73, 76, 80–83
software development plan, 168, 169, 172, 223, 225
solution levels, 207, 209, 263
solution oriented, 65, 66, 78–82, 97, 99, 135–140
sponsor's reputation, 269
Step 1, 4, 66, 89, 99–103, 108–110, 113, 115, 128, 131, 142, 147, 152–155, 163, 171, 181, 185–187, 190, 198, 202, 206, 209, 213, 219, 234, 238, 241, 244, 247, 248, 262
Step 1 revisit, 109
Step 2, 4, 66, 89, 101–103, 107–110, 113, 142, 147, 152, 155, 156, 172, 185, 187, 191, 199, 202, 209, 213, 234, 238, 241–247, 262

strict adherence, 54, 187, 191, 268
success elements, 5–8, 18–20, 28, 29, 33, 35, 38, 63–65, 102, 113

T

team assignments, 95, 185
team code, 109, 118, 239–242
team rhythm, 214, 217, 226, 263
Theory X, Theory Y, 42, 43, 49
three-dimensional attribution, 42, 49
tools, 14, 21, 22, 42, 89, 96, 158, 160, 170–172, 175, 192–194, 225, 226
traditional, 6, 8, 12, 14, 28, 43, 51–55, 60, 62, 66–69, 83, 86, 89, 96, 167, 168, 175, 207, 209, 218
two books, 180
two-step execution, 66, 113

V

valuable documents, 221, 227

Printed in the United States
by Baker & Taylor Publisher Services